POSTMODERN EDUCATION

POSTMODERN EDUCATION
POLITICS, CULTURE, AND SOCIAL CRITICISM

STANLEY ARONOWITZ
AND
HENRY A. GIROUX

UNIVERSITY OF MINNESOTA PRESS
MINNEAPOLIS • OXFORD

1991

39.95 (34.36)

B+T

4/93

Copyright © 1991 by the Regents of the University of Minnesota
All rights reserved. No part of this publication may be reproduced, stored
in a retrieval system, or transmitted, in any form or by any means,
electronic, mechanical, photocopying, recording, or otherwise, without the
prior written permission of the publisher.

Published by the University of Minnesota Press
2037 University Avenue Southeast, Minneapolis, MN 55414
Printed in the United States of America on acid-free paper

Library of Congress Cataloging-in-Publication Data

Aronowitz, Stanley.
    Postmodern education: politics, culture, and social criticism /
Stanley Aronowitz and Henry A. Giroux.
        p.   cm.
    Includes bibliographical references and index.
    ISBN 0-8166-1879-8   ISBN 0-8166-1880-1 (pbk.)
    1. Education–United States–Aims and objectives. 2. Educational
sociology–United States. 3. Politics and education– United States.
I. Giroux, Henry A.
LA209.2.A78 1991
370.19'0973–dc20   90-42909
                                                        CIP

A CIP catalog record for this book is available from the British Library

The University of Minnesota
is an equal-opportunity
educator and employer.

To our children:

Nona Brett Willis-Aronowitz
Brett Brady Giroux
Christopher Brady Giroux
Jack Brady Giroux

CONTENTS

ACKNOWLEDGMENTS

Some of the articles appearing in this volume have appeared elsewhere in modified form. Stanley Aronowitz wrote chapters 1, 6, and 7. Henry A. Giroux wrote chapters 3, 4, and 5. Chapters 2 and 8 were co-authored. Henry A. Giroux would like to thank Donaldo Macedo, Candy Mitchell, Martin O'Neill, Honor Fagan, Peter McLaren, and Ralph Page for having read and commented on substantial sections of this book and for providing invaluable criticisms.

Chapter 2 originally appeared in a different form as Stanley Aronowitz and Henry A. Giroux, "Schooling, Culture, and Literacy in the Age of Broken Dreams: A Review of Bloom and Hirsch," *Harvard Educational Review*, 58, 1988, 172-94. Copyright © 1988 by the President and Fellows of Harvard College. All rights reserved. Chapters 3 and 5 in this volume are modified versions of two articles by Henry Giroux that appeared under the titles "Postmodernism and the Discourse of Educational Criticism" and "Border Pedagogy in the Age of Postmodernism" in the *Journal of Education*, 170, 3 (1988), 5-30 and 162-81.

POSTMODERN EDUCATION

CHAPTER 1
INTRODUCTION:
CLASS, RACE, AND GENDER
IN EDUCATIONAL POLITICS

Running against the 1960s has become nearly a sure-fire prescription for political success in the United States today. Whether the target is drugs, rock music, or the liberal arts curriculum in public schools, the new wisdom, sometimes called the "new puritanism," seems to accord with everyday life, which is experienced by many as tougher, more competitive, and more dangerous. In a recent poll 86 percent of those surveyed agreed that drugs were the number one domestic priority in the United States. It was taken after six months of a media assault urging Americans, especially youth, to "just say no to drugs," a gaggle of TV specials on the deleterious effects of crack, even among children of the middle class, and a newly elected president's sober declaration that he had made getting rid of the supply and the demand for illegal drugs his administration's top domestic priority. Still, the *Wall Street Journal* (September 8, 1989) reported from Omaha's black ghetto that "many people think that the chances of victory are slight" unless the emphasis shifts from law enforcement to the war's most intractable problem: "the alienated youth." Huge quantities of crack are produced and shipped from Colombia and Peru; much of its distribution is in the hands of local teenagers coordinated in a nationwide network by two Los Angeles youth gangs. Ben Gray, an Omaha television producer, thinks the problem is that "these kids feel locked out of the system." Like many others who despaired of sharing in the mainstream's structure of economic and social opportunities, they created a second economy—an alternative business environment that was empowering, at least compared to the lack of training, decent jobs, and a vision of a better future offered by the mainstream. But that's not how the Establishment sees the issue. Underscoring these profound differences is the perception by representatives of the "first economy" that refusing to work for fast-food retailers at or near minimum wage was a "cop-out" for young people who find they can earn three hundred dollars in an afternoon selling drugs. For young drug dealers, making and serving Big Macs is a "dead-end street," a step just above jail. The *Journal* story concludes that these black youth are not "dumb." They see the scandal in the Department of Housing and Urban Development of the federal government, the virtual freedom won by Colonel Oliver North and dozens of other corrupt and convicted Reagan administration officials. They know that in this country "politics is a money thing" and "money talks." Freedom can be purchased only at a high price. Ironically, the protagonist of this tale, seventeen-year-old Robert Penn, quit running a $10-million-a-year crack business to work part-time in a television studio where he takes home $121 a week. Despite his cynical view of the Establishment, Penn has completely bought into the middle-class cultural ideal: "What I want is to be happy . . . a big house, a pool, horses, satellite television—to see China, and Mexico—the American dream."

It is not completely fortuitous that Reagan's former secretary of education, William Bennett, is the chief architect of President Bush's drug "strategy." In a militant refusal to address drugs from the point of view of youth alienation, the linch-pin of Bennett's antidrug campaign is the creation of an overwhelming climate of public opinion in favor of strengthening the police, courts, and prisons. Congress and state legislatures will see no alternative but to fund retributive programs even if it means that other approaches to drugs, especially social programs such as income maintenance and job training, will have to be sacrificed. The underlying philosophy of the administration's drug crusade hovers between moral condemnation of users (even if they have been dehumanized, they are moral agents and therefore to be blamed for their weakness) and adherence to the traditional view that addiction inheres in crack's chemical effects on the body. In these times, there is absolutely no room in the public discussion of drugs for the idea that addiction is produced psychologically and socially as much as by any other factor. Unless these influences are admitted, policy is bound to draw closer to morally loaded remedies. In a series of television interviews, drug czar Bennett placed the burden on the victims to act like "human beings" in order to earn society's respect. The administration's drug policy reproduces Bennett's earlier education strategy in that the Bush proposals are resolutely anti-innovative. Instead, the key proposals open up, in the guise of a moral crusade, another front in the ideological campaign against freedom. For if children and youth are regarded as repositories of evil, the antidote to which is to beat the devil out of them in jails and work camps, appeals to human rights are likely to fall on deaf ears.

Bennett's education offensive stubbornly insisted that "throwing money" at schools, even those with leaky roofs and broken boilers, was not the solution to what he termed the "crisis of excellence." Rather, he urged a massive curriculum revision, the central features of which were resuscitating math and science education, concentrating on transmitting the canonical works of Western civilization as a required part of the undergraduate curricula of elite colleges and universities, and emphasizing values such as respect for authority, especially in the family, as well as patriotism and other aspects of moral education, in the early grades. Bennett's curriculum strategy was more than a way to avoid frequent demands for more federal financial support for schools; it was a profound attack on many reforms of the 1960s, when students obtained from reluctant administrators more curriculum choice than was enjoyed by any generation of secondary and university students in recent educational history.

During the late 1960s and early 1970s many colleges reduced the number of so-called breadth requirements, especially languages; students won both the right to initiate new courses and a greater voice in educational governance, and they spurred the formation of a plethora of new programs in black, Latino, and women's studies. These were both demeaned by the traditional disciplines as academically "unrigorous" and regarded as a threat to school authorities' prerogatives. Education history of the later 1970s and 1980s can be told in terms of a student disempowerment.

Wrapped in the mantle of the Enlightenment and armed with the rhetoric of education excellence, neoconservatives have turned the wheel at least ninety degrees. Schools have added required courses at all levels, eliminating or sharply reducing the number and extent of electives, especially at the secondary and preprofessional undergraduate levels. Where school officials refused to acknowledge the ideological character of these "reforms" they blamed the growing fiscal crisis for the changes. But Bennett's tenure at the Department of Education provided clear direction for those who had always been uncomfortable with student power. The routinization of reform, a phrase that signifies, among other things, the incorporation of once controversial proposals into bureaucratic procedures, also entails the process by which such proposals are severed from the political struggles that gave practical life to these ideas. The student movement, lacking a broad ideological vision for reasons we will make clear below, was never sufficiently powerful, intergenerationally, to protect most of its gains. Where educational innovations survive they have been watered down to their symbolic value, but they occupy no secure place in the system. For example, many public universities, especially in states with large minority populations, have retained, for political reasons, open admissions policies according to which high school graduates or GED holders may gain admission regardless of grades or academic skills. Simultaneously, legislatures have systematically reduced funds available for reading and writing programs intended to provide the preconditions for academic success. The bureaucratic incorporation of innovations born of sit-ins, mass demonstrations, and alternative universities formed during student strikes, appeared to have been made permanent. But genuine legitimation was really never granted to student-generated courses, tutorials (really an adaptation of the British elite university's core pedagogy), and, most important, courses in marginal and subaltern discourses such as are represented by women's studies, African-American programs, and Puerto Rican and Hispanic studies. School authorities sanctioned pedagogical diversity only so long as the political pressure from within and from outside the universities was powerful.

These programs were made possible by the success of the most radical of the education reforms, particularly the one that is still the chief object of scorn and the main candidate for dismantling: open admissions. The racial and ethnic composition of public colleges and universities was rapidly transformed in the 1970s and remains in the 1980s the target of the educational counterrevolution. Financial aid, fellowships, and other scholarship programs have been drastically cut back by federal and state governments. The Reagan approach to equal opportunity permits only the most economically deprived to avail themselves of these benefits. Students of low- or middle-income families are forced to take out tuition loans while many others are disqualified from these low-interest loans by their income. The assault has also been marked by profound funding reductions in remedial programs; the increasing rigidity of the higher education tracking system, which has made it more difficult for community college graduates to enter four-year institutions; and, most egregiously, frequent state-level "budget crises," resulting in funding cuts that whittle away at the infrastructure of public higher education, particularly at community colleges and the four-

year universities created in the late 1960s to accommodate open enrollment. Bennett led the charge against open admissions, which in
retrospect must be seen in the context of the relatively new 1980s federal policy of dealing with such problems as international economic
competition from Europe and Japan, stagnation, inflation, and the like
by redistributing the pain in favor of the most privileged sectors of the
society.

Institutionalized racism, a permanent feature of many of our systems of public order, especially education, labor, and criminal justice,
is today exacerbated by economic uncertainty. World economic restructuring and its effects on working-class lives has produced more
overt racism among those white workers who, metaphorically, rub
shoulders with blacks and Latinos typically locked into insecure economic niches or in the second economy. For the dirty secret of the past
decade is that white "ethnics," especially those of eastern and southern European origins who occupied well-paid industrial jobs after the
war, have suffered significant deterioration of their living standards.
Capital flight, technologically induced labor displacement, and the
growth of the predominantly nonunion service and industrial sectors
have served as grim reminders that prosperity is not forever. For a large
portion of the 1980s generation of Italian and Polish youth, the last decade has been a disaster; where twenty years earlier jobs were usually
waiting alongside their fathers on a truck, the docks, in steelmills, auto
plants, or in the telephone or gas and electric company, now the mills
are closed down and automation has drastically reduced the demand
for untrained manual labor in many other industries where workers
have been reduced to watchers, or where they maintain highly complex machinery but are not needed as operators. The white kids who
enter neither the military nor police and fire services, half of whom
drop out of high school or do not go on to college, finally get jobs, but
not good ones (unless they manage to get a place in one of the dimin-
ishing number of federally sponsored formal apprenticeship programs, take up a service skill in technical college, or get into a relative's
business). Otherwise they land nonunion retail jobs, jobs as construction laborers rehabilitating houses or building roads, or find their way
into the second economy selling dope of one kind or another.

To their sorrow and amazement many whites have learned about
economic insecurity in the 1980s. But lacking a movement capable of
providing a clear analysis of how and why unemployment, wage reductions, and inflation have conspired to erode their living standards, they
are prone to blame the Japanese, poor blacks, or themselves. After all,
for two generations educational achievement was not understood to

be the basic condition for achieving a decent standard of living. For blue-collar workers unions provided the moral and political equivalent of professional credentials. Then the bottom dropped out.

While it may be true that the past rests like a dead weight on the shoulders of the future and, as Sartre has argued, achieves a factual existence that is hard to overcome, we are helped as much as weighed down by tradition.[1] There are multiple pasts, not a single past that is the object for memory. For example, many black workers whose sons and daughters were forced to enter the second economy can remember how they got jobs in the plant and earned wages that enabled them to own homes, drive late-model cars, and even save for their children's education. Their economic and cultural ideals are formed by these experiences and the victories of the civil rights movement as much as by the collective black experiences of discrimination, poverty, and repression. The cultural program of those who wish to turn back the clock must rely on eliminating these contradictory and multiple pasts both from institutional life and from memory. This is why the civil rights acts of 1965 and 1968 are currently systematically vitiated by the administration's drug war, just as the 1954 Supreme Court decision banning school segregation has been violated as much as implemented for the past thirty-five years.

Aided by compliant state legislatures and courts, executive and police authorities have succeeded in making casual drug use as well as sale a felony, a measure that has contributed centrally to the swollen prison population while depriving drug rehabilitation programs of adequate resources. Drugs have become the occasion for providing police with new powers of search and seizure. The Bush proposals expand funds for more police and enforcement technologies, while cutting the money available for education and rehabilitation. The new retributive framework provides a legal mechanism for controlling black and Latino communities as well as the drug-using educated middle class. Bush, who during his victorious 1988 campaign announced he wanted to be the "education president," has found in the drug war a better political weapon.

The educational policy of the Bush administration, in concert with its drug policy, is to centralize federal power through the exercise of ideological hegemony rather than fiscal policy. This is to be achieved by the creation of a set of national educational standards to which the local school district and its constituent schools are held responsible. These norms are upheld by a series of student performances on standardized tests measuring reading, math, and writing skills. In addition, school administrators and teachers are expected to transmit a checklist of positive "values," chiefly those of work and family linked to the religion of the American way: patriotic, nationalistic signifiers such as free enterprise, American-style democracy, and obedience to constituted authority, that is, law and order and its official bearers. Oppositional or alternative goals such as student empowerment, individuation, creativity and intellectual skepticism embodied in art and music, student participation in curriculum and school governance, and unconventional learning styles and subject matter are to be excluded from approved pedagogical or curricular mandates. In short, the official policy is to wage an ideological offensive to persuade local school authorities to see themselves as moral agents of intellectual standardization.

As with any standard, those who fail to measure up are consigned to subordinate niches in the economic and status order; in our culture this also designates them as morally inferior. The trouble with this regime of social sorting is that it assumes the truth of a now outstripped reality. Until the mid-1970s, black and white school leavers without technical or academic credentials occupied different places in work hierarchies from those possessing credentials, but many shared pieces of an expanding pie. Labor shortages during the Second World War and the postwar economic expansion, especially in production industries, combined with a high level of union seniority protections to afford black men a fairly secure place in factories. This state of affairs was sharply contrasted to the black industrial exclusions that marked the post-Civil War period when employers preferred the labor of immigrants to that of native-born blacks. By 1960, the days when blacks entered an industrial plant only as strikebreakers and laborers remained a bitter memory for black men, but this bitterness was softened by the expectation that their sons would have dignified jobs at the plant.

However, in an age when factories stand empty amid the rubble of the cities, and credentials remain an important rite of passage to entry-level technical and managerial jobs as well as being an absolute precondition of professional occupations, a student's failure to meet approved academic standards is tantamount to a sentence from a court of law. The accused is condemned to what some political economists term the secondary labor market: industries in highly competitive markets, with low technological development, and offering nonunion wages and working conditions. Or, alternatively, such youths enter the informal or underground economy, the leading activities of which are drugs, prostitution, and gambling. In both cases, the child is imprisoned in the inner city. Thus the close link between the philosophy and objectives of the drug war and those of education policy. From the point of view of the drug warriors, the righteous wages of academic failure—jail—accrue with the consequence of entering the second economy.

Public discourse on social issues, abetted by the martial intonations of the drug war, has all but abandoned the language of hope, even the feeble efforts of liberal predecessors who recognized the obligation of the established order to address the problem of alienation. Twenty years ago the dominant ideology recognized that the formation of the second economy was a structural consequence of inequality, the most overt manifestation of which is poverty. Thus, although individuals (anomalously not the economic system) remained the object of social policy, and treatment (everything from therapy, schooling, and income to methadone maintenance or job training), remained the method, the state expanded the scope of the welfare state, rather than that of police forces, to buttress its legitimacy. This policy proved to be merely a brief interlude in an otherwise unrelieved program to coerce the poor into obedience, and for this reason cannot be attributed primarily to the liberalism of the post-New Deal Democratic party, to the unpopularity of the war in Southeast Asia, or even to postwar prosperity, although these elements were part of the constellation that led to change. A sufficient explanation for the crisis of state legitimation that urged this policy may be found in the black freedom explosion of 1955-68, especially the escalation of this movement from the search for legal sanctions for antidiscrimination practices, to nonviolent protest, to the urban insurgencies of the mid-1960s (which were derisively named "riots").

The genius of Lyndon Johnson for handling protest and opposition before this explosion was never better displayed than in his skillful management of the split in the civil rights movement that accompanied the 1964 Democratic convention. There the incipient black militants and their white allies demanded that the convention seat an alternate delegation to that of the official Mississippi Democratic party. A "compromise" was put over on the dissenters, but there was no question of not supporting Johnson's renomination even after he had vehemently opposed seating the Freedom Democrats, as the integrated civil rights party was called. The militants were isolated in this skirmish; Johnson seemed to have discovered a formula for co-opting the civil rights mainstream, which would also be seen in his sponsorship of the Civil Rights Act of 1964. The formula consisted in his resistance to structural reforms, while at the same time sponsoring legal remedies for racial discrimination, and education and training to ameliorate economic inequality. For a time the strategy of dealing with racism through enlarging mainstream opportunities for blacks seemed to work for some, and proponents could safely argue that, given more resources, poverty would become a bitter but distant memory by the end of the century. However, the fires of anger among black youth had never been banked. By 1968, portions of a dozen American cities were in ruins and the glorious anticommunist war in Asia was going badly, forcing the administration to pour ever-increasing resources of armed forces and equipment into losing battles. The Great Society, Johnson's version of post-New Deal statism, was falling apart, a victim of the escalation of the war (except for the inadequate but lingering income, training, and education programs). Amid the din of disapproval, Johnson discreetly retired, but not before he had sponsored the greatest period of government-initiated social reform since the 1930s. During his administration billions of dollars were spent on a gaggle of programs ostensibly aimed at helping the poor enter the mainstream. The most dramatic achievement of the Great Society was to have substantially enlarged the size of the black middle class. Many cities employed black professionals to head antipoverty agencies; a new generation of black elected officials emerged from these programs and from the small but growing black managerial elite within large corporations; and affirmative action legislation produced some major shifts in the admissions policies of professional schools.

Parallel to the established drug maintenance programs attached to hospitals, all over the country drug rehabilitation centers and halfway houses were funded by federal and state agencies but usually run and staffed by ex-addicts. At first, the core idea of the centers was to reproduce the spirit of the counterculture—which despite many shortcomings was and is far more democratic and inclusive than the larger society. The guiding theory of these programs was that many addicts refused to abandon drugs not only because they craved the substance but, more to the point, because they craved the community around drugs, which effectively addressed the need for intimacy even as mainstream culture rewarded only achievement and held up the nuclear family as the institution of preference. The centers recognized that as early as the 1950s, suburbanization, redevelopment of the increasingly black center cities, and other forms of rationalization were dividing people from themselves. Even when the "therapy" was entirely authoritarian insofar as it denied in theory and practice one of the bases of the drug culture—pleasure—the ideological commitment of most of these "houses" was to create or re-create group life as the crucial antidote, rather than accepting as inevitable the alternatives of synthetic drugs or jail.

The 1960s were also a time for educational change, especially for kids, rich and poor, for whom the system had no room. We do not want to equate the needs of the two major constituents of alternative schools: poor kids and alienated kids of the middle class. The poor kids, most of them of color, opted out of school success nearly as much as they were rejected by school authorities for reasons that parallel traditional working-class rejections of school knowledge: to surrender to the curriculum entails more than choosing to acquire cultural capital. That is, school knowledge is loaded in class terms. It frequently signifies the eventual severance of the individual from her or his community, after an uneasy elementary school experience during which friendships are strained by academic achievement ("smart" boys are often labeled "fags" "ass-kissers," and other culturally disapproved categories when they do well in class; working-class girls suffer similar ostracism).[2] Needless to say, as for many kids of white working-class backgrounds, the marginality of poor kids of color is coded in their speech and their different conceptions of the function of language. From the perspective of those who believe in and teach standard English, to belong to the speech communities of subaltern classes and races is a crucial signifier, not merely of difference but also of exclusion. For a poor or working-class kid to achieve high grades in school environments necessarily involves massive code switches. Since the child commonly speaks one of the many versions of the vernacular, he or she learns standard English as a second language. Gradually the successful student who accepts the baggage of social mobility and professionalization that comes with buying into the curriculum must give up her or his first language, a procedure reminiscent of the turn-of-the-century practice of melting linguistic and cultural difference. In contrast, alternative schools are places where young people may discover a public voice without making many compromises. Many of these schools overtly recognized that kids had the right to their own vernacular without suffering stigmatization, and they encouraged kids' indigenous communities as crucial sites where social identity is forged.

Concomitant to the emergence of the movements for education reform that were inspired by black freedom ideology, linguists and anthropologists challenged the conventional scientific wisdom according to which possessing an expanded vocabulary, and imbibing the official version of syntactical and grammatical rules, was identical to possessing the capacity for complex thinking. Accordingly, black and working-class speech, which some social linguists coded as "restricted" to the functions of unskilled and semiskilled labor and cultural communities built around factories and ghettos, was no longer construed to signify a naturalistic or even a socially constructed absence of intelligence.[3]

In contrast, many liberal educators who accepted the intimate link between speech, language, and class and thereby rejected genetic explanations for the failure of working-class and black school leavers to master the curriculum, nevertheless retained explanatory models that preserved the correlation between class and school intelligence. Liberals were prepared to accept that kids of working-class backgrounds and of color suffered deficits in acquiring legitimate school knowledge because of discrimination and economic and social inequality, but were unprepared for the claims of subaltern groups and their advocates that legitimate intellectual knowledge bore the marks of the class and race system. For even sympathetic educators, any position that questioned the utter rationality of the canon or indicated that the canon signified something other than the progressive achievements of the human mind was blasphemous. Here the distinction between progressivism and postmodernism in education becomes most stark: unlike conservatives who blame the victims for their failure to meet established educational standards, the progressives want to make room for the excluded within the established culture; in contrast, postmodernism asserts no privileged place, aside from power considerations, for the art works, scientific achievements, and philosophical traditions by which Western culture legitimates itself.

Dell Hymes, William Labov, and their colleagues have produced a theoretical and empirical counterweight to the dominant progressive views. Labov's detailed linguistic ethnographics purport to demonstrate the equivalence of black speech patterns at the logical plane with those of standard discourse. He claims to show that Basil Bernstein's distinction between the restricted and elaborated code cannot be articulated to the deficits conventionally associated with class and race. Drawing from dialogic speech of lower-class black communities, Labov displays the complexity of vernacular speech acts. In effect, he claims that black speech is a different language from English, but that it observes the syntactic and semantic rules of any language in Western culture. Further, the universality of both language and its logical rules, a characteristic claim of structural linguistics, is reasserted in terms of the ethnographic procedures of sociolinguistics. Armed with these results, many black and Latino educators opposed both the neoracist genetic arguments for black inferiority of William Shockley and David Hernnstein and Oscar Lewis's conventional "culturalist" explanation for intergenerational poverty.[4]

The 1960s witnessed the emergence of an educational theory that argued that preserving the richness of black culture entailed preserving black language. Accordingly, postmodern educators tried to legitimate subaltern literary and other cultural works as intellectual equivalents of so-called high culture. Black scholars proposed an alternative black literary and musical canon; similarly, the rising feminist movement of the same period spawned a canon of women's literature that dated from Sappho of Lesbos and was enriched by works by contemporary black as well as white women writers. Simultaneously, Latinos began proselytizing the idea of "the Americas," and proposed the works of the "Boom" as the most vital literary movement of the postwar era. In the 1970s, the literary public as well as critics became aware of names such as García Márquez, Fuentes, Cortázar, and Vargas Llosa; the 1980s brought works by Puig and Valenzuela into translation.[5] But Western xenophobia dies hard. After twenty years during which these works have been widely read and praised, mainstream literary scholarship has made little effort to incorporate them into the twentieth-century canon alongside Joyce, Eliot, Pound, Kafka, Faulkner and other modernists (with the possible exception of Borges and García Márquez).

All of these efforts remained partially constrained by modernist assumptions: artists, scholars, and critics wanted to establish the ground for inclusion of subaltern discourses within academic precincts as well as in publishing and the art world. Thus, women and people of color fashioned their assault on hegemonic culture in terms of the demand for a place in its ample sun. Just as the civil rights movement felt obliged, throughout the 1960s, to simultaneously assert black autonomy and inclusion into the white world, educational and art movements moved in contradictory directions: on the one hand, they attempted to develop aesthetic and social conceptions incommensurable with the mainstream; on the other, they asserted equivalence and demanded to be recognized and rewarded by the dominant world.

The strategy of school reform that refused to accept the superiority of standard (white) middle-class English need not signify the reproduction of class difference. Rather, the schools at all levels were obliged to recognize the preservation of cultural difference, not as an intellectual and economic deficit, but as a human right (if not an intellectual and aesthetic equivalent) to which political and economic institutions must adapt. Having asserted linguistic equivalence (whose theoretical basis was a reading of structuralist linguistics), educational pluralists recognized that kids of color and working-class kids needed to study English as a second language, to master the dominant codes of commercial, professional, and political discourse for the purposes of survival. This latter objective was not, however, confused with genuine education. Rather it was conceived as a training objective of public schools and plainly subordinate to providing to black and Latino youth (and later to girls and women) the cultural signifiers of identity without which the concept of moral and political agency is not possible.

The 1960s witnessed the beginnings of an approach to education that radically diverged from the progressive tradition, even if many of the tenets of this new approach built on progressive ideas, some elements of which we choose to name "postmodern." With progressives, especially those who trace their lineage to John Dewey, postmodern educators demanded of theoretical knowledge that it demonstrate its relevance to practice, and insisted on the importance of practice and everyday culture for the constitution of theoretical knowledge. While it can be shown that this position is close to one facet of John Dewey's educational philosophy,[6] the leading edge of progressive education had interpreted the relation between knowledge and practice in a different way. For progressives, practice was the test of truth, and was understood as a vital pedagogical tool, but they largely ignored its transformative role. Following from the dialectical relationship between knowledge and practice, postmodern educators believe the curriculum can best inspire learning only when school knowledge builds upon the tacit knowledge derived from the cultural resources that students already possess. For example, electronically mediated popular culture, which, it can be shown, is produced from a constellation of influences of which black speech is a crucial element, is treated by postmodern education as a legitimate object of knowledge. In contrast to practices that uncritically transmit apparently unrelated disciplines of math, literature, geography, and history, organized in discrete time periods of the school day, the teacher attempts to integrate these knowledges within a series of projects chosen jointly with students. The project may be a study of rap music, sports, the Civil War, neighborhoods, youth in society, race relations, sexuality, or almost anything else.

For postmodern education it is not a question of substituting popular culture for traditional, high-culture topics. Instead, the traditional curriculum must meet the test of relevance to a student-centered learning regime where "relevance" is not coded as the rejection of tradition but is a criterion for determining inclusion. It is the task of the teacher to persuade students that these knowledges contribute to helping them learn what they want to know. In any case the canons are no longer taught as self-evident repositories of enlightenment. Rather, the teacher is obliged to encourage students to interrogate the values underlying a work of literature, or a traditional history, the bulk of which are devoted to the contributions of Great Men or are narratives of canonical events.

Under this regime, educators are forced to rethink the nature of legitimate knowledge—to ask, for example, what is the significance, apart from sorting, of the predominant operational approach to mathematics? For it must be admitted that math teaching has rarely been oriented to the concepts of the various branches of the field. Learning the procedures helps students to solve prefigured problems, and the exercise surely measures, to some degree, students' mental discipline and their ability to abstract from particulars. But math pedagogy as currently practiced does not necessarily develop an ability to use and discover mathematical concepts among nonspecialists. On the contrary, it encourages the student to learn the logical processes that follow from accepting the axioms of the discipline and its postulates. As opposed to the intellectual claims made on behalf of math education by those who insist on expanding the role of these subjects in primary and secondary schools, math is generally taught as an applied discipline, not as an intellectual pursuit. It is interesting to note here that these issues are rarely if ever addressed by neoconservative proponents of "excellence."

Now there are many pleasures in mathematics that commend the discipline to dedicated study, but to include math as part of a developmentally oriented curriculum requires rationale and elaboration beyond the spurious claims made for it in the current campaigns to strengthen its role in education. Similarly, while knowledge of the main currents of scientific thought can assist students to become citizens in the determination of public policies in this vital arena, school authorities "sell" science as high-class knowledge without explaining its importance for daily life. Not unexpectedly, absent a rationale for subjecting themselves to the rigors of natural scientific knowledge, high school students, especially girls, are often intimidated by the formulaic law-like pedagogy of even the most dedicated teachers. In recent years, a counterweight to this abstract approach has entered the debate. Some teachers center science learning on ecological issues and try to demonstrate the importance of theoretical knowledge for solving one of the most pressing social and political questions of our day: the degree to which the domination of nature by industrial and consumer society distorts our interaction with the environment and may threaten human survival. Thus the criterion of relevance is not to be construed as a way to weaken "rigorous" education, but it does challenge the instrumentalism characteristic of science and math pedagogies.

We describe this educational strategy as an important aspect of the postmodern intellectual shift that occurred in the late 1960s and early 1970s in the wake of the rise of new social movements of youth, race, and feminism. As the members of these movements ineluctably turned to the education system because of its perceived centrality to their life chances, they were confronted with a canon of Great Works constituted as Wisdom, which asserted its superiority to their own cultures. In the panoply of knowledges, intellectual knowledge as interpreted by the academy is privileged over other types: practical knowledge, "useless" knowledge, gossip, folk wisdom, and so on.[7] Moreover, popular knowledges do not count as intellectual knowledge because they are ungrounded in an explicit philosophy and methodology that can be evaluated from a foundational perspective. For this reason, one position argues that contemporary popular culture can become an object of legitimate intellectual inquiry in the same way that ethnomusicology was invented to collect and classify folk songs and other traditional musical expressions, but only if it is integrated into one of the accepted disciplines—aesthetics, sociology, history, and so on—and, further, is subjected to methodological rigor.[8]

While the move away from an exclusive preoccupation with the high-cultural canon is surely welcome, it is different from a postmodern perspective, which interrogates the priority of canonicity itself. More particularly, postmodern education deconstructs the canon in crucial ways: in the humanities, the idea of a "universal" aesthetics against which art may be judged has come under attack. Postmodern criticism shows that the category of aesthetics presupposes a social hierarchy whose key is the description of exclusions, which are imbedded in the compositional conventions employed in the works, not only in the institutions of artistic dissemination.

Perhaps more controversial is the fostering by postmodernists of the claims to intellectual validity of marginal discourses in the sciences and social sciences, especially those that refuse, on philosophical or ideological grounds, to observe accepted algorithms of inquiry. At issue is the question of diversity in ways of producing knowledge and, more broadly, the validity of the distinction between legitimate intellectual knowledge and other kinds of knowledge. For example, the privileged status of quantitative methods of research in the life sciences and increasingly in the social sciences, is not generally subject to dispute. Without substantial argument from mainstream scholars, models derived from physics and particularly statistical mechanics have been applied to these sciences, and those who remain wedded to evolutionary or other historical and experimental frameworks are rapidly being marginalized.

Even more controversial for the social sciences is the status of social knowledge that is acquired through "informal" means, such as are provided by various oral traditions whose characteristic form is the narrative and whose "scientific" community is constituted by friendship rather than professional networks. As is well known, it is precisely the issue of its universality that is put in question by postmodernism. As with black speech, we argue that popular knowledge, even if it does not possess the same apparatus of inquiry that has marked legitimate academic knowledge, is nevertheless a form of intellectual knowledge. Jazz buffs, rock music fans, and those who closely follow various professional and college sports are required to abstract from the particular to find commensurable and incommensurable features of various genres within their fields. The degrees of specialization that mark the discourses of popular culture are no more parochial than those of academic disciplines. In "legitimate" social sciences, for example, there is an increasing tendency to affirm the integrity of the disciplinary canon over the effort to cross over among the intellectual canons of the five major disciplines. Moreover, the respective master narratives of the disciplines have typically broken down over the past twenty years, so that, for example, the professional associations in sociology and psychology are constituted mostly by "sections," each having a canon not shared by others within their own field.

A case in point is the reception of the work of Sigmund Freud, which is widely read among cultural and social theorists and remains powerfully influential among psychoanalytic clinicians, but has lost its impact on newer clinical models. Moreover, Freudian categories have almost no importance for the majority of experimental, social, or cognitive psychologists for whom the pyschoanalytic paradigm of human behavior, particularly the regulative function of the unconscious, has only historical interest. One could demonstrate the same development in American sociology, where the "classical" tradition of Marx, Weber, and Durkheim is elaborated by some, but ignored by most, for whom an antitheoretical statistical or ethnographic empiricism suffices to comprehend social life. Thus debates within social sciences center increasingly upon competing methodologies for aggregating and analyzing survey data. For much of contemporary social science there simply are no canonical theoretical works, since theory itself is under a shadow. Instead, theory is subsumed under "value orientations," really research ideologies in which metacategories are tacitly employed but rarely if ever acknowledged.[9]

This development illustrates the ambivalence of postmodern conditions. The continuity between an emancipatory postmodernism and modernism is that they share a critical, reflexive approach to knowledge. The challenge to foundational or master narratives does not relieve postmodern knowledge communities of the obligation to answer for their choices, even as these choices are provisional and viewed skeptically and even ironically. Right-wing postmodernism verges on a nihilistic renunciation of engaged intellectual and political activity. In the recent past, the post-Marxist shift to this version of postmodernism has produced a widespread impression that this right-wing version is identical with what we mean by "the postmodern." However, we have tried to show that in education, social inquiry, and philosophy this characterization is, to say the least, incomplete. It best describes the fate of intellectual communities and individuals whose Marxism was as uncritical as their post-Marxism is despairing.

These cases illustrate our claim that the once-powerful cultural ideal of science, with its elaboration of axiomatic foundations and leading postulates, is to say the least in disarray in academic social science. Needless to say, parallel examples could be drawn in the humanities. In Anglo-American philosophy since the war we have witnessed the displacement of once-dominant American pragmatism in favor of analytic philosophy, but the monopoly scientific philosophy enjoyed until the late 1970s is today under siege by a revival of ethics and the antipositivisms of neo-Marxist, neopragmatist, feminist, and other perspectives.[10] Rather than rejecting analysis, competing paradigms have tried to effect a synthesis, and have won significant constituencies among philosophers. There is no question of a new paradigm replacing the older one, as Kuhn describes the history of science. Instead, it is more likely that philosophy, which has traditionally aspired to join physics in unifying the sciences, must settle for the presence of a plurality of philosophical discourses, radically decentered within the profession. At the same time, as we argue in chapter 6, the integrity of the disciplines is being challenged in theory and research: on the one hand, there is greater integration of once discrete discursive positions; on the other, the disciplines are themselves rent so that what is meant by integration cannot be equated with the formation of new master narratives.

Of course, the state of the arts and sciences bears on issues of curriculum not just in the United States but throughout the world. Dialectical and historical materialism and its leading texts and concepts, especially in social sciences and the humanities, have dominated Soviet, Eastern European, Chinese, and Cuban schooling and professional life for two generations. Today, the universalist claims of Marxist science are targets of both an action-critique and a serious intellectual challenge. Is the outcome likely to destroy or completely delegitimate Marxism in the countries of "really existing" socialism? Probably not. Instead, these societies have already witnessed the emergence of a plurality of discourses—social and ethical theories, philosophical perspectives, aesthetic criteria—none of which will be in a position to impose its particular vision as a universal standard. Under these circumstances, Marxism is already obliged to contend with the claims of competing paradigms. For the first time since achieving state power, communism is obliged to persuade students, intellectuals, and workers, rather than asserting the truth of its leading concepts; to fight for intellectual and moral leadership instead of merely imposing it— provided, that is, these societies enter into a democratic period in which human rights, especially of speech and publication, are guaranteed.

The difficulties currently experienced by subaltern discourses in the United States have highlighted the unity of conservative and liberal cultural ideologies: with notable exceptions, the possibility of aesthetics itself is never challenged, nor is the possibility of universal sciences of humans and of nature, the validity of which may be established by experimental and logical proofs. The modernists may grant the right of marginal science and art to be heard but would restrict the obligation of the state to support work that is deemed by recognized leaders to be outside or against the mainstream. This hypocritical stance is like that of the Congress that remains unable to abolish legal abortions but denies to poor women the means to obtain them.

This prompts us to return to an earlier theme: By what means should school curricula be determined? Where are the appropriate sites of curriculum development? In most cases, the authority to decide what constitutes legitimate and necessary knowledge is vested by legislative bodies in special school authorities who decide requirements with respect to which areas of knowledge must be studied as well as textbook selection. This power corresponds to standardized tests to determine competence, which are devised, in most cases, by experts working under the supervision of state and local authorities.

One can imagine a postmodern high school. One of its more distinctive features is that what is to be studied is a matter for local decision making. Higher bodies—state and local school boards, principals and department chairs—may propose courses, texts, and pedagogies. And parents may express their concerns and try to influence what is taught and how. But the students and teachers have final authority. The accountability criteria established by legislatures, according to which curricula must conform to standards established by administrative and political bodies, are rescinded. There are no requirements imposed from above. Instead, students and teachers negotiate which courses, if any, are to be required. Students may propose courses and pursue them as self-studies and teachers may offer courses. Whether students choose to study math, science, literature, or any other course or sequence of courses is subject to extensive planning in which they have an equal role with teachers. Moreover, they engage in curriculum discussions with teachers during which teachers and administrators try to persuade them to follow a regimen of study. The classroom is not routinely organized in the traditional monovocal format, with a lecture, questions and answers after the lecture, and workbooks. In fact, the normal class (the length and frequency of which are indeterminate) now resembles an open classroom where small groups of students are simultaneously studying different aspects of the course subject matter, and others are engaged in individual tutorials with the teacher or another knowledgeable person. Frequently, these groups are to be found in a library or doing field work. And they are obliged to study fewer things than are required by the typical secondary school curriculum. They may study deeply in one or two areas of knowledge for an entire year. The teacher employs a wide variety of pedagogic styles, including lectures to the entire group or to small groups. Perhaps the most difficult aspect of this pedagogy is to find ways to articulate the sciences with the humanities.

The difficulty consists in this: the leading philosophical premise of both the natural and the human sciences is the incommensurability of their respective discourses, except those social sciences that try to reduce the object of inquiry to particles or systems, in which case they naturalize the social rather than finding a meeting ground. This tradition may be traced to the *Geisteswissenschaften* school of Dilthey and Ranke in the late nineteenth century, to Bergson, and to contemporary theorists such as Foucault, as well as to the social psychology emanating from Mead and the phenomenologists. Despite their differences, the philosophers of the human sciences have resisted reduction, but have also resisted comparison with natural sciences. Habermas goes so far as to claim that, just as work creates, in many ways, objects for appropriation, the study of nature similarly refers to such objects, while the human sciences address interaction. Natural science rests its claim to incommensurability on its claim to precision, at least in comparison to the extreme methodological confusion of the human sciences. In any case, this split has led to educational segregation, as well as providing the ideological basis for establishing hierarchies of knowledge according to which mathematics and physics rest at the pinnacle.

The fundamental requirement of an adequate challenge to the acceptance of incommensurability consists in a critique of the epistemological foundations of the sciences, with respect to their claim to represent in logical forms the real world, and with respect to the efficacy and validity of observation and experimental proof, which provide the grounds for regarding all knowledge as ultimately empirically based. We not only must show the effects of scientific knowledge *cum* technology on the social world and "nature" but also must make problematic the assumptions upon which the truth claims of science are grounded. These critiques can be woven into curricula without undermining the value or the relevance of scientific knowledge. It seems possible that scientific knowledge can be made available and accessible to all students if it is removed from its absolutist pedestal.

The values that constitute postmodern education are those of empowerment in the most profound meaning of the term. Students can appropriate the canon of legitimate thought without a prior pledge of reverence. In fact, the power of these texts may stimulate religious fervor in some and skepticism in others. This attitude violates some recent defenses of the Western canon by some educators who claim mastery is awarded to those who submit themselves to the pleasures of canonical texts. Postmodern educators grant the wisdom contained in such texts but suspend judgment as to their power of universal persuasion in our heterodox social environment. Freedom consists in the capacity of people and groups to transform knowledge in accordance with their own plans.

Obviously, we realize that these reflections imply profound changes in the goals, systems of governance, and curricula of schools. To formally empower parents, teachers, and students without an extensive debate on what we want of our schools is to prepare for likely failure. On the other hand, without a vision of transformed power relations within schools and the larger society, education reforms will inevitably be reversed or used to maintain the existing authorities. Under these circumstances the immediate losers are the kids, from whom the education enterprise derives its legitimacy. Schools may not measure up to the claims made for them by educators of all ideological persuasions. They may not be our frontline in the struggle against social disintegration; many writers have shown that schools are not unambiguously distinct from those forces that produce social relations. Nevertheless, to the degree schools are viewed as special institutions in which practices are not obliged to mimic those of either the workplace or the state, they provide, at least potentially, the space for difference if not opposition. In short, schools may be arenas for contesting increasing regimentation, according to which all public institutions are obliged to subordinate themselves to centralized authority. The special place of schools derives from the "other tradition" of democracy and popular political and social power, in which the existence of public schools is, historically, one of the great victories. These traditions have been weakened in the past forty years, but are by no means dead. The new educational movements for parent,teacher, and student power over curriculum in evidence in Chicago, New York, and many smaller communities attest to the vitality of these traditions in schools. Remarkably, after a decade of conservative battering, the cultural ideal of democratic schooling articulated in new languages of possibility has returned. As did our previous book *Education under Siege*, this book tries to advance the discussion of some of the theoretical and practical aspects of this new movement.

Notes

1. Jean-Paul Sartre, *Critique of Dialectical Reason* (London: New Left Books, 1976).

2. The classic study that discuses the practical consequences for working-class kids of obedience to or rebellion against school authority is Paul Willis, *Learning to Labor* (New York: Columbia University Press, 1981).

3. See especially William Labov, *Language in the Inner City* (Philadelphia: University of Pennsylvania Press, 1972); *Sociolinguistic Patterns* (Philadelphia: University of Pennsylvania Press, 1972); Dell Hymes, "The Ethnography of Speaking," in T. Gladwin and Dell Hymes, eds., *Anthropology and Human Behavior* (The Anthropological Society of Washington, n.d.).

4. Oscar Lewis, *La Vida* (New York: Random House, 1966).

5. Gabriel García Márquez, *One Hundred Years of Solitude, Autumn of the Patriarch*, and other works; Carlos Fuentes, *Terra Nuestra*; Julio Cortázar, *Hopscotch* and also *Manual for Mañuel*; Mario Puig, *Betrayed by Rita Hayworth, A Buenos Aires Affair, Kiss of the Spider Woman*; Mario Vargas Llosa, *Green House, Conversations in a Cathedral*, and other works; Jorge Luis Borges, *Labyrinths*.

6. John Dewey, *Democracy in Education*, Middle Works, vol. 9 (Carbondale: Southern Illinois University Press, 1980).

7. Fritz Machlup, *The Production and Distribution of Knowledge in the United States* (New York: Columbia University Press, 1962, 1969).

8. A standard and intelligent version of empirically based theorizing is Arthur I. Stinchcombe, *Constructing Social Theories* (New York: Harcourt, Brace and World, 1968).

9. Perhaps the leading philosopher of this movement is Richard Rorty. See his *Philosophy and the Mirror of Nature* (Princeton: Princeton University Press, 1979) and *Consequences of Pragmatism* (Minneapolis: University of Minnesota Press, 1982).

10. Stanley Aronowitz and Henry A. Giroux, *Education under Siege* (South Hadley, Mass.: Bergin & Garvey Press, 1985).

CHAPTER 2

TEXTUAL AUTHORITY, CULTURE, AND THE POLITICS OF LITERACY

Since the second term of the Reagan administration, the debate on education has taken a new turn. Now, as before, the tone is principally set by the right, but its position has been radically altered. The importance of linking educational reform to the needs of big business has continued to influence the debate, while demands that schools provide the skills necessary for domestic production and expanding capital abroad have slowly given way to an overriding emphasis on schools as sites of cultural production. The emphasis on cultural production can be seen in current attempts to address the issue of cultural literacy, in the development of national curriculum boards, and in reform initiatives bent on providing students with the language, knowledge, and values necessary to preserve the essential traditions of Western civilization.[1] The right's position on cultural production in the schools arises from a consensus that the problems faced by the United States can no longer be reduced to those of educating students in the skills they will need to occupy jobs in more advanced and middle-range occupational levels in such areas as computer programming, financial analysis, and electronic machine repair.[2] Instead, the emphasis must be switched to the current cultural crisis, which can be traced to the broader ideological tenets of the progressive education movement that dominated the curriculum after the Second World War. These include the pernicious doctrine of cultural relativism, according to which canonical texts of the Western intellectual tradition may not be held superior to others; the notion that student experience should qualify as a viable form of knowledge; and the idea that ethnic, racial, gender, and other relations play a significant role in accounting for the development and influence of mainstream intellectual culture. On this account, the 1960s proved disastrous to the preservation of the inherited virtues of Western culture. Relativism systematically downgraded the value of key literary and philosophical traditions, giving equal weight to the dominant knowledge of the "Great Books" and to an emergent potpourri of "degraded" cultural attitudes. Allegedly, the last twenty years have witnessed the virtual loss of those revered traditions that constitute the core of the Western heritage. The unfortunate legacy that has emerged has resulted in a generation of cultural illiterates. In this view, not only the American economy but civilization itself is at risk.

Allan Bloom (1987) and E. D. Hirsch (1987) represent different versions of the latest and most popular conservative thrust for educational reform. Each, in his own way, represents a frontal attack aimed at providing a programmatic language with which to defend schools as cultural sites, that is, as institutions responsible for reproducing the knowledge and values necessary to advance the historical virtues of Western culture. Hirsch presents his view of cultural restoration through a concept of literacy that focuses on the basic structures of language, and applies this version of cultural literacy to the broader consideration of the needs of the business community, as well as to the maintenance of American institutions. His view of literacy represents an attack on educational theories that validate student experience as a key component of educational formation and curriculum development. For Hirsch, the new service economy requires employees who can write a memo, read within a specific cultural context, and communicate through a national language composed of the key words of Western culture. In the same spirit, Bloom offers a much wider critique of education. Advancing a claim that schools have contributed to the instrumentalization of knowledge and that the population has fallen victim to rampant relativism and anti-intellectualism, Bloom proposes a series of education reforms that privileges a fixed idea of Western culture organized around a core curriculum based on the old Great Books:

> Of course, the only serious solution [for reform in higher education] is almost universally rejected: the good old Great Books approach, in which a liberal education means reading certain generally recognized classical texts, just reading them, letting them dictate what the questions are and the method of

approaching them—not forcing them into categories we make
up, not treating them as historical products, but trying to read
them as their authors wished them to be read. . . . But one
thing is certain: wherever the Great Books make up a central
part of the curriculum, the students are excited and satisfied,
feel they are doing something that is independent and
fulfilling, getting something from the university they cannot get
elsewhere. The very fact of this special experience, which leads
nowhere beyond itself, provides them with a new alternative
and a respect for study itself. (344)

This propensity for making sweeping claims without even a shred of
evidence raises serious questions about the nature of Bloom's position
as well as the quality of his own scholarship. Moreover, Bloom's position is hardly novel. It has been with us since the Enlightenment and
has long been invoked as an argument for the reproduction of elites. It
is a position that advocates a social system in which a select cadre of
intellectuals, economically privileged groups, and their professional
servants are the only individuals deemed fit to possess the culture's sacred canon of knowledge, which assures their supremacy.

Both of these books represent the logic of a new cultural offensive,
one of the most elaborate conservative educational manifestos to appear in decades. But it is important to recognize that this offensive represents a form of textual authority that not only legitimates a particular
version of Western civilization as well as an elitist notion of the canon,
but also serves to exclude all those other discourses, whether from the
new social movements or from other sources of opposition, which attempt to establish different grounds for the production and organization of knowledge. In effect, the new cultural offensive is not to be understood simply as a right-wing argument for a particular version of
Western civilization or as a defense for what is seen as a legitimate academic canon; instead, both of these concerns have to be seen as part
of a broader struggle over textual authority. In this case, the notion of
textual authority is about the right-wing shift from the discourse of
class to the broader relationship between knowledge and power, and
the struggle to control the very grounds on which knowledge is produced and legitimated. What is at issue here is not simply how different discourses function to reference particular forms of intellectual,
ethical, and social relations but how power works as both a medium
and outcome of what we might call a form of textual politics.

Textual authority is both pedagogical and political. As a social and
historical construction, textual authority offers readers particular subject positions, ideological references that provide but do not rigidly

determine particular views of the world. As a pedagogical practice, the text has to be read not simply as a study in the production of ideology but as part of a wider circuit of power that calls into play broader institutional practices and social structures. In effect, textual authority represents the medium and outcome of a pedagogical struggle over the relationship between knowledge and power as well as a struggle over the construction and the development of the political subject. Needless to say, Bloom and Hirsch represent forms of textual authority linked to a cultural practice that have broad implications for educational reform and for the wider crisis in democracy. We intend to analyze, in this chapter, the ideological and pedagogical content of these books in the context of the current debates, beginning with an analysis of Bloom's *The Closing of the American Mind*.

Bloom's critique of American education does not address the indifference of schools to the realities of the international marketplace, as in the old technicist discourse that reduces schooling to job training. Instead, Bloom attacks modernity, especially what he considers the rampant relativism that marks the last one hundred years of Western history. Like José Ortega y Gasset, his illustrious predecessor, Bloom seeks to restore the dominance of Platonism—that is, the belief in the transhistorical permanence of forms of truth—to education. Where President Reagan's secretary of education, William Bennett, and the older elitists reiterated the call for "excellence," but never succeeded in articulating its substance, Bloom presents his proposals in more concrete terms.

Bloom's attack on liberal educational practice and the philosophy that underlies it is a sobering reminder that political and social analyses, which have identified themselves with modernity as a critique of advanced industrial societies, constitute powerful weapons in the hands of both the right and the left. Here we have all the elements of an elitist sensibility: abhorrence of mass culture; a rejection of experience as the arbiter of taste and pedagogy; and a sweeping attack on what is called "cultural relativism," especially on those who want to place popular culture, ethnic and racially based cultures, and cultures grounded in sexual communities (either feminist or gay and lesbian) on a par with classical Western traditions. For conservatives, each of these elements represents a form of anti-intellectualism that threatens the moral authority of the state. Consequently, much more than economic survival is at stake: at issue is the survival of Western civilization as it represents itself through 2,500 years of philosophy, historiography, and literature.

Bloom's sweeping agenda intends to eliminate culture as a serious object of knowledge. According to Bloom, the culturalist perspective is what Plato meant by the allegory of the cave. We are prevented from seeing the sunlight by culture, which is the enemy of what Bloom calls "openness." Although vaguely apologetic on the subject, Bloom ends up arguing that Western tradition is superior to non-Western cultures precisely because its referent is not "cultural" but is the universal and context-free love of wisdom; for the underlying ethic of Western civilization, according to Bloom, is its capacity to transcend the immediate circumstances of daily life in order to reach the good life. Lower cultures are inevitably tied to "local knowledge"—to family and community values and beliefs, which are overwhelmingly context-specific. As it happened in the course of history, the Greeks managed to teach some thinkers—Bloom being one—the way to universal truth.

For Bloom, the teachings of Plato and Socrates provide the critical referents with which to excoriate contemporary culture. Bloom systematically devalues the music, sexuality, and pride of youth, and traces what he envisions as the gross excesses of the 1960s (the real object of his attack) to the pernicious influence of German philosophy from Nietzsche to Heidegger as refracted through the mindless relativism of modernizers. Feminism is equated with "libertinism," or making sex easy; "affirmative action now institutionalizes the worst aspects of separatism"; and rock music "has the beat of sexual intercourse" and cannot qualify, according to Bloom's Socratic standard, as a genuinely harmonic reconciliation of the soul with the passions of the body. Instead, rhythm and melody are viewed as a form of barbarism when they take on the explicit sexual coloration of modern rock music. For Bloom, popular culture, especially rock music, represents a new form of barbarism whose horror he conjures up in the image of a thirteen-year-old boy watching MTV while listening to a Walkman radio:

> He enjoys the liberties hard won over centuries by the alliance
> of philosophic genius and political heroism, consecrated by the
> blood of martyrs; he is provided with comfort and leisure by
> the most productive economy ever known to mankind; science
> has penetrated the secrets of nature in order to provide him
> with the marvelous, lifelike electronic sound and image
> reproduction he is enjoying. And in what does progress
> culminate? A pubescent child whose body throbs with orgasmic
> rhythms; whose feelings are made articulate in hymns to the
> joys of onanism or the killing of parents; whose ambition is to
> win fame and wealth in imitating the drag-queen who makes

the music. In short, life is made into a nonstop, commercially prepackaged masturbational fantasy. (75)

Bloom's sentiments, in this case, have been shaped by what he perceives as indications of a serious moral and intellectual decline among American youth: a challenge to authority formed by the student movements of the 1960s and the leveling ideology of democratic reform characteristic of radical intellectuals.[3]

These judgments merely provide a prologue to a much more forceful and unsparing attack on nihilism, which, according to Bloom and his political and intellectual peerage, consistently devalues scholarship, or, in its more universal aspect, the life of the mind. Nihilism in Bloom's philosophy is a code word for the glorification of action and power and represents the real threat to contemporary civilization. Nihilism has a number of historical roots: the modernism of the good life that stresses pluralism and diversity; the vacillations of democracy that permit the ignorant a degree of freedom that, in four undergraduate years, students are not prepared to use; a fragmentation born out of the uncertainties of a moral order that cannot present to the young either a unified worldview or goals to overcome the greed of modern life; and, in a more politically charged context, the decade of the 1960s, which was marked by a flagrant disrespect for authority, especially the authority of the intellect. Here we have more than the usual tepid porridge of conservative discourse. Bloom invokes images of "chaos and decay" in the moral fabric of our society. However, the sources of decay are rarely seen to be economic and political. Indeed, there is not a whisper of criticism of capitalism. In fact, capitalism appears only as a sidelight in Bloom's rather indirect discussion of Marxism.

This brief description does not exhaust the breadth of Bloom's hyperbolic tirade. Our concern, of course, is focused on Bloom's vision of the crucial role schools can perform in correcting the current state of academic and public national culture he so roundly despises. Naturally, Bloom does not expect all schools to participate in reversing our country's spiritual malaise. The task falls to the literally twenty or thirty first-rate colleges and universities that are blessed with the best students but are regrettably frittering away their mission to restore to the West the mantle of greatness.

Commanding his minions to revise radically the curriculum, to purge it of allusions to student experience (which, in any case, is mired in ignorance), Bloom seeks to rid the classroom of cultural relativism and of all those areas of study that do not venerate the traditions of the past. Bloom's call for curriculum reform is clear: End the sham of the sexual, racial, and cultural revolution that animated the generation who confronted the white men at the Pentagon and at other institutions of economic, political, and cultural power twenty years ago. Reinstate Latin as the lingua franca of learning and transmit Western civilization through the one hundred greatest books that embody its system of values.

Of course, the state universities and colleges are now populated by the casualties of contemporary culture: large numbers of children of divorced parents, who are portrayed by Bloom as unfortunate—even tragic—products of current conditions; blacks and other minorities whose university experience is "different from that of other students" because of their history of "disadvantage," and whose dedication is, except in rare instances, not to learning but to practical advantage; and dispirited faculty members whose dreams of living in a community of scholars have been destroyed by the "interruptions" of modern social problems. For Bloom, these conditions disqualify the state universities and colleges as appropriate sites for professors and students to experience the awe and wonder of confronting the "great minds" of the ages.

It would be too easy to dismiss this frankly aristocratic vision of education as simply an effort to establish a new status quo conforming to Clark Kerr's model: a three-tier postsecondary education system in which theoretical knowledge is confined to the Ivy League institutions and major state universities—principally the University of California and some of the Big Ten—and private institutions such as Chicago, Duke, and Emory. But this would not do justice to the political intention in the neoconservatives' attack on higher education, or comprehend the danger and novelty of their argument.

For, unlike Irving Kristol's rantings against the 1960s New Left (who were trying to create an "adversary culture" in opposition to the supremely democratic and capitalist society that had become America), Bloom joins Hilton Kramer and the professors of the Cold War intelligentsia of the 1950s in advocating a return to the age of the medieval Schoolmen, or at least to the high European culture of the nineteenth century. Rather than praising democracy, he yearns for the return of a more rigidly stratified civilization in which the crowd is contained within the land of the marketplace and its pleasures are confined to the rituals of the carnival. What he wants to exclude are the majority of the population from the precincts of reason. At the same time, he would drive the vox populi from the genuine academy where the Absolute Spirit should find a home, but does not, because of the confusion that reigns amidst the dangerous and flabby influence of the discourses of social commitment, politics, and equality. Bloom identifies the impulse to egalitarianism as the chief culprit in the decay of higher learning, as well as the worst impasse of democracy. But university administrators bear equal responsibility for pandering to these base motives. Instead of feeling bound by tradition to transmit the higher learning, which, after all, is the repository of what is valuable in schooling, they gave away the store. Universities lost their way in the scandal that is culture.

Pluralists and democrats might dismiss these elitist ruminations without grasping the valid elements of the complaint. For there can be no doubt that the reception that Bloom's book has enjoyed signifies that he has struck the elitists' collective nerve. Intellectuals are uneasy about their role as teachers because their own experiences, interests, and values seem profoundly at odds with the several generations they have taught since the 1960s. But even more searing is their growing feeling of irrelevance, not only with respect to the process of education, but also with respect to their role in public life.

In Bloom's exegesis, the past must play a crucial role in the formulation of the future. Intellectuals are to join in a classical evocation of a mythically integrated civilization that becomes the vantage point from which to criticize the current situation. In all of its versions, the integrated past is marked by the existence of a community of the spirit; it is a time when at least a minority was able to search for the good and the true, unhampered by temporal considerations such as making a living. For the idyllic past is always constructed in the images of leisure, or, to be more fair, in an environment where society provides a sufficient social surplus to support a priest class, or their secular equivalents. In contrast, the contemporary construction of the intellectual is on the model of technical thought rather than pure reason. The intellectual transmits algorithms rather than ideas, and orients students to careers rather than criticizing the social structure.

Bloom's attack on higher education conveniently excludes the degree to which the existing arrangements of social and economic power have contributed to the shaping of the intellectual life that he so stridently laments. What Bloom fails to mention in his attack on the servants of higher education is that the disappearance of political intellectuals corresponds to the passing of politics from "public" life. Educational institutions, once charged with the task of providing a little learning to ruling elites and providing them with a mandarin class, have assumed a crucial place in the economic and cultural order. Their task is no longer to preserve civilization as it has been defined by the Greek and Roman aristocracies; these institutions are now filled with knowledge-producers, who, in advanced capitalist societies, have become part of the process of material and social reproduction. The idea of the intellectual as adversary of the dominant culture is utterly foreign to current arrangements (for example, the president of Barnard College, a former corporate lawyer, appeared on television commenting as an insider on the stock market crash and barely referred to her role as educator except to observe that students were calling home and nervously asking their parents, "How are we doing?").

In his last chapter Bloom alludes to business civilization and describes negatively the way economics has overwhelmed the social sciences in "serious" universities (taking the place once held by sociology in the days when students desired to help other people rather than looking out for themselves). Sounding like a member of the Frankfurt school of critical theory, Bloom even manages to criticize the belief, common among natural scientists, that their disciplines yield the only "real" knowledge. Characteristically, Bloom appeals to the elite schools to introduce philosophy as a key component of liberal education in order to counter the threat to higher education being posed by the rigid empiricisms of economics and natural science.

The tension between tradition and innovation plagues all who are seriously concerned with education. But Bloom refuses to go beyond scapegoating to ask how classical texts have failed to address the generations that came into postsecondary education after the Second World War: why Latin and Greek were no longer deemed essential for even the elite university curricula; why students, administrators, and the overwhelming majority of faculty came to view universities as degree mills, at worst, or at best as places where the enterprising student could be expected to receive a good reading list. These questions cannot be addressed, much less answered, by invective.

The conservative appeal to the past becomes an ideological flag carried against the future. It is not that the relativists, of both left and liberal persuasions, want to destroy the spirit and form of Western cultural heritage. Rather, they seek to reveal how such a heritage has often been employed as a weapon against those who would democratize institutions, who would change relations of power. Every achievement of civilization—the pyramids, great works of Greek philosophy and science, the wonderful representations of the human body and the soul that emerged during the Renaissance—has been built on the backs of slaves, or on the labor of a faraway peasantry, in short, on a material foundation that undermines the notion of an uncomplicated marriage between high culture and humanism. Ignoring this fact, as Walter Benjamin reminds us, helps to sustain the culture and civilization in general.[4] For this reason, the rebellion against privilege is frequently accompanied by an attack against the intellectuals. What oppressed people understand better than most is that intellectuals are typically servants of the mighty; they often provide legitimacy for deeds of state, private violence, and exploitation. This, of course, is the meaning of the argument that every achievement of high culture is preceded by the blood of those who make it possible.

When Bloom calls for reviving Latin as a requirement for educated youth, he opposes one of the crucial reforms of the eighteenth- and nineteenth-century democratic revolutions: the establishment of the vernacular as the language not only of commerce and manufacture but also of public life, literature, and philosophy. His fealty to classical texts excludes the Presocratics and Aristotle and focuses instead on Socrates and his disciple Plato precisely because of their attempt to separate truth from knowledge. Truth in Plato's *Symposium* requires no external object for its justification but refers instead to itself, particularly to purity of form. Knowledge is always one-sided, referring to an external object. It constitutes a representation of things and not, in Plato's terms, the things themselves. This distinction was challenged during the Enlightenment, when, increasingly, truth and knowledge began to have the same external referent; subjectivity was removed from the realm of science and occupied, as did ethics, psychology, and philosophy, a quasi-religious margin.

The virtue of Bloom's tirade, despite its reactionary content, is to remind us of what has been lost in the drive for rationalization, for the supremacy of science over philosophy, history over eternal essences. That is, a twentieth-century obsession, to both define and celebrate history as an evolutionary mode of ideological and material progress produced through the marriage of science and technology, has resulted in a refusal to give primacy to the important and problematic relationship of truth, power, and knowledge. From the point of view of a conservative for whom the past is all that is worth preserving, the consequences of Enlightenment ideology find their apogee in the brutality of the cultural revolutions of 1789 and 1968; but of course he forgets to mention the response of traditional Schoolmen to Galileo's discoveries. The intellect, in this case, defends itself by threatening to obliterate its adversaries.

The historical legacy of technicization has been to turn universities into training institutions, which creates few spaces for intellectuals. Within the ranks of the democratic professoriate, a debate often rages between those who spurn the elitism that emanates from the new conservative attack on affirmative action, open admissions, and student-centered learning, and others who would try to extract some self-serving half-truths from Bloom's critique of contemporary postsecondary education (for example, open admissions is detrimental to quality education, affirmative action is unfairly discriminatory, and so forth).

What must be accepted in Bloom's discourse is that anti-intellectualism in American education is rampant, influencing even those whose intentions are actually opposed to closing the doors to genuine learning. We know that the environment in most universities is inimical to broadly based, philosophically informed scholarship and dialogue concerning burning questions of politics and culture. In a few places, liberal and radical intellectuals are building microinstitutions (centers, institutes, programs) within the universities as outposts that attempt to resist the larger trends toward instrumentalized curricula. These programs wisely accept that they are engaged in an intellectual as well as a political project; but, for the most part, their influence is confined to the already initiated.

On the front lines, some teachers, buffeted and bewildered, continue to maintain fresh creative and critical approaches to their tasks. In doing so, they receive little or no sustenance from the intellectuals. The challenge, in our view, is to combine the intellectual work of cultural reclamation with the work of pedagogy. This would entail a deliberate effort to avoid the tendency toward exclusivity on the part of intellectuals; to refuse the temptation to reproduce the "community of scholars" that is the heart of Bloom's program, even if the scholars are democratic intellectuals. The intellectuals who boldly announce that the search for truth and the good life is not the exclusive property of the right and, in fact, is largely opposed to the conservative sensibility, would be required to engage with students—to start, not from the new great texts, much less from the old great texts, but from the texts of the vernacular experience: from popular culture, not only in its written forms but in its visual artifacts as well. As Bertolt Brecht quipped, "Let's start not from the good old things but from the bad new things."

This need not imply leaving aside any consideration of the tradition. But the task of reworking it might be explicitly combined with current concerns. For if tradition is to become part of a popular canon, it would have to justify itself either by its claim to pertinence or as a sociological and historical trace of the culture against which the present contends. In this connection, it is instructive to follow the fate of scientific texts. Except for historians, practicing physicists and their students rarely, if ever, read the works of Newton, Galileo, Kepler, and Copernicus. Similarly, Darwin is left to the scholars. Surely, one would not want to construct a curriculum in which this rich past was left to gather cobwebs. Science has no need for a literary canon, because it has long since abandoned the search for truth, and is intent on discovery. In other words, science is interested only in knowledge that can be derived from mathematics and experiment. Consequently, with few exceptions, it discourages the focus on meaning that still dominates the humanities. Like the social sciences, the natural sciences are content with explanation, and have forgotten that any object of knowledge is grasped not only quantitatively or by perception, but also historically.

The relationship between literary tradition and history is the most important one. For, unless we are to take the position made popular by Henry Ford that "history is bunk," we are obliged to take a historical perspective on the present and the future. That is to say, what we know is conditioned by historical precedents, and our natural and social world is constituted rather than merely given. For this reason, both knowledge and the truths of subjects themselves presuppose the elements of their formation. The danger lies in taking the position that the present is absolutely determined by the past, in which case nothing ever really happens; events are reworkings of their antecedents. Instead, we propose that both disruption and continuity are characteristic of the nature of things. "Disruption" is a name for the proposition that things are constituted by interactions: constituted, in the first place, by intersubjective relations, but also by the relations of what humans produce in the present and the past, which appear as a part of the "natural" order. To critique the reification of the social as an unproblematic category does not dissolve everything into intersubjective relations—including our own "nature," since our relation to what is taken as nature is part of human formation. This double relation has a history that is, to a great extent, embodied in literature and philosophy, and in folk narratives that are incorporated into popular cultural forms.

While it is possible to make a strong case that reading classic texts is necessary even today because they continue to speak to our condition, we must take into account the massive shift that has occurred in the terms of the discourse: vernacular speech and popular language are now deeply embedded in the collective imagination. Thus any effort to displace this language must be perceived as an imposition from on high, an effort by professional intellectuals to destroy or ignore what has happened in the last two hundred years. We do not want to argue that none of the privileged texts of Western culture should be incorporated into the curriculum. Nor are we defending anti-intellectualism, even as we explain some of its democratic impulses. But the responsibility of intellectuals for the current state of affairs must be acknowledged before the tension between tradition and modernity or postmodernity can be ameliorated. When intellectuals, whose alliance with the established order is their last best hope to save their status, make proclamations about educational reform, they must remain suspect. For what Bloom means by reform is nothing less than an effort to make explicit what women, minorities, and working-class students have always known: the precincts of higher learning are not for them, and the educational system is meant to train a new mandarin class. Their fate is tied to technical knowledge. This is Bloom's program. In part, this becomes clear not only in Bloom's complaint that "Harvard, Yale, and Princeton are not what they used to be—the last resorts of aristocratic sentiment within the democracy" (89), but also in his attack on ethnicity and subordinate cultures. According to Bloom,

> When one hears men and women proclaiming that they must preserve their culture, one cannot help wondering whether this artificial notion can really take the place of the God and country for which they once would have been willing to die. The "new ethnicity" or "roots" is just another manifestation of the concern with particularity, evidence not only of the real problems of community in modern mass societies but also of the superficiality of the response to it, as well as the lack of awareness of the fundamental conflict between liberal society and culture. . . . The "ethnic" differences we see in the United States are but decaying reminiscences of old differences that caused our ancestors to kill one another. (192–93)

In commenting on the "sample" of students Bloom uses to construct his view of university life, Martha Nussbaum provides an illuminating insight into Bloom's treatment of students who do not inhabit the world of elite universities, particularly subordinate groups who make up the black, ethnic, and white working class.

> [Bloom's students who] are materially well off and academically successful enough to go to a small number of elite universities and to pursue their studies there without the distraction of holding a job are equated with those having "the greatest talents" and the "more complex" natures. They are said to be the people who are "most likely to take advantage of a liberal education," and to be the ones who "most need education." It would seem that the disadvantaged, as Bloom imagines them, also have comparatively smaller talents, simpler natures, and fewer needs. But Bloom never argues that they do. He simply has no interest in the students whom he does not regard as the elite—an elite defined, he makes plain, by wealth and good

fortune as much as by qualities of the mind that have deeper value.[5]

For Bloom, philosophy after Hegel abandons the search for truth, becoming the servant of technical knowledge and thereby losing its claim to wisdom. But whereas Bloom wants to reconstruct the category of truth through an unproblematic, quasi-essentialist, and elitist reading of history, we believe that recovering a notion of truth grounded in a critical reading of history that validates and reclaims democratic public life is fundamental to the project of educational reform. Consciousness must take itself as its object, recognize that the process of forging an identity should be tied not to representations of what should be the goals to which students should aspire, but to what students themselves want, what they think and feel, and—most important—what they already know. The assumption that a student is a tabula rasa upon which the teacher, armed with the wisdom of ages, places an imprint, is the basis of the widespread distrust of education among today's students. The elite professoriate is recruited from that tiny minority of every generation for whom the life of the mind represents the pinnacle of life. Such ideals are by no means shared by the preponderance of professors, much less by their students.

We are arguing for the parity of canonical text and popular text as forms of historical knowledge. In fact, high cultural texts often originated as popular novels (the works of Dickens, Dostoevsky, and Rabelais are just a few examples). Their narratives were inevitably drawn from the everyday lives of their readers, as well as from the lives of those who had not yet gained their own voices, either in the public sphere or in literature. The novelist, argues Mikhail Bakhtin, creates a narration worthy of canonization when a multiplicity of voices, analogous to a polyphonic musical work, are placed in dialogic relation to one another.[6] Among these, one can discover the popular, if by that term we mean those excluded from literate culture; this self-discovery of the voices of the popular was a basic feature of the early bourgeois epoch. In this example, we read literature as a social semiotic, as a string of signifiers that illuminate our past, that reveal ourselves, that provide us with a heritage for our own times. But the rediscovery of the popular is not the only treasure that can be scrounged from the established canon. We may discover in Gustave Flaubert's *Madame Bovary*, in Mark Twain's *Huckleberry Finn*, and in Theodore Dreiser's *Chronicles of American Plunder*—descriptions of the human sacrifices that were made for the sake of progress at the turn of the century—the modern tragedies and comic narratives that are the dark side of middle-class and native history or philosophy. In short, we may take literature as social knowledge, but the knowledge is not of an object—it is a part of the truth about ourselves.

We are sure that Bloom would find this program objectionable because it preserves what should be destroyed—historicity: placing our lives in relation to our times, seeing history as less than the unfolding of the Absolute Spirit, but instead, as the deconstruction of the myths of "civilization." The democratic use of literary canons must always remain critical. Above all, the canon must justify itself as representing the elements of our own heritage. In the final instance, it is to be appropriated rather than revered—and, with this appropriation, transformed. The canon, then, is to be pressed into the service of definite ends--which frees us from the yoke of acknowledging it as the unquestioned embodiment of Truth, even as it remains unread.

At first glance, Hirsch's *Cultural Literacy* has little in common with Bloom's work. Bloom directs his attack against a number of institutions, social practices, and ideologies that challenge the dominant assumptions of contemporary social life. As we have mentioned, his targets include cultural relativism, higher education, popular culture, Nietzsche, the left, feminism, rock music, and the social movements of the 1960s. Hirsch's focus is narrower; he argues for a view of cultural literacy that serves both as a critique of many existing theories of education and as a referent for a reconstructed vision of American public schooling. Whereas Bloom attacks the notion of culture as a referent for self- and social formation, Hirsch attempts to enlist the language of culture and the culture of literacy as bases for rethinking the American past and reconstructing the discourse of public life. But the differences that characterize these two positions are minor compared to the ideological and political project that they have in common.[7] In the most general sense, Hirsch and Bloom represent different versions of the same ideology, one that is deeply committed to cleansing democracy of its critical and emancipatory possibilities.

At the same time, Hirsch and Bloom share a common concern for rewriting the past from the perspective of the privileged and the powerful. In this view, history becomes a vehicle for endorsing a form of textual and cultural authority that legitimates an unproblematic relationship between knowledge and truth. Both disdain the democratic implications of pluralism, and each argues for a form of cultural uniformity in which difference is consigned to the margins of both history and everyday life. From this perspective, culture, along with the authority it sanctions, is not a terrain of struggle: it is merely an artifact, a warehouse of goods, posited either as a canon of knowledge or a canon of information that has simply to be transmitted as a means for promoting social order and control. Learning, for both Hirsch and Bloom, has little to do with dialogue and struggle over the meanings and practices of a historical tradition. On the contrary, learning is defined primarily through a pedagogy of transmission, and knowledge is reduced to a culture of great books or unrelated catalogues of shared information. As we indicated earlier, their positions are both part of the most recent effort by the aristocratic traditionalists to restore knowledge as a particular form of social authority, pedagogy, and discipline in the classroom in order to replace democratic educational authority. Each position espouses a view of culture removed from the trappings of power, conflict, and struggle, and in doing so, each attempts to legitimate a view of learning and literacy that not only marginalizes the voices, languages, and cultures of subordinate groups but also degrades teaching and learning to the practice of implementation and mastery. Both of these discourses are profoundly antiutopian, and correspond with a more general vision of domination and control as it has been developed during the Reagan era. Specifically, Bloom and Hirsch represent the most popular expression of the resurgent attempt on the part of right-wing intellectuals and ruling groups to undermine the basis of democratic public life as we have known it over the last two decades. In what follows, we analyze in greater detail some of these assumptions through an analysis of the major themes presented in Hirsch's version of the conservative educational credo.

Hirsch has entered the debate on the nature and purpose of public schooling by way of a discourse that has gained public attention within the last ten years. In the manner of conservatives such as William Bennett, Diane Ravitch, Chester Finn Jr., and Nathan Glazer, Hirsch begins with the assumption that a state of crisis exists in the United States that reflects not only the demise of public schooling but also the weakening of a wider civic and public culture. Schools in this view are frontline institutions that have reneged on their public responsibility to educate students into the dominant traditions of Western culture.

Appropriating the radical educational position that schools are agencies of social and cultural reproduction, conservatives such as Hirsch defend this position rather than criticize it, and make it a measure for defining both the quality of school life and that of society at large. Implicit in this position is the notion that schools represent a preparation for and legitimation of particular forms of social life; they are cultural institutions that name experience, and in doing so presuppose a vision of the future. It is in these terms that Hirsch's book becomes important. For Hirsch insists that schools be analyzed as sites of learning in which knowledge, not merely skills, constitutes the most important consideration, if public schooling is to fulfill its imperative as a transmitter of civic and public culture. To Hirsch's credit, he enters the debate regarding public schooling by arguing for a particular relation between culture and power on the one hand and literacy and learning on the other. In doing so, he not only provides an important corrective to the view that the curriculum in general and learning in particular should be organized around the developmental organization of learning skills; he also argues for a definition of literacy that embraces a particular relationship between knowledge and power. Knowledge, in this case, is not only the basis for learning; it also enables entrance into the social and economic possibilities that exist in the wider society. These issues have been analyzed critically by a number of educational traditionalists as key referents for challenging some of Hirsch's major assumptions. To pursue this analysis we will examine Hirsch's view of the crisis in education, his reading of history and tradition, his construction of the relationship among culture, language, and power and its contribution to a view of literacy, and finally, the implications of *Cultural Literacy* for teachers and classroom pedagogy.

Reiterating the arguments of Bennett, Ravitch, and Finn, Hirsch identifies the crisis in education through the general level of cultural ignorance exhibited in recent years by American students. In this view, students lack the knowledge necessary to "thrive in the modern world" (xiii). Relying heavily on the declining test scores of college-bound students, particularly those of the Scholastic Aptitude Test (SAT) and the National Assessment of Educational Progress, as well as on anecdotal evidence, Hirsch argues that there is indeed a literacy crisis in the United States. For Hirsch, the SAT is essentially a "test of advanced vocabulary," and as such is a "fairly sensitive instrument for measuring levels of literacy" (4). In these assertions, the relationship between ignorance and learning, between knowledge and ideology, first becomes evident in Hirsch's book. At issue is a definition of literacy that is organized within categories that favor knowledge as a shared body of information, and a definition of learning as the appropriation of this information. For Hirsch, the defining character of this knowledge is that it represents the unifying facts, values, and writings of Western culture. In this instance, the relationship between knowledge and power is legitimated through claims to a body of information that resides beyond the sphere of historical conflict and the shifting terrain of ideological struggle. Authority and meaning come together within a view of history that appears unproblematic and unchangeable in its determining influence on the present and the future. What you see is what you get.

More important, Hirsch's view of history is the narrative of the winners. It is the discourse of the elites in history that constitutes the fund of cultural knowledge that defines literacy. Assured by his son, who taught high school Latin, Hirsch recognizes that students do in fact know something. Ignorance, for Hirsch, is not merely the absence of information. At stake is *what* the students know. Literacy and illiteracy are defined by the information students possess regarding the canon of knowledge that constitutes, for Hirsch, the national culture. Hirsch characterizes the crisis in literacy by the lack of familiarity students have with Western culture's canon, bequeathed by history as a series of facts—dates of battles, authors of books, figures from Greek mythology, and the names of past presidents of the United States. In effect, the crisis of literacy is defined primarily as an epistemological and political problem. In the first instance, students cannot read and write adequately unless they have the relevant background information, a particular body of shared information that expresses a privileged cultural currency with a high exchange value in the public sphere. In the second instance, students who lack the requisite historical and contemporary information that constitutes the canon of Western tradition will not be able to function adequately in society. In Hirsch's terms, the new illiteracy is embodied in those expanding ranks of students who are unable either to contextualize information or to communicate with each other within the parameters of a wider national culture.

Hirsch does more than rely on the logic of verification and personal anecdote to signal the new illiteracy. He also attempts to analyze the causes for its emergence in the last half of the twentieth century. Hirsch begins by arguing that schools are solely responsible for the current cultural blight plaguing contemporary youth. If students lack the requisite historical and literary knowledge, it is because both schools of education and the public schools have been excessively influenced by the theoretical legacies of the early progressive movement of the 1920s. Influenced by the theories of John Dewey and the liberal ideas embodied in the 1918 Cardinal Principles of Education, public schooling is alleged to have historically shifted its concern from a knowledge-based curriculum to one that has emphasized the practical application of knowledge. The result has been, according to Hirsch, the predominance in public schools of a curriculum dominated by concern for developmental psychology, student experience, and the mastery of skills. Within this line of reasoning, progressive educational theory and practice have undermined the intellectual content of the curriculum and further contributed to forms of public schooling marked by an increasing loss of authority, cultural relativism, lack of discipline, poor academic performance, and a refusal to train students adequately to meet the demands of the changing industrial order.

Hirsch is not content merely with criticizing the public schools. He is also intent on developing a programmatic discourse for constructing curriculum reform. Hirsch's message is relatively simple. He believes that since literacy is in a decline caused by an overemphasis on process at the expense of content, schools should begin to subordinate the teaching of skills to what he calls common background knowledge. For Hirsch, this common background knowledge consists of information from mainstream culture represented in standard English. Its content is drawn from what Hirsch calls the common culture, which in his terms is marked by a history and contemporary usefulness that raises it above issues of power, class, and discrimination. In Hirsch's terms, this is "everybody's culture," and the only real issue, as he sees it, is that we outline its contents and begin to teach it in schools. For Hirsch, the national language, which is at the center of his notion of literacy, is rooted in a civic religion that forms the core of stability in the culture itself. "Culture" in these terms is used in a descriptive rather than an anthropological and political sense; it is the medium of conservation and transmission. Its meaning is fixed in the past, and its essence is that it provides the public with a common referent for communication and exchange. It is the foundation upon which public life interacts with the past, sustains the present, and locates itself in the future. Psycholinguistic research and an unchallenged relationship among industrialization, nationalism, and historical progress provide the major referents mobilized in the name of cultural literacy. The logic underlying Hirsch's argument is that cultural literacy is the precondition for industrial growth, and that with industrial growth comes the standardization of language, culture, and learning. The equation is somewhat baffling in its simplicity, and Hirsch actually devotes whole chapters to developing this particular version of historical determinism. The outcome of his Hegelian rendering of history and literacy is a view of Western culture that is both egalitarian and homogeneous.[8] Hirsch dismisses the notion that culture has any determinate relation to the practices of power and politics, or that it is largely defined as a part of an ongoing struggle to name history, experience, knowledge, and the meaning of everyday life in one's own terms. Culture for Hirsch is a network of information shrouded in innocence and goodwill. This is in part reflected in his reading of the relationship between culture and what he describes as nation building:

Nation builders use a patchwork of scholarly folk materials, old songs, obscure dances, and historical legends all apparently quaint and local, but in reality selected and reinterpreted by intellectuals to create a culture upon which the life of the nation can rest. (83)

There is a totalitarian unity in Hirsch's view of culture that is at odds with the concept of democratic pluralism and political difference. In fact, where difference is introduced by Hirsch, as in reference to multiculturalism or bilingualism, it appears to vacillate between the categories of a disrupting discourse and a threat to the vitality and strength of the Western cultural tradition. Hirsch's defense of a unified version of Western tradition ideologically marks his definition of cultural literacy as more than a simplistic call for a common language and canon of shared information. Hirsch's argument is that to be culturally literate is "to possess the basic information needed to thrive in the modern world," and that mastering the standard literate language will make us "masters of communication, thereby enabling us to give and receive complex information orally and in writing over time" (3). This argument is not merely a prescription for a particular form of literacy and schooling. It is part of a hegemonic discourse that is symptomatic of the crisis in history currently facing this nation, and is a threat to democracy itself.

We will analyze some of the major arguments made by Hirsch in defense of his notion of cultural literacy. In doing so we will not restrict our analysis to the defining ideas that Hirsch develops, but will also analyze the significant gaps in Hirsch's view of history, literacy, culture, and schooling. We hope to show that Hirsch's argument is more than a popular and politically innocent treatise on educational reform, but rather serves at best as a veiled apology for a highly dogmatic and reactionary view of literacy and schooling. At worst, Hirsch's model of cultural literacy threatens the very democracy he claims to be preserving.

For Hirsch, the starting point for the crisis in literacy and education is the decline of student achievement as measured by the SAT and similar tests. Hirsch and other conservatives presume that the test scores accurately measure academic proficiency, and that progress in educational reform can be accurately inferred from an upturn in SAT scores. In recent times this wisdom has been highly disputed. Not only is the validity of the SAT and other national measurement schemes being questioned despite the alleged objectivity of such tests, but it is also being strongly argued that the reliance on test scores as a measure of school success contains in itself an ideology that is highly detrimental to improving the quality of school life and providing the basis for critical learning.[9]

We believe that Hirsch's reliance on such scores to analyze the nature of the problems public schools currently face in this country is theoretically impoverished and politically visionless. This position ignores the wider complex of social and political forces that deeply influence the way schools are structured to benefit some students at the expense of others. For instance, this position is silent regarding the ways that tracking, the hidden curriculum, the denial of student experience as a valid basis for knowledge, and school practices predicated on racial, sexist, and class interests discriminate against students. Nothing in Hirsch's position speaks to the 50 to 80 percent dropout rate of high school students in inner-city schools, or to the fact that in major cities like Chicago, schools with over a 50 percent black and Hispanic enrollment manage to retain only 39 percent of the entering freshmen by their senior year.[10] These figures highlight a number of problems that cannot be accounted for or even understood through analysis of so-called aptitude tests. Hirsch's reliance on test scores also ignores the effect that the technical rationality of this position has had on the deskilling of teachers, particular women, within the last decade.[11] State-mandated efforts to raise test scores, especially in the areas of reading and writing, have been part of a much broader educational reform movement tied to instrumentalizing teaching and learning around a variety of accountability schemes. As Linda Darling-Hammond reports, the results have had very little to do with genuine reform and a great deal to do with teacher disempowerment and despair:

> Viewing teachers as semiskilled, low-paid workers in the mass production of education, policymakers have sought to change education, to improve it, by "teacher-proofing" it. Over the past decade we have seen a proliferation of elaborate accountability schemes that go by acronyms like MBO (management by objectives), PBBS (performance-based budgeting systems), CBE (competency-based education) . . . and MCT (minimum competency testing) . . . we learned from teachers that in response to policies that prescribe teaching practices and outcomes, they spend less time on untested subjects . . . they use less writing in the classrooms in order to gear assignments to the format of standardized tests; they resort to lectures rather than classroom discussion in order to cover the prescribed behavioral objectives without getting "off

the track"; they are precluded from using teaching materials that are not on prescribed textbook lists, even when they think these materials are essential to meet the needs of some of their students; and they feel constrained from following up on expressed student interests that lie outside the bounds of mandated curricula. . . . And 45 percent of the teachers in this study told us that the single thing that would make them leave teaching was the increased prescriptiveness of teaching content and methods—in short, the continuing deprofessionalization of teaching.[12]

Hirsch appears unaware that the politics of verification and empiricism that he supports frame his own agenda for reform in a way that is at odds with an ethical and substantive vision of what schools might be with respect to their potential for empowering both students and teachers as active and critical citizens. Hirsch's reliance on narrow models of psycholinguistic research forces him to use absolute categories, that is, categories that appear to transcend historical, cultural, and political contingencies. By ignoring a wide range of sociological, cultural, and historical research on schooling, Hirsch wrongly names the nature of the crisis he attempts to address. He completely ignores those theories of schooling that in recent years have illustrated how schools function as agencies of social and cultural reproduction.[13] He completely ignores existing critical research that points to how working-class and minority children are discriminated against through various approaches to reading;[14] he exhibits no theoretical awareness of how schools frequently silence or discriminate against students;[15] and he completely ignores the research that points out ways in which the state and other social, economic, and political interests bear down on and shape the daily practices of school organization and classroom life.[16] Consequently, Hirsch's analysis and prescriptions are both simplistic and incorrect. The crisis in education is not about the background information that young people allegedly lack, or the inability of students to communicate in order to adapt more readily to the dictates of the dominant culture. Rather, it is a crisis framed in the intersections of citizenship, historical consciousness, and inequality, one that speaks to a breakdown at the heart of democratic public life.

The limitations of Hirsch's view of the crisis are evident not only in the research he selects to define the problem, but also in the factors he points to as causes of the crisis in literacy and schooling. Among the chief historical villains in Hirsch's script are the progressive principles embodied in the work of John Dewey. Hirsch holds Dewey responsible for promoting a formalism in which the issues of experience and process become a substitute for focusing on school knowledge in the school curriculum. Hirsch argues that Dewey is the major theoretical architect of a content-neutral curriculum (as if such a thing ever existed). Dewey's crime in this view is that he has influenced later generations of educators to take critical thinking seriously, as opposed to learning the virtues of having students accumulate information for the purpose of shoring up the status quo.

Hirsch misinterprets Dewey's work. Even the most casual reading of Dewey's *The Child and the Curriculum* and *The School and Society* reveals a blatant refusal to accept any division between content and process or between knowledge and thinking. Rather than support this bifurcation, Dewey argued that the attempt to impart information without the benefit of self-reflection and context generally resulted in methods of teaching in which knowledge was cut off from its organic connection to the student's experiences and the wider society. Dewey was not against facts, as Hirsch argues; he was against the mere collection of facts both uninformed by a working hypothesis and unenlightened by critical reflection. He was against the categorization of knowledge into sterile and so-called finished forms. We are certainly not suggesting that Hirsch's misreading of Dewey represents an act of intellectual dishonesty; more probably, since Dewey's views are so much at odds with Hirsch's theory of learning and schooling, it was easier for him to misread Dewey than to engage his ideas directly on specific issues. For example, Hirsch's claim that memorization is a noble method of learning, his refusal to situate schooling in broader historical, social, and political contexts, and his belief that public culture is historically defined through the progressive accumulation of information represent major ideas that Dewey spent a lifetime refuting as educationally unsound and politically reactionary. But Hirsch refuses to argue with Dewey on these issues; instead, he cavalierly attributes to Dewey a series of one-dimensional ideas that Dewey never advocated. This is not merely a distortion of Dewey's work; it also represents a view of history and causality that is, as we explain below, deeply flawed. Moreover, Hirsch reproduces in this view of educational history and practice a slightly different version of Bloom's profoundly antidemocratic tirade.

Underlying Hirsch's view of the major causes of the problems with American education is a notion of history that is reductionist and theoretically flawed. It is reductionist because it assumes that ideas are the determining factor in shaping history, somehow unfolding in linear fashion from one generation to the next. There is no sense of how these ideas are worked out and mediated through the ideological and material conditions of their times, or of how history is shaped through the changing patterns of communication, technology, language conflicts, struggles between different social groups, and the shifting parameters of state power. Hirsch's history lacks any concrete political and social referents, its causal relations are construed through a string of ideas, and it is presented without the benefit of a substantially argued historical context. While ideas are important in shaping history, they cannot be considered so powerful as to alter history beyond the density of its material and social contexts. Ideas are not so powerful that they exist, as Hirsch believes, in an autonomous real, independent of human activity.[17]

Hirsch practices historical inquiry not as a form of social memory but as a form of repression. It is history stripped of the discourse of power, injustice, and conflict. For instance, the struggle over curriculum in the United States emerged in the first half of the twentieth century amid an intense war of ideological positions, each attempting to stamp its public philosophy and view of learning on the curriculum of the public schools. As Herbert Kliebard points out, curriculum represented a terrain of struggle among different groups over questions regarding the purpose of schooling, how children learn, whose knowledge was to be legitimated, and what social relations would prevail.[18] The contending groups included social efficiency advocates whose priorities were based on the interests of corporate ideology, humanists who were advocates of the revered traditions of Western cultural heritage, developmentalists who wanted to reform the curriculum around the scientific study of child development, and finally, social meliorists who wanted to shape the curriculum in the interests of social reform. Kliebard not only provides a complex and dense history of the struggle for control of the curriculum in the public schools, he also argues that the most important force in shaping curriculum in the United States came not from the progressives but from the social efficiency movement. Given the history of public schooling since the rise of the Cold War and the launching of Sputnik, there can be little doubt that the efficiency and accountability models for curriculum have carried the day.

History for Hirsch is not a terrain of struggle;[19] it is a museum of information that merely legitimates a particular view of itself as a set of sacred goods designed to be received rather than interrogated by students. We have stressed Hirsch's view of history, because it influences every category he relies upon to develop his major arguments. We began our criticism of his work by arguing that his discourse on crisis and cultural restoration missed the point. We want to return to this issue and argue that the real crisis in American schooling can be better understood through an analysis of the rise of scientism and technocratic rationality as a major ideological force in the 1920s; the increasing impingement of state policy on the shaping of school curricula; the anticommunism of the 1950s; the increasing influence of industrial psychology in defining the purpose of schooling; the rise of individualism and consumerism through the growth of the culture industry, in which the logic of standardization, repetition, and rationalization defines and shapes the culture of consumption; the gendered nature of teaching as manifested in the educational labor force and in the construction of school administration and curriculum; the racism, sexism, and class discrimination that have been reinforced through increasing use of tracking and testing; and the failure of teachers to gain sufficient control over the conditions of their labor. While this is not the place to discuss these issues, they need to be included in any analysis of the problems that public schools are now facing. Moreover, these issues point to a much broader crisis in the schools and the wider society than Hirsch is willing to recognize.[20] It is a crisis that has given rise to cynicism about the promise of democracy, to a vast and unequal distribution of ideological and material resources both in the schools and in the wider society, and to the repression of those aspects of our history that carry the voices and social memories of groups who have been marginalized in the struggle for democratic life.

Central to Hirsch's concept of literacy is an understanding of the relationship between culture and literacy that warrants close theoretical scrutiny. For Hirsch, culture, which is the central structuring category in his approach to literacy and learning, appears as a mythic category that exists beyond the realm of politics and struggle. It is systematically reduced to a canon of information that constitutes not only a fund of background knowledge but also a vehicle for social and economic mobility:

> Literate culture has become the common currency for social and economic exchange in our democracy, and the only available ticket to full citizenship. Getting one's membership card is not tied to class or race. Membership is automatic if one learns that background information and the linguistic conventions that are needed to read, write, and speak effectively. (22)

There is a false egalitarianism defining Hirsch's view of culture, one that suggests that while it is possible to distinguish between mainstream and what he calls ethnic culture, the concept of culture itself has nothing to do with struggle and power. Culture is seen as the totality of the language practices of a given nation, and merely "presents" itself for all to participate in its language and conventions. Hirsch refuses to acknowledge how deeply the struggle for moral and social regulation inscribes itself in the language of culture. He makes no attempt to interrogate culture as the shared and lived principles of life characteristic of different groups and classes as these emerge within unequal relations of power and struggle. Not unlike Bloom's position, Hirsch's view of culture expresses a single, durable history and vision, one at odds with the notion of difference, and maintains an ominous ideological silence—an ideological amnesia of sorts—regarding the validity and importance of the experiences of women, blacks, and other groups excluded from the narrative of mainstream history and culture. Thus there emerges no sense of culture as a field of struggle, or as a domain of competing interests in which dominant and subordinate groups live out and make sense of their given circumstances and conditions of life. This is an essentialist reading of culture. It deeply underestimates the central feature of cultural relations in the twentieth century. That is, by failing to acknowledge the multilayered relations between culture and power, Hirsch ignores how the ideological and structural weight of different cultural practices operates as a form of cultural politics. In this case, he not only ignores how domination works in the cultural sphere, he also refuses to acknowledge the dialectic of cultural struggle between different groups over competing orders of meaning, experience, and history.

The failing of Hirsch's view of culture is most evident in his analysis of public schools. He provides little, if any, understanding of the forms of struggle that take place in schools over different forms of knowledge and social relations. This is best exemplified in the research on culture and schooling that has emerged within the last twenty years both in the United States and abroad. Theorists such as Pierre Bourdieu, Basil Bernstein, Paulo Freire, Michael Apple, and others have investigated the relationship between power and culture, arguing that the culture transmitted by the school is related to the various cultures that make up the wider society, in that it confirms and sustains the culture of dominant groups while marginalizing and silencing the cultures of subordinate groups of students.[21] This is evident in the way in which different forms of linguistic and cultural competency, whether they are manifested in a specific way of talking, dressing, acting, thinking, or presenting oneself, are accorded a privileged status in schools. For example, Ray Rist, Jean Anyon, and Hugh Mehan have demonstrated that white middle-class linguistic forms, modes of style, and values represent honored forms of cultural capital and are accorded a greater exchange rate in the circuits of power that define and legitimate the meaning of success in public schools.[22] Students who represent cultural forms that rely on restricted linguistic codes, working-class or oppositional modes of dress (long hair, earrings, bizarre patterns of clothing), who downplay the ethos of individualism (and who may actually share their work and time), who espouse a form of solidarity, or who reject forms of academic knowledge that embody versions of history, social science, and success that are at odds with their own cultural experiences and values, find themselves at a decided academic, social, and ideological disadvantage in most schools.

A more critical understanding of the relationship between culture and schooling would start with a definition of culture as a set of activities by which different groups produce collective memories, knowledge, social relations, and values within historically constituted relations of power. Culture is about the production and legitimation of particular ways of life, and schools often transmit a culture that is specific to class, gender, and race. By depoliticizing the issue of culture, Hirsch is unable to develop a view of either literacy or pedagogy that acknowledges the complex workings of power as they are produced and mediated through the cultural processes that structure school life. Thus Hirsch ends up with a view of literacy cleansed of its own complicity in furthering cultural practices and ideologies that reproduce the worst dimensions of schooling.

Given Hirsch's view of culture, it is not surprising that he espouses a clothesline-of-information approach to literacy that ignores its function as a technology of social control, as a feature of cultural organization that reproduces rather than critically engages the dominant social order. When the power of literacy is framed around a unifying logic consistent with the imperatives of the dominant culture, those groups outside the dominant tradition are often silenced because their voices and experiences are not recognized as legitimate. Hirsch's view of literacy decontextualizes learners, both from the culture and mode of literacy that give their voices meaning, and from that which is legitimated as knowledge in the name of the dominant version of literacy. Literacy for Hirsch is treated as a universal discourse and process that exists outside "the social and political relations, ideological practices, and symbolic meaning structures in which it is embedded."[23] Not only is the notion of multiple literacies (the concept of cultural difference) ignored in this formulation, but those who are considered "illiterate" bear the burden of forms of moral and social regulation that often deny their histories, voices, and sufferings. To argue for a recognition of the dialectical quality of literacy—that is, its power either to limit or enhance human capacities as well as the multiple forms of expression it takes—is a deeply political issue. It means recognizing that there are different voices, languages, histories, and ways of viewing and experiencing the world, and that the recognition and affirmation of these differences is a necessary and important precondition for extending the possibilities of democratic life. June Jordan has captured the importance of this issue in her comments regarding the problems in a democratic state:

> If we lived in a democratic state our language would have to hurtle, fly, curse, and sing, in all the common American names, all the undeniable and representative and participating voices of everybody here. We would not tolerate the language of the powerful and, thereby, lose all respect for words, per se. We would make our language conform to the truth of our many selves and we would make our language lead us into the equality of power that a democratic state must represent.[24]

To acknowledge different forms of literacy is not to suggest that they should all be given equal weight. On the contrary, it is to argue that their differences are to be weighed against the capacity they have for enabling people to locate themselves in their own histories while simultaneously establishing the conditions for them to function as part of a wider democratic culture. This represents a form of literacy that is not merely epistemological but also deeply political and eminently pedagogical. It is political because literacy represents a set of practices that can provide the conditions through which people can be empowered or disempowered. It is pedagogical because literacy always involves social relations in which learning takes place; power legitimates a particular view of the world, and privilege, a specific rendering of knowledge.[25]

This view of culture, knowledge, and literacy is far removed from the language and ideology of Hirsch and Bloom. The refusal to be literate in their terms means that one has refused to appropriate either the canon of the Great Books or the canon of information that characterizes the tradition of Western culture. In this view, refusal is not resistance or criticism; it is judged as ignorance or failure. This view of culture and literacy is also implicated in the theories of pedagogy put forth by Bloom and Hirsch. Both subscribe to a pedagogy that is profoundly reactionary and can be summed up in the terms "transmission" and "imposition." Both authors refuse to analyze how pedagogy, as a deliberate and critical attempt to influence the ways in which knowledge and identities are produced within and among particular sets of social relations, might address the reconstruction of social imagination in the service of human freedom. The categories of meaning that students bring to the classroom and that provide them with a basis for producing and interpreting knowledge are simply denied by Bloom and Hirsch as viable categories of learning. Pedagogy, for both Bloom and Hirsch, is an afterthought. It is something one does to implement a preconstituted body of knowledge. The notion that pedagogy represents a method or technique for transmitting information, as well as an essential dynamic in the production and exchange of knowledge, necessitates that educators attend to the categories of meaning that students bring to the classroom as well as to the fundamental question of why they should want to learn anything in the first place. This is an especially important consideration for those students in the public schools who know that the truth of their lives and experiences is omitted from the curriculum. A pedagogy that takes their lives seriously would have to begin with a question that June Jordan has suggested such students constantly pose to teachers through their absences and overt forms of school resistance: "If you don't know and don't care about who I am then why should I give a damn about what you say you do know about."[26] To legitimate or address a question of this sort would constitute for Bloom and Hirsch not merely bad teaching, but a dangerous social practice.

Read against the recent legacy of a critical educational tradition, the perspectives advanced by both Bloom and Hirsch reflect those of the critic who fears the indeterminacy of the future and who, in an attempt to escape the messy web of everyday life, purges the past of its contradictions, its paradoxes, and ultimately, of its injustices. Hirsch and Bloom sidestep the disquieting, disrupting, interrupting problems of sexism, racism, class exploitation, and other social issues that bear down so heavily on the present. This is a form of textual authority and discourse produced by pedagogues who are afraid of the future, who are strangled by the past, and who refuse to address the complexity, terror, and possibilities of the present. Most important, it is a public philosophy informed by a crippling ethnocentrism[27] and a contempt for the language and social relations fundamental to the ideals of a democratic society. It is, in the end, a desperate move by thinkers who would rather cling to a tradition forged by myth than work toward a collective future built on democratic possibilities. There is no sense in Bloom and Hirsch of a notion of textual authority that recognizes the need to engage in a living dialogue with diverse traditions that because of their partiality and historical limits need to be reread and recreated as part of an ongoing struggle for democratic public life. In the end,

Bloom and Hirsch cling to a notion of textual authority that neither produces critical citizens nor provides the foundation for pedagogy in which the conditions of learning become possible for the vast majority of diverse peoples who live in this society. What we are left with is the philosophy and pedagogy of hegemonic intellectuals cloaked in the mantle of academic enlightenment and literacy.

Notes

1. For an example of this position, see William Bennett, " 'To Reclaim a Legacy': Text of Report on Humanities in Higher Education," *Chronicle of Higher Education*, November 28, 1984, 16–21; Diane Ravitch and Chester Finn, Jr., *What Do Our 17-Year-Olds Know?* (New York: Harper & Row, 1988); for an excellent critique of this position, see Robert Scholes, "Aiming a Canon at the Curriculum," *Salmagundi*, 72 (Fall 1986), 101–17.

Publication information for the two works that are the primary subjects of this chapter is as follows: Allan Bloom, *The Closing of the American Mind* (New York: Simon & Schuster, 1987), and E. D. Hirsch, Jr., *Cultural Literacy: What Every American Needs to Know* (Boston: Houghton Mifflin, 1987).

2. This issue is taken up in Martin Carnoy and Henry M. Levin, *Schooling and Work in the Democratic State* (Stanford: Stanford University Press, 1985).

3. Given Bloom's tirade on popular culture and rock music, it is both somewhat surprising and ironic that when a reporter asked him if he had anticipated the popular success of *The Closing of the American Mind*, he responded with, "Sometimes I can't believe it. . . . It's like being declared Cary Grant, or a rock star. All this energy passing through you." Maybe Bloom has missed the contradiction here, but it appears that his newfound energy undermines both his own critique of the affective value of popular culture, and his own need to interrogate the underlying dichotomy he constructs between pleasure and learning. He may be surprised to find that the terrain of pleasure may be more complex and contradictory than he first imagined. See Henry A. Giroux and Roger I. Simon, "Popular Culture and Critical Pedagogy," *Cultural Studies* 2 (1988), 294–320. Bloom's comment is taken from James Atlas, "Chicago's Grumpy Guru: Best-Selling Professor Allan Bloom and the Chicago Intellectuals," *New York Times Magazine*, January 3, 1988, 25.

4. See Walter Benjamin, "Theses on the Philosophy of History," in Hannah Arendt, ed., *Illuminations* (New York: Schocken Books, 1963), 253–64.

5. In Martha Nussbaum, "Undemocratic Vistas," *New York Review of Books*, November 5, 1987, 22.

6. Mikhail Bakhtin, *The Dialogic Imagination*, ed. Michael Holquist, trans. Caryl Emerson and Michael Holquist (Austin: University of Texas Press, 1981).

7. Robert Scholes provides an illuminating commentary on the conservative agenda underlying the differences and commonalities that characterize the Bloom and Hirsch books:

> Hirsch wants to save us through information. He thinks that knowing about things is more important than knowing things. Bloom, on the other hand, thinks that the only thing that can save us is a return to really knowing and experiencing the great books, especially the great works of political and social philosophy that follow in the train of Plato's *Republic*. Hirsch concerns himself with what every American student should know, whereas Bloom is concerned only about a tiny elite.

Together, they set the conservative agenda for American education. Hirsch will make sure that everyone knows what the classics are and respects them, while Bloom will see to it that an elite can be defined by actually knowing these classics. In this way, the masses will be sufficiently educated to respect the superior knowledge of their betters, who have studied in a few major universities. Both Hirsch and Bloom emphasize certain kinds of traditional learning, but it is important to recognize that the attitude they take toward this learning is very different. For Bloom nothing less than a prolonged, serious engagement with the great books themselves can save the souls of our students. For Hirsch, just knowing the names of the great books and authors will suffice. Both Hirsch and Bloom share, however, a nostalgia for a not very closely examined past in which things were better. (Robert Scholes, "Three Views of Education: Nostalgia, History, and Voodoo," *College English, 50* [1988], 323–24)

8. The simplicity, ignorance, and political interests that often inform this particular view of Western culture are analyzed and deconstructed in James Clifford, *The Predicament of Culture: Twentieth-Century Ethnography, Literature and Art* (Cambridge, Mass.: Harvard University Press, 1988).

9. For a criticism of this form of testing, see Allan Nairn and Associates, *The Reign of ETS: The Corporation That Makes Up Minds* (Washington, D.C.: Ralph Nader, 1980); David Owen, *None of the Above: Behind the Myth of Scholastic Aptitude* (Boston: Houghton Mifflin, 1985); Peter Schrag, "What the Test Scores Really Mean," *The Nation*, October 4, 1986, 311–14; Peter Schrag, "Who Wants Good Teachers?" *The Nation*, October 11, 1986, 332–45.

10. For both a statistical and a theoretical analysis of these problems, see National Coalition of Advocates for Students, *Barriers to Excellence: Our Children at Risk* (Boston: Author, 1985).

11. Michael W. Apple, *Teachers and Text: A Political Economy of Class and Gender Relations* in Education (London: Routledge & Kegan Paul, 1986).

12. Linda Darling-Hammond, "Valuing Teachers: The Making of a Profession," *Teachers College Record, 87* (1985), 210.

13. For a review of this literature, see Henry A. Giroux, *Theory and Resistance in Education* (South Hadley, Mass.: Bergin & Garvey Press, 1985).

14. See, for example, Patrick Shannon, "The Use of Commercial Reading Materials in American Elementary Schools," *Reading Research Quarterly, 19* (1983), 68–85; Patrick Shannon, "Reading Instruction and Social Class," *Language Arts, 62* (1985), 604–11; Kenneth S. Goodman, "Basal Readers: A Call for Action," *Language Arts, 63* (1986), 358–-63.

15. See, for example, Michelle Fine, "Silencing in Public Schools," *Language Arts, 64* (1987), 157–74; Henry A. Giroux, *Schooling and the Struggle for Public Life* (Minneapolis: University of Minnesota Press, 1988).

16. Martin Carnoy and Henry M. Levin, *Schooling and Work in the Democratic State* (Stanford: Stanford University Press, 1985); Ira Katznelson and Margaret Weir, *Schooling for All: Class, Race, and the Decline of the Democratic Ideal* (New York: Basic Books, 1985); Stanley Aronowitz and Henry A. Giroux, *Education under Siege* (South Hadley, Mass.: Bergin & Garvey Press, 1985).

17. Hirsch's view of history represents what Harvey J. Graff calls a radically idealist conception of historical causation, in which one speaks "in historical claims without studying or interpreting any range of historical evidence or [presumes] the universality

and power of ideas without inquiring into them and their actual or alternative historical contexts or consequences." Harvey J. Graff, "A Review of *The Closing of the American Mind: How Higher Education Has Failed Democracy and Impoverished the Souls of Today's Students*," *Society, 17* (November/December, 1987), 101.

18. Herbert M. Kliebard, *The Struggle for the American Curriculum 1893–1958* (New York: Routledge & Kegan Paul, 1986).

19. Hirsch's view of history is strikingly similar to that expressed by William J. Bennett in his "To Reclaim a Legacy." In this view, as Harvey J. Kaye has pointed out, history is not conveyed as a "sense of the conflicts between social and political groups over ideas, values, and social relations. Nor does it posit the necessity of examining the distance between 'ideal' and 'experience' in Western Civilization and world history." In Harvey J. Kaye, "The Use and Abuse of the Past: The New Right and the Crisis of History," in Ralph Miliband, Leo Panitch, and John Saville, eds., *Socialist Register 1987* (London: Merlin Press, 1987), 354.

20. Hirsch argues for a notion of cultural literacy that suffers both from a misplaced faith in its social and economic possibilities and a refusal to take seriously how a pedagogy might be constructed that is consistent with the aims of this particular form of literacy. In the first instance, Hirsch argues that literacy is an essential precondition for eliminating just about every social and economic evil that plagues contemporary industrial societies. In this view, literacy becomes an independent variable that operates as part of a simple cause and effect relationship to produce particular outcomes. The issue here is not simply that Hirsch claims more for literacy than it can actually do as an ideological and social practice; more important, Hirsch presents an argument for literacy that both ignores and mystifies the role that wider cultural, historical, and social forces play in defining both the different forms of literacy and in supporting particular political and economic inequities. Hirsch's view of literacy is one that is silent about the wider problems and inequities that plague American society, problems that are rooted in configurations of power and structural relations that call into question not simply the dominant forms of literacy but the political, economic, and social fabric of the society itself. This issue is discussed in Harvey Graff, *The Literacy Myth: Literacy and Social Structure in the Nineteenth-Century City* (New York: Academic Press, 1979); see also Colin Lankshear with Moira Lawler, *Literacy, Schooling and Revolution* (New York: Falmer Press, 1987). But Hirsch does more than mystify the nature and effects of literacy, he also completely ignores the issue of what makes students want to learn, to be interested, or to listen to pedagogues such as himself. As we point out in the latter section of this essay, pedagogy for Hirsch is an unproblematic and uncritical construct, a technique to be employed after one has decided on the content to be taught. Given the wide gap between what Hirsch expects from his view of literacy and the simplistic and reactionary view of pedagogy he employs, it is not surprising that he ends up with what Scholes has called "voodoo education." (See Scholes, "Three Views of Education," 327.)

21. This literature is extensively reviewed in Giroux, *Theory and Resistance in Education*.

22. Ray Rist, "On Understanding the Process of Schooling: The Contribution of Labeling Theory," in J. Karabel and A. H. Halsey, eds., *Power and Ideology* (New York: Oxford University Press, 1977); Jean Anyon, "Social Class and the Hidden Curriculum of Work," in Henry A. Giroux, Anthony Penna, and William Pinar, eds., *Curriculum and Instruction* (Berkeley: McCutchan, 1981); Hugh Mehan, *Learning Lessons* (Cambridge: Harvard University Press, 1979).

23. Kathleen Rockhill, "Gender, Language and the Politics of Literacy," *British Journal of Sociology of Education, 8* (1987), 158.

24. June Jordan, *On Call: Political Essays* (Boston: South End Press, 1987), 30.

25. The notion of literacy as a form of cultural politics that embodies a particular pedagogical practice is most evident in the works of Paulo Freire. See, for example, Paulo Freire, *Pedagogy of the Oppressed*, trans. Myra Bergman Ramos (New York: Seabury Press, 1968); Paulo Freire and Donaldo Macedo, *Literacy: Reading the Word and the World* (South Hadley, Mass.: Bergin & Garvey, 1987).

26. Jordan, *On Call*, 29.

27. Martha Nussbaum's comment on the narrowness of Bloom's reading of the fruits of Western civilization is worth repeating:

> His special love for these books [the old Great Books of the ancient philosophers] has certainly prevented him from attending to works of literature and philosophy that lie outside the tradition they began. For he makes the remarkable claim that "only in the Western nations, i.e., those influenced by Greek philosophy, is there some willingness to doubt the identification of the good with one's own way." This statement shows a startling ignorance of the critical and rationalist tradition in classical Indian thought, of the arguments of classical Chinese thinkers, and beyond this, of countless examples of philosophical and nonphilosophical self-criticism from many parts of the world. (Nussbaum, "Undemocratic Vistas," 22)

CHAPTER 3

POSTMODERNISM AND THE DISCOURSE OF EDUCATIONAL CRITICISM

Genealogical practice transforms history from a judgment on the past in the name of a present truth to a "counter-memory" that combats our current modes of truth and justice, helping us to understand and change the present by placing it in a new relation to the past.
Jonathan Arac, *Postmodernism and Politics*

The Crisis of Modernism in the Postmodern Age

Educational theory and practice have always been strongly wedded to the language and assumptions of modernism. Educators as diverse as John Dewey (1916), Ralph Tyler (1950), Herb Gintis (Bowles and Gintis, 1976), John Goodlad (1984), and Martin Carnoy (Carnoy and Levin, 1985) have shared a faith in those modernist ideals that stress the capacity of individuals to think critically, to exercise social responsibility, and to remake the world in the interest of the Enlightenment dream of reason and freedom. Central to this view of education and modernity has been an abiding faith in the ability of individuals to situate themselves as self-motivating subjects within the wider discourse of public life. For many educators, modernism is synonymous with "the continual progress of the sciences and of techniques, the rational division of industrial work, and the intensification of human labor and of human domination over nature" (Baudrillard, 1987, 65–66). A faith in rational-

57

ity, science, and technology buttresses the modernist belief in permanent change, and in the continual and progressive unfolding of history. Similarly, education provides the socializing processes and legitimating codes by which the grand narrative of progress and human development can be passed on to future generations.

The moral, political, and social technologies that structure and drive the imperatives of public schooling are drawn from the modernist view of the *individual* student and educator as the guarantor of the delicate balance between private and public life, as the safeguard who can guarantee that the economy and the democratic state will function in a mutually determining manner. Within the discourse of modernism, knowledge draws its boundaries almost exclusively from a European model of culture and civilization. Civilization in this script is an extension of what Jean-François Lyotard (1984) calls the "great story" of the Enlightenment. In addition, modernism has been largely drawn from cultural scripts written by white males whose work is often privileged as a model of high culture informed by an elite sensibility that sets it off from what is often dismissed as popular or mass culture. While it is not the purpose of this chapter to write either the story of modernism[1] or its specific expressions in the history of educational theory and practice, it is important to note that modernism in both its progressive and reactionary forms has provided the central categories that have given rise to various versions of educational theory and practice. To question the most basic principles of modernity redefines the meaning of schooling, and also calls into question the very basis of our history, our cultural criticism, and our manifestations and expressions of public life. In effect, to challenge modernism is to redraw and remap the very nature of our social, political, and cultural geography. It is for this reason alone that the challenge currently being posed by various postmodernist discourses needs to be taken up and examined critically by educators.

In this chapter, we want to argue that the challenge of postmodernism is important for educators because it raises crucial questions regarding certain hegemonic aspects of modernism and, by implication, how these have affected the meaning and dynamics of present-day schooling. Postmodern criticism is also important because it offers the promise of deterritorializing modernism and redrawing its political, social, and cultural boundaries, while simultaneously affirming a politics of racial, gender, and ethnic difference. Moreover, postmodern criticism does not merely challenge dominant Western cultural models with their attendant notion of universally valid knowledge; it also resituates us within a world that bears little resemblance to the one that inspired the grand narratives of Marx and Freud. In effect, postmodern criticism calls attention to the shifting boundaries related to the increasing influence of the electronic mass media and information technology, the changing nature of class and social formations in postindustrialized capitalist societies, and the growing transgression of boundaries between life and art, high and popular culture, and image and reality.

We will argue in this essay that postmodern criticism offers a combination of reactionary and progressive possibilities, and that its various discourses have to be examined with great care if we are to benefit politically and pedagogically from its assumptions and analyses. We will also argue that a critical pedagogy is not to be developed on the basis of a choice between modernism and postmodernism. As Ernesto Laclau (1988) aptly states, "Postmodernism cannot be a simple rejection of modernity; rather, it involves a different modulation of its themes and categories" (65).[2] Moreover, both discourses as forms of cultural criticism are flawed; they need to be examined for the ways in which each cancels out the worst dimensions of the other. They each contain elements of strength, and educators have an opportunity to fashion a critical pedagogy that draws on the best insights of each. Most important, we will argue that those ideals of the project of modernity that link memory, agency, and reason to the construction of a democratic public sphere need to be defended as part of a discourse of critical pedagogy within (rather than in opposition to) the existing conditions of a postmodern world. At issue here is the task of delineating the broader cultural complexities that inform what we shall call a postmodern sensibility and criticism. Such a delineation needs to take place within the boundaries of a pedagogy and politics that reclaims and reinvigorates, rather than denies or is indifferent to, the possibilities of a radical democracy (Giroux, 1991).

The argument that is developed here unfolds as follows: first, we will provide some theoretical groundwork for developing a broad map of what constitutes the meaning of postmodernism, and what can be called the postmodern condition. Briefly put, the postmodern condition refers to the various discursive and structural transformations that characterize what can be called a postmodern culture in the era of late capitalism. Second, we will articulate some of the central and most critical themes that have emerged from the various discourses on postmodern theory. In this section we will examine the conservative and radical implications of these positions. Third, we will argue that in order to develop a more adequate theory of schooling as a form of cultural politics it is important that contemporary educators integrate the central theoretical features of a postmodernism of resistance with the more radical elements of modernist discourse.

The Meaning of Postmodernism

Though postmodernism has influenced a wide variety of fields that include music, fiction, film, drama, architecture, criticism, anthropology, sociology, and the visual arts, there is no agreed-upon meaning for the term.[3] In keeping with the multiplicity of difference that it celebrates, postmodernism is not only subject to different ideological appropriations, it is also marked by a wide variety of interpretations. This can be illustrated by briefly looking at the different views of postmodernism articulated by two of its leading theorists, Jean-François Lyotard (1984) and Fredric Jameson (1984).

Lyotard has described postmodernism as a rejection of grand narratives, metaphysical philosophies, and any other form of totalizing thought. In his view, the meaning of postmodernism is inextricably related to the changing conditions of knowledge and technology that are producing forms of social organization that are undermining the old habits, bonds, and social practices of modernity. For Lyotard, the postmodern is defined through the diffusion throughout Western societies of computers, scientific knowledge, advanced technology, and electronic texts, each of which accents and privileges diversity, locality, specificity, and the contingent against the totalitizing narratives of the previous age. According to Lyotard, technical, scientific, and artistic innovations are creating a world where individuals must make their own way without the benefit of fixed referents or traditional philosophical moorings. Total mastery and liberation are dismissed as the discourses of terror and forced consensus. In its place postmodernism appears as an ideological and political marker for referencing a world without stability, a world where knowledge is constantly changing and where meaning can no longer be anchored in a teleological view of history.

Fredric Jameson's (1984, 1988) writings on postmodernism challenge the nihilism implicit in many such theories. Jameson defines postmodernism as the "cultural logic" that represents the third great stage of late capitalism, as well as the new cultural dominant of the times in Western societies. For Jameson (1984), postmodernism is an epochal shift that alerts us to the present remapping of social space and the creation of new social formations. If postmodernism represents new forms of fragmentation, the creation of new constellations of forms, and the emergence of new technological and artistic developments in capitalist society, Jameson does not respond by calling for the death of grand narratives or by celebrating the electronic spectacles that substitute images for reality. Instead, he argues for new cognitive maps, different forms of representation that provide a systematic reading of the new age.

Douglas Kellner (1988) is right in arguing that Jameson's view of postmodernism is quite different from that of Lyotard and a number of other prominent theorists of the postmodern. Kellner writes:

> In any case, one sees how, against Lyotard, Jameson employs the form of a grand narrative, of a totalizing theory of society and history that makes specific claims about features of postmodernism—which interprets as "the cultural logic of capital" rather than as a code word for a new (post)historical condition—as do Lyotard and Baudrillard (however much they reject totalizing thought). Obviously, Jameson wishes to preserve Marxism as the Master Narrative and to relativize all competing theories as sectorial or regional theories to be subsumed in their proper place within the Marxian Master Narrative. (262)

Postmodernism's refusal of grand narratives, its rejection of universal reason as a foundation for human affairs, its decentering of the humanist subject, its radical problematization of representation, and its celebration of plurality and the politics of racial, gender, and ethnic difference have sparked a major debate among conservatives, liberals, and radicals in an increasingly diverse number of fields. For example, conservative cultural critics such as Allan Bloom (1987) argue that postmodernism represents "the last, predictable stage in the suppression of reason and the denial of the possibility of truth" (379). In a similar fashion, conservatives such as Daniel Bell (1976) claim that postmodernism extends the adversarial and hedonistic tendencies of modernism to destructive extremes. For a host of other conservatives, postmodernism as it is expressed in the arts, music, film, and fiction is pejoratively dismissed as "a reflection of . . . the present wave of [destructive] political reaction sweeping the Western world" (Gott, 1986, 10).

Liberals such as Jürgen Habermas and Richard Rorty take opposing positions on the relevance of postmodernism. Habermas (1983) sees it as a threat to the foundations of democratic public life, while Rorty (1985) appropriates its central assumptions as part of the defense of liberal capitalist society. Among left-wing radicals, postmodernism runs a theoretical gamut that ranges from adulation to condemnation to a cautious skepticism. Radical critics such as Terry Eagleton (1985), Perry Anderson (1984), and Barbara Christian (1987) see postmodernism as either a threat to or a flight from the real world of politics and struggle. Hal Foster (1983), Andreas Huyssen (1986), Stuart Hall (in Grossberg, (1986), and a number of feminist critics such as Teresa de Lauretis (1987), Meaghan Morris (1988), and Nancy Fraser and Linda Nicholson (1990), approach the discourse of postmodernism cautiously by interrogating critically its claims and absences. Radical avant-garde theorists such as Jean Baudrillard (1988) and Jean-François Lyotard (1984) utilize postmodern discourses as a theoretical weapon to articulate either the nihilism of capitalist society and its alleged collapse of meaning or the tyranny implicit in the totalizing narratives characteristic of modernity.

While it would be easy to dismiss postmodernism as simply a code word for a new theoretical fashion, the term is important because it directs our attention to a number of changes and challenges that are a part of the contemporary age. For some social theorists, postmodernism may be on the verge of becoming an empty signifier, while others credit it with a theoretical and heuristic relevance deriving from its capacity to provide a focus for a number of historically significant debates. As Dick Hebdige (1986) points out, there can be little doubt that the term "postmodern" appears to "have occupied a semantic ground in which something precious and important was felt to be embedded" (79). The discourse of postmodernism is worth struggling over, and not merely as a semantic category that needs to be subjected to ever more precise definitional rigor. Rather, it is important to mine its contradictory and oppositional insights for possible use in the service of a radical cultural politics and a critical theory of pedagogy. At the same time, to provide a basis for understanding its cultural and political insights, we want to argue that postmodernism in the broadest sense refers to an intellectual position, a form of cultural criticism, as well as to an emerging set of social, cultural, and economic conditions that have come to characterize the age of global capitalism and industrialism. In the first instance, postmodernism represents a form of cultural criticism that radically questions the logic of foundations that has become the epistemological cornerstone of modernism. In the second instance, postmodernism refers to an increasingly radical change in the relations of production, the nature of the nation-state, the development of new technologies that have redefined the fields of telecommunications and information processing, and the forces at work in the growing globalization and interdependence of the economic, political, and cultural spheres. All of these issues will be taken up below in more specific detail.

Before enumerating what we think are the basic assumptions that the various discourses of postmodernism have in common, we want to briefly elaborate on some of the conditions that have come to characterize what can be called a postmodern age. We don't believe that postmodernism represents a drastic break or rupture from modernity as much as it signals a shift toward a set of social conditions that are reconstituting the social, cultural, and geopolitical map of the world, while simultaneously producing new forms of cultural criticism. Such a shift represents a break away from certain definitive features of modernism, "with the emphasis firmly on the sense of the relational move away" (Featherstone, 1988, 197). At the same time, we believe that the various discourses of postmodernism have underplayed the continuities that mark the transition from one age to another within the current capitalist countries. Modernism is far from dead—its central categories are simply being written within a plurality of narratives that are attempting to address the new set of social, political, technical, and scientific configurations that constitute the current age. Stuart Hall (in Grossberg, 1986) captures the complexity of the relationship between modernity and postmodernism in the following comment:

> But I don't know that with "postmodernism" we are dealing
> with something totally and fundamentally different from that
> break at the turn of the century. I don't mean to deny that
> we've gone through profound qualitative changes between
> then and now. There are, therefore, now some very perplexing
> features to contemporary culture that certainly tend to outrun
> the critical and theoretical concepts generated in the early
> modernist period. We have, in that sense, to constantly update
> our theories and to be dealing with new experiences. I also
> accept that these changes may constitute new subject-positions
> and social identities for people. But I don't think there is any
> such absolutely novel and unified thing as the postmodern
> condition. It's another version of that historical amnesia
> characteristic of American culture—the tyranny of the New. (47)

In what follows we will discuss some of the major features of the postmodern condition. In doing so, we will draw on a variety of different theoretical perspectives regarding the nature and meaning of these conditions.

The postmodern condition has to be seen as part of an ongoing shift related to global structural changes as well as a radical change in the way in which culture is produced, circulated, read, and consumed. Such shifts cannot be seen as part of the old Marxist base/superstructure model. Instead, they have to be viewed as part of a series of uneven developments that have emerged out of the conflict between traditional economic models and new cultural formations and modes of criticism, on the one hand, and related discourses that mark out the terrains of certain aspects of modernism and postmodernism on the other. On an ideological level, the deterritorialization and remapping characteristic of the postmodern condition can be seen in the effort by many theorists and critics to challenge and rewrite in oppositional terms the modernist ideals of rationality, totality, certainty, and progress along with its "globalizing, integrative vision of the individual's place in history and society" (Richard, 1987/1988, 6). But the struggle against the ideals of modernity is not limited to the rewriting of its major texts and assumptions. For example, such a struggle cannot be seen exclusively as a matter of challenging a privileged modernist aesthetic, which calls into question the oppressive organization of space and experience that characterizes institutions such as schools, museums, and the workplace; nor can the struggle against modernity be read simply as a call to open up texts to the heterogeneity of meanings they embody and mediate. These sites of struggle and contestation are important, but the postmodern condition is also rooted in those fundamental political and technological shifts that undermine the central modernist notion that there exists "a legitimate center—a unique and superior position from which to establish control and to determine hierarchies" (Richard, 1987/1988, 6). This center refers to the privileging of Western patriarchal culture, with its representations of domination rooted in a Eurocentric conception of the world, and to the technological, political, economic, and military resources that once were almost exclusively dominated by the Western industrial countries. In effect, the basic elements of the postmodern condition have been created by major changes in the global redistribution of political power and cultural legitimation, the deterritorialization and decentering of power in the West, the transformations in the nature of the forces of production, and the emergence of new forms of cultural criticism. In what follows, we will spell these out in greater detail.

The economic and political conditions that have come about in the Western nations since the Second World War have been extensively analyzed by theorists such as Stanley Aronowitz (1987/1988), Scott Lash and John Urry (1987), and Jean Baudrillard (1988). Although these theorists hold differing positions on the importance of postmodernism, each of them believes that postmodernism can only be understood in terms of its problematic relationship with central features of the modernist tradition. Each of their analyses is important. For Aronowitz

(1987/1988), modernity's faith in the nation-state is receding on a world-wide level as the forces of production that drive the global economy are increasingly dispersed through the multinationalism of corporations and the emergence of economic powers outside of the Western industrialized nations. Moreover, Aronowitz believes that the modernist legitimating narratives of public life no longer have the power of conviction or the ideological cohesiveness they once had. Ideological support has given way to bad faith. This can be seen in the various ways in which sexual and power hierarchies, electoral politics, and faith in industrialism are now under attack from a wider variety of groups at the same time that they are more deeply entrenched in elite public discourse and politics.

For Lash and Urry (1987), capitalism has become increasingly disorganized. They argue that this process, while not contributing directly to the development of postmodernist culture, represents a powerful force in the emergence of many elements making up the postmodern condition. The central changes that Lash and Urry point to include the deconcentration of capital as national markets become less regulated by national corporations; the decline in the number of blue-collar workers as deindustrialization reconstructs the centers of production and changes the makeup of the labor force; a dramatic expansion of the white-collar workforce as well as a distinctive service class; an increase in cultural pluralism and the development of new cultural/ethnic/political formations; and demographic changes involving the financial collapse of inner cities and the growth in rural and suburban populations. And, finally, though they touch on a number of other considerations, Lash and Urry emphasize the appearance of an ideological/cultural apparatus in which the production of information and symbols not only becomes a central aspect of the making and remaking of everyday life, but contributes to the breakdown of the division between reality and image.

In Jean Baudrillard's (1988) discourse, the postmodern condition represents more than a massive transgression of the boundaries that are essential to the logic of modernism; it represents a form of hyperreality, an infinite proliferation of meanings in which all boundaries collapse into models of simulation. In this perspective, there is no relevance to an epistemology that searches out the higher elevations of truth, exercises a depth reading, or tries to penetrate reality in order to uncover the essence of meaning. Reality is on the surface. Ideology, alienation, and values are all jettisoned in this version of postmodern discourse, and are subsumed within the orbit of a society saturated with media messages that have no meaning or content in the rationalist sense. In this view, information as noise is passively consumed by the masses, whose brutish indifference obliterates the ground of mediation, politics, and resistance. In emphasizing the glitter of the everyday as spectacle, Baudrillard points to the new forms of technology and information that have become central to a reproductive order that blurs the lines between past and present, art and life, and commitment and experience.

But Baudrillard's (1988) society of simulations, a society in which "signs replace the logic of production and class conflict as key constituents of contemporary capitalist societies" (Kellner, in press, 11), translates less into a provocative analysis of the changing contours and features of the age than it does into a nihilism that undermines its own radical intent. Fatalism replaces struggle, and irony resigns itself to a "mediascape" that offers the opportunity for a form of refusal defined simply as play. Foundationalism is out, and language has become a signifier, floating anchorless in a terrain of images that refuse definition and spell the end of representation. In Baudrillard's postmodern world, history is finished, subsumed in a vertigo of electronic fantasy-images that privilege inertia as reality. For theorists like Baudrillard, the masses have become the black hole into which all meaning simply disappears. Domination now takes place through the proliferation of signs, images, and signifiers that envelop us without a hint of either where they come from or what they mean. The task is not to interpret but to consume—to revel in the plurality of uncertainties that claim no boundaries and seek no resolutions. This is the world of the spectacle and the simulacrum, a world in which the modernist notion of the "aura" of a work, personality, or text no longer exists (Benjamin, 1969). Everything is a copy, everything and everyone is networked into a communication system in which we are all electronically wired, pulsating in response to the simulations that keep us watching and consuming. In Baudrillard's world, the postmodern condition is science fiction, meaning is an affront to reality, and pedagogy vanishes except as form because there are no more experts.

In spite of the different politics and analyses presented by each of these positions, they all respectively concede that we are living in a transitional era in which emerging social conditions call into question the ability of old orthodoxies to name and understand the changes that are ushering us into the twenty-first century. Whether these changes suggest a break between modernity and postmodernity may not be as important an issue as understanding the nature of the changes and what their implications might be for reconstituting a radical cultural politics appropriate to our own time and place. We need to understand more clearly what changes are taking place in various artistic, intellectual, and academic spheres regarding the production, distribution, and reception of various theories and discourses. We also need to understand better how a broader shift in the balance of power in the wider cultural sphere either opens up or restricts the possibilities for developing a discourse of public life, one that can draw from both a critical modernism and a postmodernism of resistance. Finally, we need to understand how the field of the everyday is being reconstituted not simply as a commodity sphere but as a site of contestation that offers new possibilities for engaging the memories, histories, and stories of those who offer not simply otherness but an oppositional resistance to various forms of domination. All of these concerns and changes involve pedagogical and political issues, because they focus on the ways in which power is being redistributed and taken up by different social formations making new and radical demands both within and outside societies, and also because they illuminate the need to understand how these changes are actually taken up by different groups in particular historical and cultural contexts.

Postmodern Problematics: Reactionary versus Progressive Appropriations

In what follows, we shall address productive contradictions inherent in important thematic considerations that cut across a number of postmodernist discourses. Following Linda Hutcheon (1988), we maintain that the various theories and practices that constitute the postmodern field represent what can in effect be called postmodern problematics: "a set of problems and basic issues that have been created by the various discourses of postmodernism, issues that were not particularly problematic before but certainly are now" (Hutcheon, 1988, 5). The problematics that will be analyzed below make clear some of the major paradoxes of postmodernist discourse; they also illuminate the difficulties and possibilities for rereading and rewriting the major categories of educational theory and cultural criticism.

Postmodernism and the Crisis of Totality and Foundationalism

> We have paid a high enough price for the nostalgia of the whole and the one, for the reconciliation of the concept and the sensible, of the transparent and the communicable

> experience. . . . Let us wage war on totality; let us be witnesses
> to the unpresentable; let us activate the differences and save
> the honor of the name. (Lyotard, 1984, 81–82)

In the above quotation, Lyotard articulates an antagonism that has become a central feature of postmodernist discourse. That is, postmodernism rejects those aspects of the Enlightenment and Western philosophical tradition that rely on master narratives "which set out to address a transcendental Subject, to define an essential human nature, to prescribe a global human destiny or to proscribe collective human goals" (Hebdige, 1986, 81). Within this perspective all claims to universal reason and impartial competence are rejected in favor of the partiality and specificity of discourse. General abstractions that deny the specificity and particularity of everyday life, that generalize out of existence the particular and the local, that smother difference under the banner of universalizing categories are rejected as totalitarian and terroristic.

The postmodern critique of totality also represents a rejection of foundational claims that wrap themselves in an appeal to science, objectivity, neutrality, and scholarly disinterestedness. Validity claims that rest on essentializing and transcendent metadiscourses are viewed with suspicion and skepticism, and are regarded as ideological expressions of particular discourses embodying normative interests and legitimating historically specific relations of power. This is especially true of those grand narratives that encompass sweeping global claims regarding human destiny and happiness. In this case, postmodern discourse rejects, for example, the totalizing theories of Marxism, Hegelianism, Christianity, and any other philosophy of history based on notions of causality and all-encompassing global resolutions regarding human destiny. For Lyotard (1984), totalizing narratives need to be opposed as part of the wider struggle against modernity.

> I will use the term *modern* to designate any science that
> legitimates itself with reference to a metadiscourse of this kind
> making an explicit appeal to some grand narrative, such as the
> dialectics of Spirit, the hermeneutics of meaning, the
> emancipation of the rational or working subject, or the creation
> of wealth. (xxii)

But there is more at stake here than simply an argument against the grand narrative or the claims of universal reason; there is also an attack on those intellectuals who would designate themselves the emancipatory vanguard, an intellectual elite who have deemed themselves above history only to attempt to shape it through their pretensions to what Dick Hebdige (1986) calls an "illusory Faustian omnipotence" (91). In some versions of the postmodern, totality and foundationalism do not lead to the truth or to emancipation, but to periods of great suffering and violence. The postmodernist attack on the grand narrative is simultaneously a criticism of an inflated teleological self-confidence, an indictment of a dangerous transcendentalism, and a rejection of the omniscient narrator (Feher, 1988, 197–98). Read in more positive terms, postmodernists are arguing for a plurality of voices and narratives— that is, for different narratives that present the unrepresentable, for stories that emerge from historically specific struggles (Welch, 1990). Similarly, postmodern discourse is attempting, with its emphasis on the specific and the normative, to situate reason and knowledge within rather than outside particular configurations of space, place, time, and power. Partiality in this case becomes a political necessity as part of the discourse of locating oneself within rather than outside of history and ideology. Stanley Aronowitz (1987/1988) captures this issue in the following comment:

> Postmodern thought . . . is bound to discourse, literally narratives about the world that are admittedly partial. Indeed, one of the crucial features of discourse is the intimate tie between knowledge and interest, the latter being understood as "standpoint" from which to grasp "reality." Putting these terms in inverted commas signifies the will to abandon scientificity, science as a set of propositions claiming validity by any given competent investigatory. What postmodernists deny is precisely this category of impartial competence. For competence is constituted as a series of exclusions—of women, of people of color, of nature as a historical agent, of the truth value of art. (103)

The postmodern attack on totality and grand narratives needs to be dialectically construed if it is to contribute to a radical theory of education and cultural politics. At one level the critique of master narratives is important because it makes us attentive to those mythic elements of foundationalism that give history, society, nature, and human relations an ultimate and unproblematic meaning. In this case, the critique of master narratives is synonymous with an attack on those forms of theoretical terrorism that deny contingency, values, struggle, and human agency. Moreover, by denying an ultimate ground upon which human action is construed, the critique of totality/master narratives opens up the possibility for a wider proliferation of discourses and forms of political action (Laclau, 1988, 78–79). In effect, this form of critique rejects totality and the master narrative as ontological notions. On the other hand, to reject all notions of totality is to run the risk of being trapped in particularistic theories that cannot explain how the various diverse relations that constitute larger social, political, and global systems interrelate or mutually determine and constrain each other. In order to retain a relationship between postmodern discourse and the primacy of the political, it is imperative that the notion of totality be embraced as a heuristic device rather than as an ontological category. In other words, we need to preserve a notion of totality that privileges forms of analysis in which it is possible to make visible those mediations, interrelations, and interdependencies that give shape and power to larger political and social systems. We need theories that express and articulate difference, but we also need to understand how the relations in which differences are constituted operate as part of a wider set of social, political, and cultural practices. Doug Kellner (1988) is incisive on this issue as he modifies the postmodernist position on totality with a more critical and dialectical view by arguing for a distinction between what he calls grand and master narratives:

> Against Lyotard, we might want to distinguish between "master narrtives" that attempt to subsume every particular, every specific viewpoint, and every key point into one totalizing theory (as in some versions of Marxism, feminism, Weber, etc.) from "grand narratives" which attempt to tell a Big Story, such as the rise of capital, patriarchy or the colonial subject. (253)

Postmodernism, Culture, and the Problematic of Otherness

Related to the critique of master narratives and theories of totality is another major concern of postmodernism: the development of a politics that addresses popular culture as a serious object of aesthetic and cultural criticism, on the one hand, and signals and affirms the importance of minority cultures as historically specific forms of cultural production, on the other. Postmodernism's attack on universalism has translated, in part, into a refusal of modernism's relentless hostility to mass culture, and its reproduction of the elitist division between high and low culture (Foster, 1983; Huyssen, 1986). Not only has postmodernism's reaffirmation of popular culture challenged the aesthetic and epistemological divisions supportive of academic disciplines and the contours of what has been considered "serious" taste, it has also resulted in new forms of art, writing, filmmaking, and types of aesthetic and social criticism.[4] Similarly, postmodernism has provided the conditions necessary for exploring and recuperating traditions of various forms of Otherness as a fundamental dimension of both the cultural and the sociopolitical spheres.

What postmodernism has done in problematizing the cultural sphere is threefold. First, it has pointed to those changing conditions of knowledge embedded in the age of electronically mediated culture, cybernetic steering systems, and computer engineering (Lyotard, 1984). Second, it has helped to raise new questions about the terrain of culture as a field of both domination and contestation. More specifically, various discourses of postmodernism have challenged the ethnocentricity that rests on the assumption that America and Europe represent universalized models of civilization and culture (Ross, 1988). In doing so postmodernism has helped to redefine the relationship between power and culture, representation and domination, and language and subjectivity. Third, postmodernism has provided a theoretical foundation for engaging the Other not only as a deterritorialized object of domination, but also as a source of struggle, collective resistance, and historical affirmation. In other words, postmodernism's stress on the problematic of Otherness has included a focus on the importance of history as a form of counter-memory (Kaplan, 1987); an emphasis on the value of the everyday as a source of agency and empowerment (Grossberg, 1988); a renewed understanding of gender as an irreducible historical and social practice constituted in a plurality of self- and social representations (de Lauretis, 1987; Morris, 1988); and an insertion of the contingent, the discontinuous, and the unrepresentable as coordinates for remapping and rethinking the borders that define one's existence and place in the world.

By pointing to the increasingly powerful and complex role of the electronic mass media in constituting individual identities, cultural languages, and social formations, the various discourses of postmodernism have provided a powerful new language that enables us to understand the changing nature of domination and resistance in late capitalist societies. This is particularly true in its understanding of how the conditions for the production of knowledge have changed within the last two decades with respect to the electronic and information-processing technologies of production, the types of knowledge produced, and the impact they have had both at the level of everyday life and in larger global terms (Kellner, in press). By incorporating these changes in the cultural sphere into its discourse, postmodernism questions the relevance of traditional discourses such as Marxism, and raises serious ideological questions about the academic boundaries that structure the organization of canons and knowledge formations. Within many postmodernist discourses, the established academic canons are criticized for ignoring the socially constructed nature of their form and content and for narrowly defining their relationship to and impact on the larger world. The importance of this form of postmodern criticism can be seen in the ways it has been taken up in the various debates on the status and ideological nature of the canon in higher education.[5]

Of course, there is no systematic theory of culture at work in postmodernism; instead, there are a variety of theoretical positions and cultural practices ranging from Baudrillard's (1988) darker vision of the collapse of meaning into simulations or simulacra to less pessimistic theoretical attempts to challenge new forms of cultural production and domination while simultaneously creating alternative artistic and cultural spheres (Foster, 1983; Kellner, 1988). At stake here are a politics and cultural analysis that provide the conditions for challenging the formalist and institutionalized boundaries of art and culture that characterize those public spheres that trade in and profit from the reproduction and production of signs, images, and representations, whether they be the museum, school, city planning commission, or the state. Similarly, there is also an increasing proliferation of pastiche, irony, and parody, forms of cultural criticism that allow us to deepen our understanding of "the kinds of men, women, and biographical experiences that the late postmodern period makes available to its members" (Denzin, 1988, 461).

The postmodern problematic of culture and Otherness is not without its ambiguities and problems. Postmodernism may display dazzling cultural criticism, but postmodern critics say very little regarding how the characteristic experiences of the postmodern are actually experienced and taken up by different groups. There is little if any sense of pedagogy in this discourse, which is overly focused on the reading of cultural texts, without a concomitant understanding of how people invest in signs, signifiers, images, and discourses that actively construct their identities and social relations. Similarly, postmodernism has a tendency to democratize the notion of difference in a way that echoes a type of vapid liberal pluralism. There is in this discourse the danger of affirming difference simply as an end in itself without acknowledging how difference is formed, erased, and resuscitated within and despite asymmetrical relations of power. Lost here is any understanding of how difference is forged in both domination and opposition. While the rediscovery of difference as an aesthetic and cultural issue is to be applauded, there is a theoretical tendency in many postmodernist discourses to abstract the primacy of the relations of power and politics from the discussion of marginalized Others. Difference in this sense often slips into a theoretically harmless and politically deracinated notion of pastiche. As Cornel West points out, the revolt "against the center by those constituted as marginals [should be viewed in terms of] an oppositional difference. . . . These American attacks on universality in the name of difference, these 'postmodern' issues of Otherness (Afro-Americans, Native Americans, women, gays) are in fact an implicit critique of certain French postmodern discourses about Otherness that really serve to hide and conceal the power of the voices and movements of Others" (Stephanson, 1988, 273).

The position that West is criticizing is best exemplified in the work of the liberal postmodernist Richard Rorty (1979, 1985). Rorty's postmodernism attempts to allow space for the diverse voices of marginalized groups by including them in conversations that expand the notions of solidarity and human community. But in Rorty's version, solidarity is given a liberal twist that removes it from relations of power, resistance, and struggle. The community in which Rorty's conversation takes place engages a notion of pluralism in which various groups appear to have equal voices. As George Yudice (1988) convincingly reveals, there is a failure within this type of thought to develop forms of social analysis, critique, or understanding of how particular voices and social formations are formed in oppositional struggle, rather than in dialogue. That is, there is little or no theoretical attempt to illustrate how dominant and subordinate voices are formed in the ideological and material contexts of real conflict and oppression. In Rorty's position there is no clear understanding of why marginalized Others may not be able or willing to participate in such a conversation. Similarly, there is little sense of how subordinate groups, as part of an oppositional cultural politics, first need to participate in the struggle to constitute themselves as both subjects and objects of history. Put another way, some versions of postmodern discourse want to recognize and privilege the marginal without engaging the important issue of what social conditions need to exist before such groups can actually exercise forms of self-and social empowerment. In similar fashion, what needs to be dealt with in postmodernist discourse regarding the problematic of Otherness is how subordinate groups can struggle collectively to create conditions that enable them better to understand how their identities have been constructed within dominant and subordinate relations of power, and what it takes to struggle for their own voices and visions while simultaneously working to transform the social and material conditions that have oppressed them (Hartsock, 1987; Yudice, 1988). There is no pure space from which to develop either a politics of resistance or a politics of identity. Indeed, the struggle for voice and collective empowerment has to be forged within, not outside, the mediating traditions and histories that link the center and the margins of late capitalism.

Within the postmodern discourses of culture and Otherness, there is a privileging of space, textuality, signs, and surfaces that runs the risk of abandoning all forms of historicity. While some critics rightly argue that postmodernism offers the opportunity to repossess those human histories barred from the script of dominant historical narratives, as well as the possibility of reworking history from another vantage point (Chambers, 1986; Feher, 1988), more often than not, such opportunities remain concretely unrealized. For in the vast territory of postmodern commentary and cultural production, history either gets lost in the effacement of boundaries orchestrated in the reworkings of pastiche or is displaced into forms of parody and nostalgia. For example, films like *Blue Velvet* and *Wetherby* depict a postmodernist experience that, while sometimes fascinating, effaces most connecting boundaries between the past and the present (Denzin, 1988). In these films, history either collapses into an attack on nostalgia that becomes synonymous with terror, as in *Blue Velvet*, or, as in *Wetherby*, dissolves in the destruction of narrative structure itself. In both films, historical understanding gives way to a pastiche in which the film characters become so free-floating as to become lost in a web of self-parody. In these films, style is subsumed into celebration of the grotesque, collapsing into a display of the strange and unrepresentable, and impeding the audience's ability to engage critically the politics of the film. In these films, style disguises rather than illuminates the underlying political machinery. For instance, *Blue Velvet* may successfully employ parody in its depiction of small-town America, but it also denigrates working-class life and women in nothing less than reactionary terms. Otherness in these films is depicted within hegemonic categories that undermine and restrict a progressive reading and do not invite identification with subordinate groups. These are films without a critical sense of history and politics. To a large extent, these films reflect some of the deeper problems characteristic of postmodern cultural forms and criticism in general.

Postmodernism and the Crisis of Language, Representation, and Agency

Perhaps the most important feature of postmodernism is its stress on the importance of language and subjectivity as new fronts from which to rethink the issues of meaning, identity, and politics. Postmodern discourse has retheorized the nature of language as a system of signs structured in the infinite play of difference, and in so doing has undermined the dominant positivist notion of language as either a permanent genetic code or simply a transparent medium for transmitting ideas and meaning. Jacques Derrida (1976), in particular, has played a major role in retheorizing language through the principle of what he calls *différance*. This view suggests that meaning is the product of a language constructed out of and subject to the endless play of differences between signifiers. What constitutes the meaning of a signifier is defined by the shifting, changing relations of difference that characterize the referential play of language. What Derrida, Laclau and Mouffe (1985), and a host of other critics have demonstrated is "the increasing difficulty of defining the limits of language, or, more accurately, of defining the specific identity of the linguistic object" (Laclau, 1988, 67). But more is at stake here than theoretically demonstrating that meaning can never be fixed once and for all. Postmodernism has also offered powerful new modes of criticism in which various cultural objects can be read textually in the manner of a socially constructed language. In effect, by constituting cultural objects as languages, it has become possible to question radically the hegemonic view of representation, which argues that knowledge, truth, and reason are governed by linguistic codes and regulations that are essentially neutral and apolitical (Cherryholmes, 1988; McLaren, 1986). The most politically charged aspect of the postmodern view of discourse is that "it challenges reason on its own ground and demonstrates that what gets called reason and knowledge is simply a particular way of organizing perception and communication, a way of organizing and categorizing experience that is social and contingent but whose socially constructed nature and contingency have been suppressed" (Peller, 1987, 30). For traditionalists, the postmodern emphasis on the contingency of language represents a retreat into nihilism, but in effect, such contingency can move against nihilism, by making problematic the very nature of language, representation, and meaning. In this view, truth, science, and ethics do not cease to exist; instead, they become representations that need to be problematized rather than accepted as received truths.

The postmodern emphasis on the centrality of discourse has also re-sulted in a major rethinking of the notion of subjectivity. In particular, various postmodern discourses have offered a massive critique of the liberal humanist notion of subjectivity that is predicated on a unified, rational, self-determining consciousness. In this view, the individual subject is the source of self-knowledge, and his or her view of the world is constituted through the exercise of a rational and autonomous mode of understanding and knowing. What postmodern discourse challenges is liberal humanism's notion of the subject "as a kind of free, autonomous, universal sensibility, indifferent to any particular or moral contents" (Eagleton, 1985/1986, 101). Chris Weeden (1987) offers a succinct commentary on postmodernism's challenge to this position:

> Language is the place where actual and possible forms of social organization and their likely social and political consequences are defined and contested. Yet it is also the place where our sense of ourselves, our subjectivity, is constructed. The assumption that subjectivity is constructed implies that it is not innate, not genetically determined, but socially produced. Subjectivity is produced in a whole range of discursive practices—economic, social and political—the meanings of which are a constant site of struggle over power. Language is not the expression of unique individuality; it constructs the individual's subjectivity in ways which are socially specific. . . . subjectivity is neither unified nor fixed. Unlike humanism, which implies a conscious, knowing, unified, rational subject [postmodernism] theorizes subjectivity as a site of disunity and conflict, central to the process of political change and to preserving the status quo. (21)

The importance of postmodernism's retheorizing of subjectivity can-not be overemphasized. In this view, subjectivity is no longer assigned to the apolitical wasteland of essences and essentialism. Subjectivity is now read as multiple, layered, and nonunitary; rather than being con-stituted in a unified and integrated ego, the "self" is seen as being, in Stuart Hall's words, "constituted out of and by difference and remains contradictory" (Grossberg, 1986, 56). No longer viewed as merely the repository of consciousness and creativity, the self is constructed as a terrain of conflict and struggle, and subjectivity is seen as the site of both liberation and subjugation. How subjectivity relates to issues of identity, intentionality, and desire is a deeply political issue that is in-extricably related to social and cultural forces that extend far beyond the self-consciousness of the so-called humanist subject. The nature of subjectivity, and its capacities for self- and social determination, can no longer be determined by the guarantees of transcendent phenomena or metaphysical essences. Seen in this perspective, the basis for a cultural politics and the struggle for power has been opened up to include the issues of language and identity.

The theoretical status and political viability of various postmodern discourses regarding the issues of language, textuality, and the subject are a matter of intense debate among diverse progressive groups. What appears to be at stake in these debates is less a matter of accepting the theoretical and political credibility of these categories than of deepening and extending their radical potential for a viable and critical theory of cultural practice. While the questions raised around these categories are important and politically necessary, what remains subject to serious criticism are the theoretical and political absences that have characterized the way in which the issues of language and subjectivity have been developed in some American versions of postmodernism. In what follows, we will develop some of the more important criticisms aimed at radicalizing rather than rejecting the notions of language and subjectivity as part of a wider discourse of educational and cultural struggle.

The postmodern emphasis on language and textuality is marked by a number of problems that need to be addressed. In the United States, the postmodern/deconstructive emphasis on treating social and cultural forms as texts has become increasingly reductionist in its overly exclusive reliance on literature as its object of analysis. Confined largely to literary and film studies, textual criticism has failed to move beyond the boundaries of the book or screen. Consequently, such analyses have become highly academicized, and have retreated into a formalism that fails to link their own semiological productions to wider institutional and social practices. By failing to incorporate the complexity of determinations that constitute the cultural, political, and economic aspects of the society, postmodern criticism often fails to confront those aspects of hegemonic power that cannot be captured in merely linguistic models. This limited focus on textual analysis runs the risk of dissolving into a kind of self-congratulatory form of academic hyperbole, one that, as many feminist theorists have noted, produces a form of sterile academic politics (Kaplan, 1988). Commenting on Jean-François Lyotard's (1984) revision of the theory of language games, Meaghan Morris (1988) offers an illuminating criticism of the postmodern emphasis on the endless deconstructive rereading and rewriting of texts:

One of the problems now emerging as a result is that as the

terms of such analyses become commodified to the point of becoming dated . . . they offer little resistance to the wearing effects of overuse. When any and every text can be read indifferently as another instance of "strategic rewriting," another illustration of an established general principle, something more (and something more specific) is needed to argue how and why a particular event of rewriting might matter. (5)

Cornel West extends this criticism by arguing that the multilevel operations of power within social practices cannot be understood exclusively with reference to language and discourse (Stephanson, 1988a, 271). There is more at stake here than simply the play of difference, the reading of a text, or an interrogation of the social construction of meaning. The limits of the linguistic model, and of discourse in general, become apparent in understanding how the operations of power work as part of a deeper, nondiscursive sense of reality. Language is not the sole source of meaning; it cannot capture, through a totalizing belief in textuality, the constellation of habits, practices, and social relations that constitute what can be called the "thick" side of human life. Those aspects of social practice in which power operates to maim and torture—and forges collective struggles whose strengths are rooted in lived experiences, felt empathy, and concrete solidarity—exceed the insights offered by linguistic models (Giroux and McLaren, 1989). Postmodernism performs a theoretical service by arguing that a new political front can be opened up in the sphere of language, but it must extend the implications of this analysis from the domain of the text to the real world, and in doing so, must recognize the limits of its own forms of analysis.

Postmodernism is deeply indebted to various poststructuralist theories of the subject. In many of these discourses, the subject is constituted through language in a number of different subject positions prescribed by various cultural texts. Unfortunately, in too many of these accounts, the subject is not only decentered—it ceases to exist. In other accounts, the construction of the subject appears to be entirely attributable to textual and linguistic operations. The subject is constructed, but bears no responsibility for agency, since he or she is merely a heap of fragments bereft of any self-consciousness regarding the contradictory nature of his or her own experience. There is little sense in many of these accounts of the ways in which different historical, social, and gendered representations of meaning and desire are actually mediated and taken up subjectively by real, concrete individuals. Paul Smith has addressed this question with more theoretical rigor than most. He argues convincingly that it is imperative that any theory of the subject address why certain subject positions offered in various ideologies that circulate in everyday life are rejected by some individuals, and how it is possible to theorize beyond the "subjugation" of the subject in order to leave room in which "to envisage the agent of a real and effective resistance" (Smith, 1988, 39). In this view, the issue of how people become agents is seen as part of a broader attempt to reconstruct a theory of cultural politics, and politics is not made subordinate to an overly structuralist theory of the subject.

It is also important to note that the postmodern emphasis on both the decentering and death of the subject has been criticized in political terms on the grounds that it makes it more difficult for of those who have been excluded from the centers of power to name and experience themselves as individual and collective agents. Nancy Hartsock (1987) is worth repeating at length on this issue:

> Somehow it seems highly suspicious that it is at this moment in history, when so many groups are engaged in "nationalisms" which involve redefinitions of the marginalized Others, that doubt arises in the academy about the nature of the "subject," about the possibilities for a general theory which can describe the world, about historical "progress." Why is it, exactly at the moment when so many of us who have been silenced begin to demand the right to name ourselves, to act as subjects rather than objects of history, that just then the concept of subjecthood becomes "problematic"? Just when we are forming our own theories about the world, uncertainty emerges about whether the world can be adequately theorized? Just when we are talking about the changes we want, ideas of progress and the possibility of "meaningfully" organizing human society become suspect? And why is it only now that critiques are made of the will to power inherent in the effort to create theory? (196)

According to theorists such as Elizabeth Fox-Genovese (1986), the death of the subject not only seems theoretically premature but also is ideologically suspect, especially since such a position is being touted principally by white male academics in mostly elite universities. In this case, some versions of postmodernism are being questioned not only because they offer a radically depoliticized notion of subjectivity, but also because they refuse to treat the issue of subjectivity in historical and political terms. Terry Eagleton (1985/1986) is right in arguing that understanding the production of certain forms of subjectivity in any society involves analyzing in historical terms the various technologies of power that are used to instill "specific kinds of value, discipline, behaviour, and response in human subjects." He adds that "what these techniques at once map and produce, for the ends of social knowledge and order, are certain forms of value and response" (97). While it is important to understand subjectivity as constructed and decentered, to extol the death of the subject and with it any notion of agency is to "jettison the chance of challenging the ideology of the subject (as male, white, and middle-class) by developing alternative and different notions of subjectivity" (Huyssen, 1986, 212).

For feminist theorists such as Teresa de Lauretis (1987), Linda Alcoff (1988), and Meaghan Morris, postmodern discourse is theoretically flawed on two related counts. First, it pays too little attention to the issue of how subjectivity can be linked to a notion of human agency in which self-reflective, capable political selves become possible. Second, by ignoring both the issue of gender and the contribution of feminists to what Morris calls the formative and enabling aspects of the postmodern debate, postmodernism becomes complicitous with other discourses that leave "a woman no place from which to speak, or nothing to say" (Morris, 1988, 15). Unwilling to explore the contributions of feminists or to articulate a concept of gendered subectivity, postmodern discourse fails to link the emphasis on difference with an oppositional politics in which the particularities of gender, race, class, and ethnicity are seen as fundamental dimensions in the construction of subjectivity and the politics of voice and agency (Kaplan, 1988; Nicholson, 1990).

Conclusion

In spite of some of its theoretical failings, postmodernism offers educators a number of important insights that can be taken up as part of a broader theory of schooling and critical pedagogy. Moreover, rather than negating the modernist concern with public life and critical rationality, postmodernism provides grounds on which to deepen and extend such concerns. Postmodern engagements with foundationalism, culture, difference, and subjectivity provide the basis for questioning the modernist ideal of what constitutes a decent, humane, and good life. Rather then celebrating the narratives of the "masters," postmodernism raises important questions about how narratives get constructed, what they mean, how they regulate particular forms of moral and social experience, and how they presuppose and embody particular epistemological and political views of the world. Postmodernism attempts to delineate how borders are named; it attempts to redraw the very maps of meaning, desire, and difference; it inscribes the social and individual body with new intellectual and emotional investments; and it calls into question traditional forms of power and accompanying modes of legitimation.

For educators postmodernism offers new theoretical tools to rethink both broad and specific contexts in which authority is defined; it offers what Richard Bernstein calls a healthy "suspiciousness of all boundary-fixing and the hidden ways in which we subordinate, exclude, and marginalize" (Bernstein, 1988, 267). Postmodernism also offers educators a variety of discourses for interrogating modernism's reliance on totalizing theories based on a desire for certainty and absolutes. In addition, postmodernism provides educators with a discourse capable of engaging the importance of the contingent, specific, and historical as central aspects of a liberating and empowering pedagogy. But in the end, postmodernism is too suspicious of the modernist notion of public life, and of the struggle for equality and liberty that has been an essential aspect of liberal democratic discourse. If postmodernism is going to make a valuable contribution to the notion of schooling as a form of cultural politics, educators must combine its most important theoretical insights with those strategic modernist elements that contribute to a politics of radical democracy. In this way, the project of radical democracy can be deepened by expanding its sphere of applicablity to increasingly wider social relations and practices; encompassing individuals and groups who have been excluded by virtue of their class, gender, race, age, or ethnic origin. What is at stake here is the recognition that postmodernism provides educators with a more complex and insightful view of the relationships of culture, power, and knowledge. But for all of its theoretical and political virtues, postmodernism is inadequate to the task of rewriting the emancipatory possibilities of the language and practice of a revitalized democratic public life. This is not to suggest that postmodernism is useless in the task of creating a public philosophy that extends the possibilities of social justice and human freedom. But it does argue that postmodernism must extend and broaden the most democratic claims of modernism. When linked with the modernist language of public life, the notions of difference, power, and specificity can be understood as part of a public philosophy that broadens and deepens individual liberties and rights *through rather than against* a radical notion of democracy.

Talk about the public must be simultaneously about the discourse of an engaged plurality and critical citizenship. This must be a discourse that breathes life into the notion of democracy by stressing a notion of lived community that is *not* at odds with the issues of justice, liberty, and the good life. Such a discourse must be informed by a postmodern concern with establishing the material and ideological conditions that allow multiple, specific, and heterogeneous ways of life. For educators the modernist concern with enlightened subjects, when coupled with the postmodernist emphasis on diversity, contingency, and cultural pluralism, points to educating students for a type of citizenship that does not separate abstract rights from the realm of the everyday, and does not define community as the legitimating and unifying practice of a one-dimensional historical and cultural narrative. The postmodern emphasis on refusing forms of knowledge and pedagogy wrapped in the legitimizing discourse of the sacred and the priestly, its rejection of universal reason as a foundation for human affairs, its claim that all narratives are partial, and its call to perform critical readings on all scientific, cultural, and social texts as historical and political constructions provide the pedagogical grounds for radicalizing the emancipatory possibilities of teaching and learning as part of a wider struggle for democratic public life and critical citizenship. In this view, pedagogy is not reduced to the lifeless methodological imperative of teaching conflicting interpretations of what counts as knowledge (Graff, 1987). Instead, pedagogy is informed by a political project that links the creation of citizens to the development of a critical democracy; that is, a political project that links education to the struggle for a public life in which dialogue, vision, and compassion are attentive to the rights and conditions that organize public life as a democratic social form rather than as a regime of terror and oppression. Difference and pluralism in this view do not mean reducing democracy to the equivalency of diverse interests; on the contrary, what is being argued for is a language in which different voices and traditions exist and flourish to the degree that they listen to the voices of others, engage in an ongoing attempt to eliminate forms of subjective and objective suffering, and maintain those conditions in which the act of communicating and living extends rather than restricts the creation of democratic public forms. This is as much a political as it is a pedagogical project, one that demands that educators combine a democratic public philosophy with a postmodern theory of resistance.

Notes

1. The now classic defense of modernity in the postmodern debate can be found in Jürgen Habermas (1983; 1987). For more extensive analyses of modernity, see Marshall Berman (1982), Eugene Lunn (1982), David Frisby (1986), David Kolb (1986), and William

Connolly (1988). An interesting comparison of two very different views on modernity can be found in Berman (1988) and Nelly Richard (1987/1988).

2. Ernesto Laclau (1988) is worth elaborating on this issue. For him, it is the ontological status of the central concepts of the various discourses of modernity that the postmodern sensibility calls into question:

> If something has characterized the discourses of modernity, it is their pretension to intellectually dominate the foundation of the social, to give a rational context to the notion of the totality of history, and to base in the latter the project of a global human emancipation. As such, they have been discourses about essences and fully present identities based in one way or another upon the myth of a transparent society. Postmodernity, on the contrary, begins when this fully present identity is threatened by an ungraspable exterior that introduces a dimension of paucity and pragmatism into the pretended immediacy and transparency of its categories. This gives rise to an unbreachable abyss between the real and concepts, thus weakening the absolutist pretensions of the latter. It should be stressed that this "weakening" does not in any way negate the contents of the project of modernity; it shows only the radical vulnerability of those contents to a plurality of contexts that redefine them in an unpredictable way. Once this vulnerability is accepted in all its radicality, what does not necessarily follow is either the abandonment of the emancipatory values or a generalized skepticism concerning them, but rather, on the contrary, the awareness of the complex strategic-discursive operations implied by their affirmation and defense. (71–72)

3. Dick Hebdige (1986) provides a sense of the range of meanings, contexts, and objects that can be associated with the postmodern:

> . . . the decor of a room, the design of a building, the diegesis of a film, the construction of a record, or a "scratch" video, a TV commercial, or an arts documentary, or the "intertextual" relations between them, the layout of a page in a fashion magazine or critical journal, an anti-teleologial tendency within epistemology, the attack on the "metaphysics of presence," a general attenuation of feeling, the collective chagrin and morbid projections of a post-War generation of Baby Boomers confronting disillusioned middle age, the "predicament" of reflexivity, a group of rhetorical tropes, a proliferation of surfaces, a new phase in commodity fetishism, a fascination for "images," codes and styles, a process of cultural, political or existential fragmentation and/or crisis, the "de-centering" of the subject, an "incredulity towards metanarratives," the replacement of unitary power axes by a pluralism of power/discourse formations, the "implosion," the collapse of cultural hierarchies, the dread engendered by the threat of nuclear self-destruction, the decline of the University, the functioning and effects of the new miniaturised technologies, broad societal and economic shifts into a "media," "consumer," or "multinational" phase, a sense (depending on whom you read) of "placelessness" or the abandonment of placelessness ("critical regionalism") or (even) a generalised substitution of spatial for temporal co-ordinates. (78)

4. A characteristic example of this work can be seen in Foster (1983), Ross (1988), in the wide-ranging essays on culture, art, and social criticism in the journal *Zone* (1/2, 1988), Wallis (1988), and in *Utopia Post Utopia* (1988), published by the Institute of Contemporary Art, Boston.

5. See, for example, Aronowitz and Giroux in chapter 2 of this book and Spanos (1987).

References

Alcoff, L. (1988). "Cultural Feminism vs. Poststructuralism: The Identity Crisis in Feminist Theory." *Signs, 13*(3), 405–36.

Anderson, P. (1984). "Modernity and Revolution." *New Left Review, 144*, 96–113.

Arac, J., ed. (1986). *Postmodernism and Politics*. Minneapolis: University of Minnesota Press.

Aronowitz, S. (1987/1988). "Postmodernism and Politics." *Social Text, 18*, 94–114.

Baudrillard, J. (1987). "Modernity." *Canadian Journal of Political and Social Theory, 11*(3), 63–72.

Baudrillard, J. (1988). *Selected Writings*, ed. M. Poster. Stanford: Stanford University Press.

Bell, D. (1976). *The Cultural Contradictions of Capitalism*. New York: Basic Books.

Benjamin, W. (1969). "The Work of Art in the Age of Mechanical Reproduction." In H. Arendt, ed. *Illuminations*. New York: Schocken Books, 217–51.

Berman, M. (1982). *All That Is Solid Melts into Air: The Experience of Modernity*. New York: Simon & Schuster.

Berman, M. (1988). "Why Modernism Still Matters." *Tikkun, 4*(1), 81–86.

Bernstein, R. (1988). "Metaphysics, Critique, and Utopia." *The Review of Metaphysics, 42*, 255–73.

Bloom, A. (1987). *The Closing of the American Mind*. New York: Simon & Schuster.

Bowles, S., and Gintis, H. (1976). *Schooling in Capitalist America*. New York: Basic Books.

Carnoy, M., and Levin, H. (1985). *Schooling and Work in the Democratic State*. Stanford: Stanford University Press.

Chambers, I. (1986). "Waiting for the End of the World." *Journal of Communication Inquiry, 10*(2), 98–103.

Cherryholmes, C. (1988). *Power and Criticism: Poststructural Investigations in Education*. New York: Teachers College Press.

Christian, B. (1987). "The Race for Theory." *Cultural Critique, 6*: 51–64.

Connolly, W. (1988). *Political Theory and Modernity*. New York: Basil Blackwell.

de Lauretis, T. (1987). *Technologies of Gender*. Bloomington: Indiana University Press.

Denzin, N. (1988). "*Blue Velvet*: Postmodern Contradictions." *Theory, Culture, and Society, 5*, 461–73.

Derrida, J. (1976). *Of Grammatology*, trans. G. Spivak. Baltimore: Johns Hopkins University Press.

Dewey, J. (1916). *Democracy and Education*. New York: Macmillan.

Eagleton, T. (1985/1986). "The Subject of Literature." *Cultural Critique, 2*, 95–104.

Featherstone, M. (1988). "In Pursuit of the Postmodern: An Introduction." *Theory, Culture and Society, 5*(2–3), 195–215.

Feher, F. (1988). "The Status of Postmodernity." *Philosophy and Social Criticism, 13*(2), 195–206.

Foster, H. ed. (1983). *The Anti-aesthetic: Essays on Postmodern Culture*. Port Townsend, Wash.: Bay Press.

Foucault, M. (1977a). *Language, Counter-memory, Practice: Selected Essays and Interviews*, ed., D. Bouchard. Ithaca: Cornel University Press.

Fox-Genovese, E. (1986). "The Claims of a Common Culture: Gender, Race, Class and the Canon." *Salmagundi*, 72, 131–43.

Fraser, N., and Nicholson, L. (1990). "Social Criticism without Philosophy: An Encounter between Feminism and Postmodernism." In L. Nicholson, ed., *Feminism/postmodernism*. New York: Routledge, 19–38.

Frisby, D. (1986). *Fragments of Modernity*. Cambridge: M. I. T. Press.

Giroux, H. A., ed. (1991). *Postmodernism, Feminism, and Cultural Politics: Redrawing the Boundaries of Educational Criticism*. Albany: SUNY Press.

Giroux, H., and McLaren, P., eds. (1989). *Critical Pedagogy, the State, and Cultural Struggle*. Albany: State University of New York Press.

Goodlad, J. (1984). *A Place Called School*. New York: McGraw-Hill.

Gott, R. (1986). "The Crisis of Contemporary Culture." *The Guardian*. December 1, 10.

Graff, G. (1987). *Professing Literature: An Institutional History*. Chicago: University of Chicago Press.

Grossberg, L. (1986). "On Postmodernism and Articulation: An Interview with Stuart Hall." *Journal of Communication Inquiry*, 10(2), 40–56.

Grossberg, L. (1988). "Putting the Pop Back Into Postmodernism" In A. Ross, ed., *Universal Abandon*. Minneapolis, Minn.: University of Minnesota Press, 167–90.

Habermas, J., (1983). "Modernity—An Incomplete Project." In H. Foster, ed., *The Anti-aesthetic: Essays on Postmodern Culture*. Port Townsend, Wash.: Bay Press, 3–16.

Habermas, J. (1987). *The Philosophical Discourse of Modernity*, trans. Frank Lawrence. Cambridge: MIT Press.

Hartsock, N. (1987). "Rethinking Modernism: Minority vs. Majority Theories." *Cultural Critique*, 7, 187–206.

Hebdige, D. (1986). "Postmodernism and 'the Other Side.' " *Journal of Communication Inquiry*, 10(2), 78–99.

Hutcheon, L. (1988). "Postmodern Problematic." In R. Merrill, ed., *Ethics/Aesthetics: Post-modern Positions*. Washington, D.C.: Maisonneuve Press, 1–10.

Huyssen, A. (1986). *After the Great Divide*. Bloomington: Indiana University Press.

Institute of Contemporary Art (1988). *Utopia Post Utopia: Configurations of Nature in Recent Sculpture and Photography*. Boston: Institute of Contemporary Art.

Jameson, F. (1984). "Postmodernism or the Cultural Logic of Late Capitalism." *New Left Review*, 146: 53–93.

Jameson, F. (1988). "Regarding Postmodernism—a Conversation with Fredric Jameson." In A. Ross, ed., *Universal Abandon?* Minneapolis, Minn.: University of Minnesota Press, 3–30.

JanMohamed, A., and Lloyd, D. (1987). "Introduction: Minority Discourse—What Is to Be Done?" *Cultural Critique*, 7, 5–17.

Kaplan E. A., ed. (1988). *Postmodernism and Its Discontents*. London: Verso Books.

Kellner, D. (1988). "Postmodernism as Social Theory: Some Challenges and Problems." *Theory, Culture and Society*, 5(2 and 3), 239–269.

Kellner, D. (in press). "Boundaries and Borderlines: Reflections on Jean Baudrillard and Critical Theory." In *From Marxism to Postmodernism and Beyond: Critical Studies of Jean Baudrillard*. Oxford: Polity Press.

Kolb, D. (1986). *The Critique of Pure Modernity: Hegel, Heidegger, and After*. Chicago: University of Chicago Press.

Laclau, E., and Mouffe, C. (1985). *Hegemony and Socialist Strategy*. London: Verso Books.

Laclau, E. (1988). "Politics and the Limits of Modernity." In A. Ross ed., *Universal Abandon?* Minneapolis: University of Minnesota Press, 63–82.

Lash, S., and Urry, J. (1987). *The End of Organized Capitalism*. Madison: University of Wisconsin Press.

Lunn, E. (1982). *Marxism and Modernism*. Berkeley: University of California Press.

Lyotard, J. (1984). *The Postmodern Condition*. Minneapolis: University of Minnesota Press.

McLaren, P. (1986). "Postmodernism and the Death of Politics: A Brazilian Reprieve." *Educational Theory*, 36(4), 389–401.

Morris, M. (1988). *The Pirate's Fiancee: Feminism, Reading, Postmodernism*. London: Verso Press.

Nicholson, L. (1990). *Feminism/Postmodernism*. New York: Routledge.

Peller, G. (1987). "Reason and the Mob: The Politics of Representation." *Tikkun*, 2(3), 28–31, 92–95.

Richard, N. (1987/1988). "Postmodernism and Periphery." *Third Text*, 2, 5–12.

Rorty, R. (1979). *Philosophy and the Mirror of Nature*. Princeton: Princeton University Press.

Rorty, R. (1985). "Habermas and Lyotard on Postmodernity." In Richard Bernstein, ed., *Habermas and Modernity*. Cambridge: MIT Press, 161–76.

Ross, A., ed., (1988). *Universal Abandon? The Politics of Postmodernism*. Minneapolis: University of Minnesota Press.

Shor, I. (1979). *Critical Teaching and Everyday Life*. Boston: South End Press.

Smith, P. (1988). *Discerning the Subject*. Minneapolis: University of Minnesota Press.

Spanos, W. (1987). *Repetitions: The Postmodern Occasion in Literature and Culture*. Baton Rouge: Louisiana State University Press.

Stephanson, A. (1988a). Interview with Cornel West. In A. Ross, ed., *Universal Abandon?* Minneapolis: University of Minnesota Press, 269–87.

Stephanson, A. (1988b). "Regarding Postmodernism: A Conversation with Fredric Jameson." In A. Ross, ed., *Universal Abandon?* Minneapolis: University of Minnesota Press, 3–30.

Tyler, R. W. (1950). *Basic Principles of Curriculum and Instruction*. Chicago: University of Chicago Press.

Yudice, G. (1988). "Marginality and the Ethics of Survival." In A. Ross, ed., *Universal Abandon?* Minneapolis: University of Minnesota Press, 214–36.

Wallis, B., ed., (1988). *Blasted Allegories*. Cambridge: M. I. T. Press.

Weeden, C. (1987). *Feminist Practice and Poststructuralist Theory*. London: Blackwell.

Welch, S. (1990). *A Feminist Ethic of Risk*. Philadelphia: Fortress Press.

Zone, 1/2 (1988).

CHAPTER 4
CULTURAL POLITICS, READING FORMATIONS, AND THE ROLE OF TEACHERS AS PUBLIC INTELLECTUALS

Introduction

During the last two decades educational critics have made a number of important gains in developing a critical theory of curriculum and education. In particular, critical theorists have begun to provide a language of critique by which to analyze and demystify the role that schools play as agencies of moral and political regulation; a programmatic language by which to understand schools as sites of critical learning and social empowerment has also arisen from their work.

Central to this project has been the more recent work of theorizing curriculum as a form of cultural politics. In this view, the relationship between knowledge and power is analyzed as part of a wider effort to define schools as places where a sense of identity, worth, and possibility is organized through the interaction among teachers, students, and texts. Accordingly, schools are analyzed as places where students are introduced to particular ways of life, where subjectivities are produced, and where needs are constructed and legitimated. The more recent work in critical theories of curriculum has focused on two general modes of inquiry. In the first and most dominant mode, radical theorists have analyzed the various ways in which knowledge and power come together to give a particular ideological bent to the form and content of curriculum knowledge. Much of this work is concerned

87

with uncovering the ideological interests at work in the content of the curriculum—that is, revealing how racist, sexist, and class-specific messages work to construct particular ideological representations and images. Equally important, but less pursued, has been the attempt to analyze the structuring principles of curriculum texts in order to more fully understand how these coding structures contribute to the ways in which knowledge is produced, mediated, consumed, and transformed as part of the overall pedagogical process.[1] In the second mode, critical theorists have focused on the historical and cultural practices of subordinate groups and the ways in which these practices give rise to particular relations of oppression and resistance in schools. In this perspective, a great deal of attention is given to analyzing how school as a cultural and social terrain organizes, legitimates, sustains, and refuses particular forms of student experience.[2] In some cases, there have been attempts within this perspective to develop the rudiments of a curriculum theory and critical pedagogy based on the incorporation of the everyday experiences, languages, histories, and values of subordinate groups into the school curriculum. Central to this perspective is the need to view schools as both instructional and cultural sites—that is, as places where knowledge and learning are deeply related to the different social and cultural forms that shape how students understand and respond to classroom work.

As important as this approach has been, it has not managed to integrate in a dialectical fashion attempts to develop theoretically and politically useful school knowledge with a similar concern for developing a critical pedagogy. On the contrary, theorists who focus on developing "ideologically correct" school knowledge often assume that questions of pedagogy can be treated as afterthoughts. They often believe that if teachers present the "right knowledge" to students, the students will automatically learn something. In this case the ideological correctness of one's position appears to be the primary determining factor in assessing the production of knowledge and exchange that occurs between students and teachers. At best, questions of pedagogy are reduced to debating whether one might use a seminar, lecture, or multimedia format. On the other hand, a number of theorists struggling with the difficult task of creating the broader outlines of what constitutes a critical theory of curriculum seem impervious to the issue of how knowledge is actually produced and authority legitimated in the encounter between particular forms of curriculum and the social relations of the classroom.

In what follows we want to argue that curriculum theory, and specifically the English curriculum, is sorely in need of a theory of textual authority that allows teachers and students to reference how both knowledge and classroom social relations are constructed in ways that may either silence or empower. Textual authority, in this approach, is developed as part of a wider analysis of the struggle over culture fought out at the levels of curriculum knowledge, pedagogy, and the exercise of institutional power. In addition, we argue for the necessity of developing a politics and pedagogy of voice as part of a theory of curriculum that opens up texts to a wider range of meanings and interpretations, while simultaneously constructing student experience as part of a broader discourse of critical citizenship and democracy. In developing these positions, we emphasize that teaching must be seen as part of a larger curriculum project related to the construction of political subjects and the formation of schools as democratic public spheres. We also develop the position that administrators and teachers need to rethink their roles as public intellectuals, and in doing so must reject the cult of knowledge, expertise, and disembodied rationality that permeates the discourse of curriculum theory. Educators need to take up the task of redefining educational leadership through forms of social criticism, civic courage, and public engagement that allow them to expand oppositional spaces—both within and outside of schools—which increasingly challenge the ideological representations and relations of power that undermine democratic public life.[3]

Beyond Curriculum and the Discourse of Simplicity

Curriculum theory has never existed as a monolithic discourse. On the contrary, it has always constituted a site of struggle, a site defined by the imperative to organize knowledge, values, and social relations so as to legitimate and reproduce particular ways of life. As introductions to such ways of life, the various discourses of curriculum theory are neither ideologically innocent nor politically neutral. Deeply entrenched in the world of politics, curriculum—as a discourse and as an organized structure of social relations—represents both expression and enforcement of particular relations of power.

In spite of the gains made by alternative views of curriculum in the last decade, the field has fallen on hard times. In many of the advanced industrial democracies, public school curriculum has come under heavy attack by various elements on the right. In some cases, school curriculum has been fashioned in the interests of an industrial psychology that attempts to reduce schools and learning to strictly economic and corporate concerns. Thus, in many of these countries, we are witnessing the development of school-business partnerships in which schools are adopted by corporate institutions and then organize their curricula so as to provide the skills necessary for domestic production and expanding capital. Under the euphemism of "investing in our children," major corporations are underwriting school curricula that link the teaching of basic skills with good work habits. In other cases, curricula are being developed around the cultural imperatives of a selected version of what is called Western Civilization. In this view, schools take on a decidedly different role: rather than being defined as vehicles for economic reform, schools are viewed as sites of cultural production, and their purpose defined by the imperatives of providing students with the language, knowledge, and values necessary to preserve the essential traditions of Western culture.

The political and strategic inadequacy of much critical and radical curriculum theory is evident in its overall refusal to engage the theoretical gains accrued by literary studies, feminist theory, poststructuralism, postmodernism, and democratic theory. Isolated from the many innovations taking place in the larger world of social theory, many curriculum theorists do not critically engage the limitations of the political projects implicit in their own work, and have resorted instead to preaching the importance of simple language and the privileging of practice over theory. The call to write curriculum in a language that is touted as clear and accessible is evidence of a moral and political vision that increasingly collapses under the weight of its own anti-intellectualism. Similarly, curriculum theory is increasingly dissolved into practice under the vote-catching call for a focus on the concrete as the source and test of educational strategy and relevance. Our argument against these practices is not meant as a clever exercise, intent on merely reversing the categories so that theory is prioritized over practice, or abstract language over the language of popcorn imagery. Nor are we merely suggesting that critical educators mount an equally reductionist argument against the use of clear language or the importance of practice. At issue here is the need to question and reject the reductionism and exclusions that characterize the binary oppositions informing these overly pragmatic sentiments. We want to pose an alternative argument.

Every new paradigm has to create its own language because the old paradigms or curriculum theories produce through their use of language particular forms of knowledge and social relations that serve to legitimate specific relations of power. Oppositional paradigms offer new languages by attempting to deconstruct and challenge dominant relations of power and knowledge legitimated through traditional forms of discourse. This opposition often reflects major changes in thinking that are mediated and produced through related shifts in new ways of speaking and writing. Oppositional languages are generally unfamiliar, provoking questions and pointing to social relations that will often appear alien and strange to many educators. What is at stake here is not the issue of "bad" writing, as if writing that is difficult to grapple with has nothing important to say. Rather, the most important point to be addressed by educators and curriculum theorists is not clarity but whether such writing offers a vision and practice for deepening the possible relations between the discourse of curriculum and the imperatives of a radical democracy.

But there is also another issue that seems to be ignored in the current debate about language and clarity, particularly as it concerns the relationship between language and the notion of domination. It seems to us that those who call themselves progressive educators, whether feminists, Marxists, or otherwise, who make the call for clear writing synonymous with an attack on critical educators have missed the role that the "language of clarity" plays in a dominant culture that cleverly and powerfully uses "clear" and "simplistic" language to systematically undermine and prevent the conditions from arising for a public culture to engage in rudimentary forms of complex and critical thinking. In effect, what is missed in this analysis is that the homogenization and standardization of language in the mass media and the schools point to how language and power often combine to offer the general public and students subject positions that are cleansed of any complex thought or insight. That progressive educators have largely ignored this issue when taking up the question of language makes suspect not only their own claims to clarity, but also the limits of their own political judgments.

There is a related issue that needs to be addressed in this argument. Many critical educators often assume a notion of audience that is both theoretically simplistic and politically incorrect. It is theoretically simplistic because it assumes that there is one public sphere, rather than a number of public spheres characterized by diverse levels of intelligibility and sophistication. Moreover, by suggesting that there is only one audience or public sphere to whom critical educators speak, there is no way by which to connect discourse with audiences marked by differences with respect to histories, languages, cultures, or everyday experiences. Such a position flattens the relationship between language and audience and cancels out the need for the author/writer to take into consideration the specific history, politics, and culture of the audience that he or she attempts to address. The politics of such a position leads one either into the terrain of elitism and vanguardism or into the political dead end of cynicism and despair.

Language is always constructed with respect to the audience it addresses, and should be judged in pragmatic terms that also refer to the theoretical and political viability of the project the language articulates. It is not the complexity of language that is at issue, but the viability of the theoretical framework such language constitutes and promotes. Moreover, the relationship between theory and practice is multifaceted and complex. Simply put, theory in some instances directly informs practice, while in others practice restructures theory as a primary force for change. In some cases theory (in the more limited sense of the practice of producing narrative and rhetoric) also provides a refuge to think beyond current forms of practice so as to envision that which is not yet. Privileging practice without due consideration of the complex interactions that mark the totality of theory/practice and language/meaning relationships is not simply reductionist; it is a form of theoretical tyranny. Theory, in this sense, becomes a form of practice that ignores the political value of theoretical discourse within a specific historical conjuncture. That is, rather than examining the language of curriculum theory as part of a wider historical moment of self-examination, and the problematizing of certainty itself, the language and politics of theory is merely reduced to an unproblematic concern with clarity. The intimacy of the dialectic between theory and practice is reduced to an opposition between theory and complexity, on the one hand, and practice and clarity on the other. This is the mark of a vapid, pragmatic anti-intellectualism, the leveling tendency of which occludes the role of language in constructing theory as a historically specific practice that makes politics and praxis possible as part of an engagement with the particular problems of a given time and place.

Curriculum theory as practice needs a critical discourse to both constitute and reorder the nature of our experiences and the objects of our concerns, so as to enhance and further empower the ideological and institutional conditions for a radical democracy. The theoretical framework presented here makes no claim to certainty; it is a discourse that is unfinished, but one that may help to illuminate the specifics of oppression and the possibilities for democratic struggle and renewal for those educators who believe that schools and society can be changed, and that their individual and collective actions can make a difference.

The appeal to language cannot justify a universal or absolute claim to either truth or meaning. Language does not have a fixed and unchanging correspondence to reality; on the contrary, as Catherine Belsey points out, it is constituted "through a system of signs which signify by means of their relationship to each other. . . . Meaning is public and conventional, the result not of individual intention but of inter-individual intelligibility. In other words, meaning is socially constructed, and the social construction of the signifying system is intimately related, therefore, to the social formation itself."[4] Therefore the construction of meaning, authority, and subjectivity is governed by ideologies inscribed in language, which offer different possibilities for people to construct their relationships to themselves, others, and the larger reality. What meanings are considered the most important, what experiences are deemed the most legitimate, and what forms of writing and reading matter, are largely determined by those groups who control the economic and cultural apparatuses of a given society. Knowledge has to be viewed in the context of power, and consequently the relationships between writers, readers, and texts have to be understood as sites at which different readings, meanings, and forms of cultural production take place. In this case, reading and writing have to be seen as productive categories, as forms of discourse that configure practices of dialogue, struggle, and contestation. This position strongly challenges the dominant view of literacy, which reduces reading and writing to essentially descriptive categories that tacitly support forms of pedagogy emphasizing individual mastery and the passive consumption of knowledge and skills.[5]

By challenging the commonsense assumptions that are inscribed in the dominant ideology of discourse and power, it becomes possible for administrators and teachers to reconstruct their own theoretical frameworks by adding new categories of analysis and by rethinking what the actual purpose of their teaching might be. Interrogating the connection between language and power is crucial for understanding how educational workers might view curriculum theory as a form of textual authority that legitimates a particular form of discursive practice. Understanding curriculum as part of a broader struggle between dominant and subordinate discourses has critical implications for the ways in which educators produce and "read" curriculum, engage the notion of student experience, and redefine critically their own role as engaged public intellectuals.[6] In other words, the emphasis on language and power provides a theoretical framework for pedagogy that reconceptualizes the ways in which historically specific relations of power and textual authority combine to produce, organize, and legitimate particular forms of knowledge, values, and community within the English curriculum. Linda Brodkey captures the spirit of this position in arguing that "theories of textuality are inevitably . . . [about] theories of reading. . . . In this society the authority that teachers are empowered to grant to or withhold from student texts derives from the theory of textuality governing their reading."[7] The issue of textual authority raises serious questions regarding how schools function as forms of social and moral regulation. Furthermore, it has important implications for developing a theory of voice and student experience as a central component in a theory of curriculum and critical pedagogy. Most important, textual authority is about the struggle over culture fought out at the level of ideological representations and the exercise of institutional power.[8]

We want to analyze how the above issues have been either ignored or rejected by exploring traditional curriculum approaches to teaching writing and literature.[9] Traditionally, the notion of literacy, defined in the larger sense of learning how to read and write, has been tied to pedagogical practices in which the student is defined primarily as a passive consumer and the teacher is reduced to a dispenser of information parading as timeless truths. Such pedagogical and ideological practices are evident in those approaches to reading and writing that argue that the meaning of a text is manifested in the intention of the author or is revealed in codes that exclusively govern the text itself.[10] In both instances, the question of pedagogy is reduced not to a dialogue and much less a dialectic between teachers and students, than to a form of pedagogical training in which teachers provide the learning conditions for students to discover the "truth" of the texts in question. Lost from this position is any notion of how textual authority both produces and constitutes particular forms of political, ethical, and social interests. Nor is there any sense of how the ideologies that inform textual authority, with its particular view of knowledge and curriculum on the one hand and teaching and learning on the other, legitimate and introduce students to particular ways of life and corresponding forms of cultural capital. For example, within dominant approaches to teaching curriculum and literacy, there is a failure to understand how such a pedagogy—with its emphasis on mastery, procedure, and certainty— functions to exclude the voices, histories, and experience of subordinate groups from the ideologies, practices, and normative orderings that constitute the symbolic hierarchies of the dominant school curriculum.[11]

In what follows, we argue first that dominant approaches to curriculum and teaching employing textual authority are forms of social and political discourse that bear significantly on the ways in which knowledge and classroom social practices are constructed in the interest of relations of domination and oppression. Second, we argue for a politics and pedagogy of voice for redefining textual authority, as part of a project of possibility that opens up texts to a wider range of meanings and subject positions while simultaneously organizing and constructing student experience as part of the broader discourse of critical citizenship and democracy. Third, we will conclude by briefly analyzing the role that administrators and teachers might play as engaged and public intellectuals whose social function is defined by their commitment to a public philosophy dedicated to the formation of democratic public spheres and critical citizens.

Curriculum as a Social Discourse

Within dominant forms of curriculum theory, learning is generally perceived as either a body of content to be transmitted or a body of skills to be mastered. In the first instance, curriculum is usually made synonymous with acquiring the cultural capital associated with the "Great Books." Within this discourse, schools are seen as cultural fronts responsible for advancing the knowledge and values necessary to reproduce the historical virtues of Western culture. In the second instance, the emphasis is on what Mary Louise Pratt calls "knowledge as technique or method."[12] Contrary to what is often claimed by academic critics, what is lost from both of these approaches is the very notion of a critical education. Rather than becoming a viable activity for students, one that enables them to refigure and reread the social and political context in which knowledge, texts, and subjectivities are constructed, criticism within the dominant approaches to teaching has been denuded of its value as a subversive force. Reading critically is reduced to appropriating so-called legitimate cultural capital, decoding texts, or authorizing the voice of the "masters." As Jim Merod points out, this is a criticism without vision or hope, one particularly suited to the social function of schooling and higher education in the age of big business:

> As it stands now, criticism is a grossly academic enterprise that has no real vision of its relationship to and responsibilities within the corporate structure of North American (for that matter, international) life. It is simply a way of doing business with texts. It is in fact a series of ways, a multiplicity of methods that vie for attention and prestige within the semipublic, semiprivate professional critical domain.[13]

It is important to acknowledge that dominant approaches to curriculum theory as manifested in various schools throughout the United States exercise forms of textual authority that not only legitimate a particular version of Western Civilization and an elitist notion of the canon, but also serve to exclude all those other discourses, whether from the new social movements or from other sources of opposition, that attempt to establish different grounds for the production and organization of knowledge. In effect, the struggle over curriculum that is taking place in the United States and many other countries involves more than a dispute over what constitutes a legitimate academic canon. It has to be seen, instead, as part of a broader struggle over textual authority.

What is at stake in the struggle over curriculum and textual authority is the struggle to control the very grounds on which knowledge is produced and legitimated. This is both a political and pedagogical issue. It is political in that the curriculum, along with its representative courses, texts, and social relations, is never value-free or objective. Curriculum, by its very nature, is a social and historical construction that links knowledge and power in very specific ways. We want to illuminate this point by focusing in particular terms on the construction of English curricula in higher education, though the principles at work here apply to public schools as well. The curricula used in English departments always represent a particular ordering and rendering of knowledge selected from the wider society. Moreover, such curricula embody "a hierarchy of forms of knowledge, to which access is socially distributed."[14] This becomes clear in the preference for courses that valorize the "Great Books" at the expense of courses organized around different writers, whether they be feminists, African-Americans, Latin Americans, or any other writers labeled "Others" because of their marginality with respect to dominant representations of power. The normative and political nature of the English curriculum is also clear in its division between courses on literature and those that focus on writing, with the teaching of writing being devalued because it is falsely defined as a pedagogy of skill acquisition rather than a "creative and genuine" form of cultural production. Curriculum does not merely offer courses and skills; it functions to name and privilege particular histories and experiences. In its currently dominant form, it does so in such a way as to marginalize or silence the voices of subordinate groups. In many English classes, the curriculum reinforces social inequality. For critical educators, then, the English curriculum has to be seen as a site of struggle, one that generates different subject positions for students around the issues of what it means to be a critical citizen rather than a good one. The distinction is central to whether we educate students to adapt to existing relations of power or to learn how to read society differently so as to apply the principles of a critical democracy to the creation of new and radical forms of community. In this case, the teaching of English must be seen as a form of citizenship education that seeks to expand rather than restrict the possibilities of democratic public life. Chantal Mouffe rightly argues that such a notion of citizenship and democratic public life "is not concerned with individual questions of morality but with our obligations as fellow members of a political community; it is the ethics of the political that is at stake. The definition of citizenship must become inseparable from a project of radical plural democracy, from the extension of the democratic principle of liberty and equality to the widest possible set of social relations."[15]

We want to argue in more concrete terms that the English curriculum has to be viewed as someone's story, one that is never innocent, and that consequently has to be interrogated for its social and political functions. This suggests not only examining the curriculum, and the textual authority that legitimates it in terms of what it includes, but also examining it in terms of its "articulated silences," that is, those forms of knowledge, stories, and ideologies that it has refused to acknowledge or represent. Such a strategy allows us to understand that knowledge is not sacred, something to be simply received and revered. It also allows teachers and students to use their own knowledge in the effort to read texts productively and critically rather than passively. In this case, texts can be questioned and challenged through the knowledge of experience that students use to give meaning to the world, and the production of knowledge itself can become part of the process of reading and rereading a text. What is at stake in this notion of curriculum is the question of how power is inscribed in the symbolic categories that actively serve to construct different disciplines and subjects, as well as student subjectivities. In other words, how is power used to legitimate the production and organization of knowledge, and what range of subject positions are offered to students within the discourses and social relations of the dominant curriculum? It is to this issue that we will turn by examining the notion of student voice in relation to the pedagogy of reading texts.

Voice, Texts, and Reading Formations

Within dominant forms of curriculum theory, texts become objects to be read independently of the contexts in which they are engaged by readers. That is, the meaning of a text is either already defined by the author, whose faithful representations have to be recovered by students, or the meaning of the text inheres in its fixed properties, which can only be understood by analyzing how the text functions formally to mobilize a particular interpretation. In both cases, though the terms vary considerably, the meaning of the text appears to exist outside of the dominant and oppositional reading formations in which the text could possibly be mobilized and engaged. The category of reading formation is crucial to understanding textual authority as a socially constructed concept that challenges the dominant view of reading and pedagogy. Tony Bennet develops this concept:

> By a reading formation, I mean a set of discursive and inter-textual determinations which organize and animate the practice of reading, connecting texts and readers in specific relations to one another in constituting readers as reading subjects of particular types and texts as objects-to-be-read in particular ways. This entails arguing that texts have and can have no existence independently of such reading formations, that there is no place independent of, anterior to or above the varying reading formations through which their historical life is variantly modulated, within which texts can be constituted as objects of knowledge. Texts exist only as always-already organized or activated to be read in certain ways just as readers exist as always-already activated to read in certain ways: neither can be granted a virtual identity that is separable from the determinate ways in which they are gridded onto one another from within different reading formations.[16]

Textual authority in the dominant curriculum discourses inscribes in the reading process classroom social relations that limit the possibilities for students to mobilize their own voices in relation to particular texts. Similarly, literacy in this view often becomes a matter of mastering technical skills, information, or an elite notion of high-status knowledge. This is a form of literacy buttressed by a refusal to engage the voices and experiences that students might produce in order to give meaning to the relationship between their own lives and school knowledge. It is important to stress that this approach to reading and writing in the English classroom is eminently political. It has little to do with a pedagogy of empowerment and possibility and a great deal to do with the production of students who learn quickly how to conform to rather than challenge the established culture of power and authority. Donald Morton and Mas'ud Zavarzadeh have argued that the dominant approach to reading and writing actually serves to silence students and construct them as willing subjects of the state:

The un-said of such a view of "reading" as receiving (to be
distinguished from "producing") meaning is the sharp
separation of "reading" from "writing." The writer is always the
creative producer while the reader is the passive consumer.
The political value of such a theory of reading for the dominant
class is that in the name of "reading" the reader is taught how
to "obey" "authority"—how, in other words, to "follow" the
instructions of the writer, who stands for authority and controls
meaning.[17]

Linda Brodkey further points out that dominant approaches to literacy, and by implication curriculum theory, are more concerned with
initiating students into an existing culture than educating them to
change it. She argues that these approaches, by denying students the
opportunity to express their own voices and interests, obscure the
wider social inequalities that, in part, construct who they are and how
they live their lives:

[Teachers] are energetic and inventive practitioners committed
to universal education. In their writing, however, that
commitment manifests itself in an approach to teaching and
learning that many educators share in this country, a view that
insists that the classroom is a separate world of its own, in
which teachers and students relate to one another undistracted
by the classism, racism, and sexism that rage outside the
classroom. Discursive hegemony of teachers over students is
usually posed and justified in developmental terms—as
cognitive deficits, emotional or intellectual immaturity,
ignorance, and most recently, cultural literacy—any one of
which would legitimate asymmetrical relationships between its
knowing subjects, teachers, and its unknowing subjects,
students.[18]

Both authors are instructive in that they link the teaching of literature and writing to two forms of silencing. For Morton and Zavarzadeh,
students are silenced in the interest of a dominant culture that wants to
reproduce citizens who are passive rather than critical and actively engaged in the reconstruction of society. For Brodkey, students are silenced by being denied the opportunity to engage texts within a context that affirms the histories, experiences, and meanings that
constitute the conditions through which students exercise their own
voices. Both of these positions are important for the ways in which
they suggest that the dominant curriculum approaches to reading and
writing function to police language, reproduce a dominant cultural

capital, and deny the contradictory and often complex voices that inform how students produce and challenge the meanings that constitute their subjectivities.

Extending these criticisms demands that we work toward developing a pedagogy organized around a language of both critique and possibility, one that offers teachers the opportunity to deconstruct their own teaching practices, and beyond this, to create pedagogical practices that take up the radical responsibility of ethics in helping students to confront evil and imagine a more just society. In part, this means creating the opportunity for students to engage the conditions that serve to legitimate particular forms of textual authority as immutable, and to assess critically how the manifestations of such authority in various texts and cultural practices function to construct and constitute readers in particular ways.

The Politics and Pedagogy of Voice

The concept of voice represents forms of self- and social representation that mediate and produce wider structures of meaning, experience, and history. "Voice" refers to the ways in which students produce meaning through the various subject positions that are available to them in the wider society. In effect, voice is organized through the cultural resources and codes that anchor and organize experience and subjectivity. It is important to stress that students do not have a singular voice, which suggests a static notion of identity and subjectivity. On the contrary, student voices are constituted in multilayered, complex, and often contradictory discourses. The concept of voice, in the most radical sense, points to the ways in which one's voice as an elaboration of location, experience, and history constitutes forms of subjectivity that are multilayered, mobile, complex, and shifting. The category of voice can only be constituted in differences, and it is in and through these multiple layers of meaning that students are positioned and position themselves in order to be the subject rather than merely the object of history. A radical theory of voice represents neither a unitary subject position unrelated to wider social formations nor the unique expression of the creative and unfettered bourgeois subject. Both of these positions depoliticize and dehistoricize voice by removing it from the arena of power, difference, and struggle. A radical theory of voice signifies the social and political formations that provide students with the experiences, language, histories, and stories that construct the subject positions that they use to give meaning to their lives. As part of a power-sensitive discourse, voice draws attention to the ideological and cultural dynamics that enable people to define themselves and speak as part of a wider social and cultural formation.[19]

To speak of voice is to address the wider issue of how people become subjects who are agents in the process of making history, or how they function as subjects oppressed and exploited within the various discursive and institutional boundaries that produce dominant and subordinate cultures in any given society. In this case, voice provides a critical referent for analyzing how people are made voiceless in particular settings by not being allowed to speak, or by being allowed to say what already has been spoken, and how they learn to silence themselves.[20] At the same time, voices forged in opposition and struggle provide the crucial conditions by which subordinate individuals and groups reclaim their own memories, stories, and histories as part of an ongoing attempt to challenge those power structures that attempt to silence them. What is important to stress here is that the notion of textual authority can be used either to silence students by denying their voices—that is, by refusing to allow them to speak from their own histories, experiences, and social positions—or it can enable them to speak by being attentive to how different voices can be constituted within specific pedagogical relations so as to engage their histories and experiences in both an affirmative and a critical way.

For example, in an American literature class it would seem appropriate to use not only texts that have played major roles in shaping the history of American literature, but also those texts that have been ignored or suppressed because they have been written from an oppositional stance, or because they were authored by writers whose work is not legitimated by a dominant Eurocentric tradition. What we are arguing for here is a deliberate attempt to decenter the American literature curriculum by allowing a number of voices to be read, heard, and used. This approach to reading and writing literature should be seen as part of a broader attempt to develop pedagogically a politics of difference that articulates with issues of race, class, gender, ethnicity, and sexual preference from a position of empowerment rather than from a position of deficit and subordination. Let us be more specific.

Let's assume that a large number of students in an English class are minority students. Central to affirming the voices of these students is the use of texts that come out of an experience that they can relate to and engage critically. Such texts allow these particular students to connect with them in the contexts of their own histories and traditions. Such texts also provide another language and voice by which other students can understand how differences are constructed, for better or worse, within the dominant curriculum. Similarly, different texts offer all students forms of counter-memory that make visible what is often unrepresentable in many English classrooms. The benefit of such a pedagogical approach can be defended from a number of positions. First, using the literature of the Other provides an organic connection to the voices of students in the class who generally cannot locate their own histories in the traditional literature that constitutes the official canon. Minority literature references the living experiences and struggles of groups whose repressed narratives provide the grounds for new ways of reading history—that is, knowledge of marginal histories represents a way of reclaiming power and identity. Second, literature of the Other provides *all* students the opportunity to identify, unravel, and critically debate the codes, vocabularies, and ideologies of different cultural traditions. What is important in this case is the opportunity for students to read texts as social and historical constructs bound up with specific discourses and forms of institutional power. Third, reading texts as part of a politics of difference that *makes a difference* must be highly discriminate in providing students with the opportunities to challenge authoritative bodies of curriculum knowledge as well as transmission models of pedagogy. That is, reading texts within an affirmation of difference does not serve merely to validate the achievements of minority cultures; it offers the broader opportunity to provide a sustained critique of the historical and institutional practices that exclude them while simultaneously engaging such texts for the possibilities they may or may not offer for democratic public life. This suggests that debates about including texts by minority authors are about more than a politics of representation. These debates are fundamentally about how power and domination are inscribed in the ideological and institutional structures of society. At the same time, the rewriting of authoritative texts and the reclaiming of excluded histories and narratives offer the possibility of constructing new communities that move outside of textuality into the world of material practices and concrete social relations. Deconstructing texts is about more than analyzing ideology as discourse; such deconstruction is also about the unrealized possibilities that exist in ideology as lived experience.

Of course, what actually happens in classrooms is that dominant and subordinate voices constantly interact to qualify and modify each other, though this occurs within relations of power that are, for the most part, asymmetrical. Though the process is more dialectical than I am suggesting, it is never simply pluralistic, in the liberal sense described by Gerald Graff, Richard Rorty, and others.[21] Difference in this sense is a category that is sensitive to the ways in which dominant forms of power circulate to refuse, silence, and oppress, and do not merely function to register plurality outside of the relations of history, and outside of class, race, and gender struggles. To speak of voice within the discourse of difference as struggle and opposition is to raise questions about how textual authority can be used to validate student experiences, and to give students the opportunity to read and write culture differently within a variety of meanings and subject positions that empower rather than disempower them.

Textual Authority and the Pedagogy of the Text

If school administrators, curriculum theorists, and teachers are going to give student experience a central place in school curricula and class-room practices, they will have to redefine curriculum not as a ware-house of knowledge merely to be passed on to waiting consumers, but as a configuration of knowledge, social relations, and values that rep-resents an introduction to and legitimation of a particular form of tex-tual authority. In other words, textual authority must be viewed as a po-litically informed referent that presupposes a specific vision of subjectivity, community, and the future. Such a concept must be ana-lyzed not only for the ways in which it enables particular forms of em-powerment, but also for the ways in which it excludes the particular voices, histories, and experiences of specific groups because of their class, race, ethnicity, and gender. At the very least it is important to rec-ognize that textual authority—that is, how teachers use power to sanc-tion the reading and writing of particular stories—must be interrogated for the partiality of its own narratives, and understood in terms that make clear what its interests and purposes might be in the construction of student voices and subject positions.

Educators need to provide students with an understanding of how knowledge and power come together in the reading and writing of texts. This means that administrators and teachers need to understand schools as places in which learning is about the production, the writ-ing, and the rewriting of texts, so as to enable students to develop a sense of place, worth, and value. It is important to reiterate that voice refers to the discursive means whereby "teachers and students attempt to make themselves present and to define themselves as active authors of their own world."[22] Central to such a notion is the need for a theory of textual authority that employs a language of both critique and pos-sibility. In the first instance, educational workers need to develop a critical language to identify and eliminate those pedagogical practices that make some students voiceless, that run the risk of reducing teachers to mere technicians, and that function so as to subvert the ethical force and possibilities of educational leadership and learning. A language of critique rereads narratives "by exposing them as historical and social constructions and then reformulates them in politically different terms."[23] Such a language attempts to read the world differently, to open up those texts and discourses that suppress the constructed nature of their own historical and social categories. Similarly, a language of critique must be able to contextualize and problematize its own ideologies and normative underpinnings. This is important if such a language is to refuse to exercise monolithic forms of analysis, which function to close down the texts it helps students to read in specifically political ways.[24] As part of the project of possibility, teachers need to make spaces in their classrooms so that their own voices, along with those of their students, can be heard as part of a wider dialogue and critical encounter with the knowledge forms and social relations that structure the classroom and articulate with forms of social and political authority at work in the dominant society.

Crucial to this argument is the recognition that it is not enough for teachers merely to dignify the grounds on which students learn to speak, imagine, and give meaning to their world. Developing a pedagogy that takes the notion of student voice seriously means developing a critically affirmative language that works both *with and on* the experiences that students bring to the classroom. This means taking seriously and confirming the language forms, modes of reasoning, dispositions, and histories that give students an active voice in defining the world; it also means working on the experiences of such students in order for them to examine both their strengths and weaknesses. Students need to recover their own voices so they can retell their own histories and in so doing "check and criticize the history [they] are told against the one [they] have lived."[25] This is not merely a pedagogical practice in which voice becomes a referent for a politics of identity that brackets out the larger social reality in favor of a search for the humanistic "self." On the contrary, it is a pedagogical practice in which the issue of ethics and politics becomes central to the process of learning. Jim Merod argues that teachers can address this pedagogical issue by focusing more deliberately on the political and social functions of education. In part this suggests that teachers must be concerned with the interrelationship of text and language as a form of cultural politics that opens up the notion of reading and writing to the study of wider considerations of institutional power and the struggle for social and economic justice. This points to using texts that validate the experiences and voices that students bring to the classroom and enhance their understanding of themselves as public actors and critical citizens. Merod is worth quoting at length:

> The object of such pedagogical renovation would be to activate the critical skills of students currently trained to professionalize their intellects. For critics this "new way" means a much greater role for the intricate demands of instructing. It goes considerably beyond the traditional task of teaching students to read and write. It implies, in sum, the need for group efforts to change institutional processes of creating, implementing, and evaluating courses so that students may be put on the troubling path of learning how to imagine society as a structure of contradictory and competing elements. Institutions, political forces, economic relations, ideologies, historical conjunctures, transitional moments can be named even as students and teachers grapple with the complexities of argumentation and representation, which divide varying accounts of the issues at stake and of the social ensemble itself. The least realized and possibly most necessary job within that effort is the clarification, both historical and theoretical, of social reality as an institutional whole without final shape or outcome: a network of institutional relationships held together by traditions and practices objectified (made available, authoritative, and rational) by institutional means.[26]

In what follows we want to take up this question by suggesting how a pedagogy can be constructed so as to enable students to read differences differently—that is, to understand how texts take on particular readings as a result of the historical and social reading formations that struggle over them as sites of meaning and possibility.

Texts are sites of pedagogical and political struggle. Politically, the presentation and study of texts raises important questions about the ideological interests at work in forms of textual authority that foster particular reading practices. That is, how are readers' choices defined and limited by the range of readings made available through particular forms of textual authority? How does power and authority articulate between the wider society and the classroom, so as to create the conditions at work in constructing particular discourses in the reading of particular texts? This is an issue that connects power to textual authority in a very specific way because it raises questions about how texts are constructed and read within relations of power that offer and legitimate specific subject positions and voices for students to inhabit. For women, minority groups, and other subordinate groups, schools rarely offer reading positions that allow texts to be read in ways that disrupt "the prevailing array of discourses through which [dominant] subject positions are formed."[27] At issue here is the argument that texts are never fixed, and how they are read is always constructed through a circulation of power that produces meaning out of the determinations that mediate the relations between reader, texts, and contexts.[28]

Pedagogically, the study of texts should be engaged as a form of writing. That is, students should be allowed to make "text mean differently by reorganizing the systems of inter-textual, ideological and cultural reference, the reading formations, within which they are constituted as objects to be read."[29] Catherine Belsey offers some general pedagogical principles that provide a starting point for developing a pedagogy of the text informed by an emancipatory notion of textual power. She argues that students must be given the opportunity to analyze the plurality of meanings in a text and to challenge the obvious ones; in addition, students should make the text a new object of intelligibility: they should read the text from the position of their own experiences while simultaneously examining the ways in which the text is constructed within dominant social relations.[30] Bill Green in a similar fashion argues that English teaching must be linked to the notions of production and praxis and hence to writing.[31] That is, students must make something *happen* in studying school subjects, and that means taking up a critical attitude toward texts by "reading" them critically through written critical analyses. In this way, reading texts becomes a concrete form of cultural production open to dialogue and argument. In this view, teachers do not teach subjects; they exercise textual power by allowing students to write texts out of their own reading formations. Robert Scholes provides an illuminating analysis of how a critical pedagogy can be organized around the notion of textual power; we will here analyze his work in detail.[32]

Scholes argues that teachers, instead of simply imparting information to students, should replace teaching texts with what he calls textuality. What this refers to pedagogically is a process of textual study that can be identified by three forms of practice: reading, interpretation, and criticism, which roughly correspond to what Scholes calls reading within, upon, and against a text. In brief, as Roland Barthes also recognized, reading within a text means identifying the cultural codes that structure an author's work.[33] But it also has the pedagogical value of illuminating further how such codes function as part of a student's own attempt "to produce written texts that are 'within' the world constructed by their reading." This is particularly important in giving students the opportunity to "retell the story, to summarize it, and to expand it."[34] Interpretation means reading a text along with a variety of diverse interpretations that represent a second commentary on the text. At issue here is the pedagogical task of helping students to analyze texts within "a network of relations with other texts and institutional practices" so as to make available to students "the whole intertextual system of relations that connects one text to others—a system that will finally include the student's own writing."[35]

The first two stages of Scholes's pedagogical practice are very important because they demonstrate the need for students to engage and disrupt the text. He wants students to read the text in terms that the author might have intended, so as to make the text not merely a mirror image of the student's own subjective position, but at the same time he wants students to open the text up to a wide variety of readings so it can be "sufficiently other for us to interpret it and, especially to criticize it."[36] Finally, Scholes wants students to explode the cultural codes of the text through assertions of the reader's own textual power, to analyze the text in terms of its absences, to free "[themselves] from [the] text [by] finding a position outside the assumptions upon which the text is based."[37] Scholes wants not only to engage texts as semiotic objects but also to distinguish between the text and the outside world. Against Fredric Jameson, he argues that the point of critical interrogation is *not* to "liberate us from the empirical object—whether institution, event, or individual work—by displacing our attention to its constitution as an object and its relationship to the other objects constituted."[38] Implicit in such a concern is the recognition that texts be construed not merely as literary objects but like any other historical and social construction that moves within various circuits of power and signification. Viewing ideological and institutional representations as discursive objects does not mean that social reality can be dissolved into textuality. Relations of meaning as they are embodied in empirical referents such as the state, the workplace, and concrete forms of suffering represent embodied economies of power that have a political gravity that far exceeds the textual and the discursive. According to Scholes, social reality may be analyzed as a text but the discursive must not be substituted for society itself.[39]

We have argued that teachers can draw upon the cultural resources that students bring to the class, in order to understand the categories students use to construct meaning and to locate themselves in history. By analyzing texts in light of diverse readings, and by interrogating such readings so as to allow students to bring their own experiences to bear on such engagements, teachers of English can better understand the histories and communities of meaning that give their students a sense of voice and multilayered identity. This suggests teaching students forms of literacy that engage their own communities and the discourse of the dominant culture; it also means teaching students how to critically appropriate the codes and vocabularies of different cultural experiences so as to provide them with some of the skills they will need in order to define and shape the modern world, rather than simply serve in it. In other words, students need to understand the richness and strengths of other cultural traditions, other voices— particularly as these point to forms of self- and social empowerment. Students need to take seriously what it means to learn how to govern critically and ethically in the broad political sense. In addition, students need to address as part of the pedagogy of the Other how representations and practices that name, marginalize, and define difference as the devalued Other are actively learned, interiorized, challenged, or transformed. At stake here is the need for administrators and teachers to address how an understanding of these differences can be used to change the prevailing relations of power that sustain them.[40]

Educational workers must also take seriously the articulation of a morality that posits a language of public life, emancipatory community, and individual and social commitment. In other words, students need to be introduced to a language of morality that allows them to think about how community life should be constructed. What is of fundamental importance here is our conception of humanity and human capacities, and our recognition of those ideological and material constraints that restrict human possibilities, especially those possibilities of improving the quality of human life for all. A discourse on morality is important because it points to the need to educate students to fight and struggle in order to advance the discourse and principles of a critical democracy, and because it provides a referent against which students can decide what forms of life and conduct are most appropriate morally amidst the welter of knowledge claims and interests they confront in making choices in a world of competing and diverse ideologies.

Teachers as Public Intellectuals

If teachers are to take an active role in raising serious questions about what they teach, how they are to teach, and the larger goals for which they are striving, it means they must take a more critical and political role in defining the nature of their work, as well as in shaping the conditions under which they work. We believe that teachers need to view themselves as public intellectuals who combine conception and implementation, thinking and practice, with a political project grounded in the struggle for a culture of liberation and justice. The category of public intellectual is important here for analyzing the particular practices in which teachers engage. First, it provides a referent for criticizing those forms of pedagogies that treat knowledge as fixed and deny students the opportunity to interrogate their own histories and voices. Second, the notion of public intellectual provides a theoretical and political basis for teachers to engage in a critical dialogue among themselves and students, in order to fight for the conditions necessary for them to reflect, read, and share their work with others, in the interest not merely of improving the life of the mind but of engaging and transforming oppressive discursive and institutional boundaries. Third, the category signifies the need for teachers to redefine their role as educational leaders in order to create programs that allow them and their students to undertake the language of social criticism, to display moral courage, and to connect with rather than distance themselves from the most pressing problems and opportunities of the times.[41]

Teachers need to provide models of leadership that offer the promise of reforming schools as part of a wider revitalization of public life. Central to this notion of leadership would be questions regarding the relationship between power and knowledge, learning and empowerment, and authority and human dignity. These questions need to be examined as part of a political discourse regarding textual authority and citizenship that organizes the energies of a moral vision, raising issues about how teachers and students can work for "the reconstruction of social imagination in the service of human freedom."[42] In short, this means providing the opportunity for teachers to engage more critically with what they know and how they come to know, enabling them to presuppose a pedagogy of democratic life that is worth struggling for. This means understanding the limits of our own language as well as the implications of the social practices we construct on the basis of the language we use to exercise authority and power. It means developing a language that can question public forms, address social injustices, and break the tyranny of the present. Finally, teachers need a language of imagination, one that insists on consideration of the critical means for developing those aspects of public life that point to its best and as yet unrealized possibilities, and acts to enable such consideration. This means struggling for a language of democratic possibilities not yet realized. In part this means that critical educators will have to move away from the mechanical, one-dimensional, interest-ridden politics that appear to be on the rise again among some factions of left and progressive educators. As public intellectuals, educators need to recognize the partiality of their own discourse, be open to engaging other positions as part of a wider dialogue and struggle over reconstructing public life, and recognize what forces are *really* responsible for undermining public education in the Age of Reagan/Bush. What is at stake here is the development of a curriculum theory forged in a political project that is open to criticism, that views difference as more than a cultural marker for asserting antagonistic relations, and relates educational reform to the broader categories of democratic community, citizenship, and social justice.

In Chapter 5, we will outline some elements of what we call border pedagogy of postmodern resistance. In effect, we will attempt to demonstrate how certain postmodern notions of culture, difference, and subjectivity—when combined with modernist concerns such as the language of public life, the notion of counter-memory, and the feminist notion of political identity—provide a number of elements for developing a more encompassing theory of schooling and critical pedagogy.

Notes

1. See, for example, Michael Apple, *Ideology and Curriculum* (New York: Routledge & Kegan Paul, 1979); Nancy Lesko, "The Curriculum of the Body: Lessons from a Catholic High School," in Leslie Roman, Linda K. Christian-Smith, and Elizabeth Ellsworth, eds., *Becoming Feminine: The Politics of Popular Culture* (New York: Falmer Press, 1988), 123–42; Philip H. Steedman, "Curriculum and Knowledge Selection," in Landon E. Beyer and Michael W. Apple, eds., *The Curriculum: Problems, Politics, and Possibilities* (Albany: SUNY Press, 1988), 119–39; Philip Wexler, "Structure, Text, and Subject: A Critical Sociology of School Knowledge," in Michael W. Apple, ed., *Cultural and Economic Reproduction in Education* (New York: Routledge & Kegan Paul, 1982), 275–303.

2. Examples of this approach can be found in Paul Willis, *Learning to Labour* (Westmead: Saxon House, 1977); Dale Spender and Elizabeth Sarah, eds., *Learning to Lose* (London: The Women's Press, 1980); Linda Valli, *Becoming Clerical Workers* (Boston: Routledge & Kegan Paul, 1986).

3. This theme is taken up in Stanley Aronowitz and Henry A. Giroux, *Education under Siege* (South Hadley, Mass.: Bergin & Garvey Press, 1985).

4. Catherine Belsey, *Critical Practice* (New York: Methuen, 1980), 42, 46.

5. The critical literature on this issue is extensive. For representative examples, see Paulo Freire and Donaldo Macedo, *Literacy: Reading the Word and the World* (South Hadley, Mass.: Bergin & Garvey Press, 1987); Harvey Graff, *The Legacies of Literacy: Continuities and Contradictions in Western Culture* (Bloomington: Indiana University Press, 1987); Colin Lankshear with Moira Lawler, *Literacy, Schooling, and Revolution* (New York: Falmer Press, 1987); Jim Gee, "Literacy, Linguistics, and Ideology: An Overview," Department of Linguistics, University of Southern California, unpublished paper, 1989; Bill Green, "Subject-Specific Literacy and School Learning: A Focus on Writing," *Australian Journal of Education*, 32:2 (1988), 156–79; Mikhail Bakhtin, *Speech Genres and Other Late Essays* (Austin: University of Texas Press, 1986); Michael Halliday, *Language, Context*

and Text: Aspects of Language in a Social-Semiotic Perspective (Geelong, Australia: Deakin University Press, 1985); Gabriel Josipovici, *Writing and the Body* (Princeton: Princeton University Press, 1982); Robert Hodge and Gunther Kress, *Social Semiotics* (Ithaca: Cornell University Press, 1988); Richard Ohmann, *Politics of Letters* (Middletown: Wesleyan University Press, 1987); Jim Berlin, "The Teacher as Researcher: Democracy, Dialogue, and Power," in Don Daiker and Max Morenberg, eds., *The Writing Teacher as Researcher* (in press); Terry Cochran, "Culture Against the State," *Boundary2* (in press).

6. Henry A. Giroux, *Schooling and the Struggle for Public Life* (Minneapolis: University of Minnesota Press, 1988).

7. Linda Brodkey, "On the Subject of Class and Gender in 'The Literacy Letters'," *College English,* 51:2 (1989), 125–26

8. We are not suggesting, in developing the notion of textual authority, that such authority embodies merely a negative notion of power. On the contrary, we are arguing that textual authority has to be understood in terms of the power relations that sanction it as a disciplinary form of legitimation. The issue here is not abandoning any kind of textual authority as much as it is developing a concept of textual authority that challenges dominating forms of power and references itself through an appeal to reclaiming and reconstructing democratic public spheres and empowering democratic social relations. Henry Giroux takes up this relationship between authority and power in *Schooling and the Struggle for Public Life*

9. The notion of textual authority and its relationship to issues of power, ideology, and struggle *is* taken up critically in a number of texts, many of which are written by feminist theorists. For example, see Carroll Smith-Rosenberg, *Disorderly Conduct* (New York: Oxford University Press, 1985); Jane Roland Martin, *Reclaiming a Conversation: The Ideal of the Educated Woman* (New Haven: Yale University Press, 1985); Elaine Showalter, Speaking of Gender (New York and London: Routledge, 1989); Judith Newton and Deborah Rosenfelt, eds., *Feminist Criticism and Social Change* (New York: Methuen, 1985); Catharine R. Stimpson, *Where the Meanings Are: Feminism and Cultural Spaces* (New York: Methuen, 1988); Sandra Harding, *The Science Question in Feminism* (Ithaca: Cornell University Press, 1986); Barbara Christian, *Black Feminist Criticism* (New York: Pergamon Press, 1985); Linda Brodkey, *Academic Writing as Social Practice*, (Philadelphia: Temple University Press, 1987); Rosemary Radford Ruether, *Sexism and God-Talk: Toward a Feminist Theology* (Boston: Beacon Press, 1983); Patricia Jagentowicz Mills, *Woman, Nature, and Psyche* (New Haven: Yale University Press, 1987). Additional critical sources include Terry Eagleton, *Literary Theory: An Introduction* (Minneapolis: University of Minnesota Press, 1982); Frank Lentricchia, *Criticism and Social Change* (Chicago: University of Chicago Press, 1983); Robert Scholes, *Textual Power* (New Haven: Yale University Press, 1987); David Bleich, *The Double Perspective: Language, Literacy, and Social Relations* (New York: Oxford University Press, 1988); Kevin Hart,ed., *Shifting/Frames: English/Literature/Writing* (Victoria, Australia: Typereader Publications No. 2, Center for Studies in Literary Education, 1988); Richard Ohmann, *English in America* (New York: Oxford University Press, 1977); Richard Ohmann, *Politics of Letters* (Wesleyan: Wesleyan University Press, 1987).

10. Allan Bloom, *The Closing of the American Mind* (New York: Simon & Schuster, 1987); for a critique of this position, see Chapter 2 of this volume.

11. This theme is taken up in articles and books too numerous to mention; for a recent commentary, see Toni Morrison, "Unspeakable Things Unspoken: The Afro American Presence in American Literature," *Michigan Quarterly Review* 28:1 (1989), 1–34; Hazel Carby, "The Canon: Civil War and Reconstruction," *Michigan Quarterly Review*, 28:1 (1989), 35–43; June Jordan, *On Call: Political Essays* (Boston: South End Press, 1987);

James Donald, "Beacons of the Future: Schooling, Subjection and Subjectification," in Veronica and James Donald, eds., *Subjectivity and Social Relations* (Milton Keynes: Open University Press, 1985), 214–49.

12. Mary Louise Pratt, "Interpretive Strategies/Strategic Interpretations: On Anglo-American Reader-Response Crticism," in Jonathan Arac, ed., *Postmodernism and Politics* (Minneapolis: University of Minnesota Press, 1986), 26–54.

13. Jim Merod, *The Political Responsibility of the Critic* (Ithaca: Cornell University Press, 1987).

14. Donald, *Subjectivity and Social Relations*, 240.

15. Chantal Mouffe, "The Civics Lesson," *The New Statesman and Society*, October 7, 1989, 31.

16. Tony Bennet, "Texts in History: The Determinations of Readings and Their Texts," in Derek Atridge, Geoff Bennington, and Robert Young, eds., *Post-Structuralism and the Question of History* (New York and London: Cambridge University Press, 1987), 70–71

17. Donald Morton and Mas'ud Zavarzadeh, "The Cultural Politics of the Fiction Workshop," *Cultural Critique*, 11 (1988–89), 158.

18. Linda Brodkey, *Academic Writing*, 139.

19. These themes are developed in Henry A. Giroux, *Schooling and the Struggle for Public Life* (Minneapolis: University of Minnesota Press, 1988); Henry A. Giroux, *Teachers as Intellectuals* (Granby, Mass.: Bergin & Garvey Press, 1988); see also Peter McLaren, *Life in Schools* (New York: Longman, 1989).

20. The issue of literacy and silencing is taken up in Brodkey, *Academic Writing*, and Kathleen Rockhill, "Gender, Language, and the Politics of Literacy," *British Journal of Sociology of Education*, 8:2 (1987), 153–67.

21. Gerald Graff, *Professing Literature* (Chicago: University of Chicago Press, 1987); Richard Rorty, *Philosophy and the Mirror of Nature* (Princeton: Princeton University Press, 1979); Mary Field Belenky et al., *Women's Ways of Knowing: The Development of Self, Voice, and Mind* (New York: Basic Books, 1986).

22. Roger Simon, "Empowerment as a Pedagogy of Possibility," *Language Arts*, 64:3 (1987), 377.

23. Ben Agger, *Fast Capitalism: A Critical Theory of Significance* (Urbana: University of Illinois Press, 1989).

24. Merod, *Political Responsibility*.

25. Fred Inglis, *The Management of Ignorance* (London: Blackwell, 1985), 108.

26. Merod, *Political Responsibility*, 32–33.

27. Bennet, "Texts in History," 68.

28. Mikhail Bakhtin, *The Dialogic Imagination*, trans. Caryl Emerson and Michael Holquist (Austin: University of Texas Press, 1981).

29. Bennet, "Texts in History," 79; Merod, *Political Responsibility*; Agger, *Fast Capitalism*.

30. Catherine Belsey, *Critical Practice* (New York: Methuen, 1980).

31. Bill Green, "Literature as Curriculum Frame: A Critical Perspective," in Hart, *Shifting/Frames*, 46–71.

32. Scholes, *Textual Power*.

33. Roland Barthes, *S/Z*, trans. Richard Miller (New York: Hill & Wang, 1974).

34. Scholes, *Textual Power*, 27.

35. Ibid., 30.

36. Ibid., 30.

37. Ibid., 62.

38. Jameson quoted in Scholes, ibid., 84.

THE ROLE OF TEACHERS AS PUBLIC INTELLECTUALS □ 113

39. Gary Peller, "Reason and the Mob: The Politics of Representation," *Tikkun* 2:3 (1987), 28–31, 92–95.

40. These issues are developed extensively in "Postmodernism and the Discourse of Educational Criticism" and "Border Pedagogy in the Age of Postmodernism," chapters 3 and 5 in this volume.

41. The literature on the role of the intellectual as a public figure is too vast to cite here, but some of the more important sources include Alvin Gouldner, *The Future of Intellectuals and the Rise of the New Class* (New York: Seabury, 1979); George Konrad and Ivan Szlenyi, *The Intellectuals on the Road to Power* (New York: Harcourt Brace Jovanovich, 1979); Stanley Aronowitz and Henry A. Giroux, *Education under Siege* (South Hadley, Mass.: Bergin & Garvey Press, 1985); Russell Jacoby, *The Last Intellectuals: American Culture in the Age of Academe* (New York: Basic Books, 1987); Paul Bové, *Intellectuals in Power* (New York: Columbia University Press, 1986); Ron Eherman, Lennart G. Svensson, and Thomas Soderqvist, eds., *Intellectuals, Universities, and the State in Western Modern Societies* (Berkeley: University of California Press, 1987); Merod, *Political Responsibility*.

42. Simon, "Empowerment," 375.

CHAPTER 5

BORDER PEDAGOGY IN THE AGE OF POSTMODERNISM

You must know who is the object and who is the subject of a sentence in order to know if you are the object or subject of history. If you can't control a sentence you don't know how to put yourself into history, to trace your own origin in the country, to vocalize, to use your voice.

Nelida Piñon, interview.

We are always living out a story. There is no way to live a storyless . . . life.[1]

Michael Novak, in I. Dienske, "Narrative Knowledge and Sciences."

Within the last two decades, the varied discourses known as postmodernism have exercised a strong influence on the nature of intellectual life in a variety of disciplines both in and out of the university. As a form of cultural criticism, postmodernism has challenged a number of assumptions central to the discourse of modernism. These include modernism's reliance on metaphysical notions of the subject; its advocacy of science, technology, and rationality as the foundation for equating change with progress; its ethnocentric equation of history with the triumphs of European civilization; and its globalizing view that the industrialized Western countries constitute "a legitimate center—a unique and superior position from which to establish control and to determine

114

hierarchies" (Richard, 1987/1988, 6). From the postmodernist perspective, modernism's claim to authority partly serves to privilege Western patriarchal culture, on the one hand, while simultaneously repressing and marginalizing the voices of those who have been deemed subordinate or subjected to relations of oppression because of their color, class, ethnicity, race, or cultural and social capital. In postmodernist terms, the political map of modernism is one in which the voice of the other is consigned to the margins of existence, recognition, and possibility. At its best, a postmodernism of resistance wants to redraw the map of modernism so as to effect a shift in power from the privileged and the powerful to those groups struggling to gain a measure of control over their lives in what is increasingly becoming a world marked by a logic of disintegration (Dews, 1987). Postmodernism not only makes visible the ways in which domination is being prefigured and redrawn, it also points to the shifting configurations of power, knowledge, space, and time that characterize a world that is at once more global and more differentiated.

One important aspect of postmodernism is the recognition it imposes that, as we move into the twenty-first century, we find ourselves no longer constrained by modernist images of progress and history. Within an emerging postmodern era, the elements of discontinuity, rupture, and difference provide alternative sets of referents by which to understand modernity as well as to challenge and modify it. This is a world in which capital no longer is restricted by the imperatives of nationalism; it is a culture in which the production of electronic information radically alters traditional notions of time, community, and history, while simultaneously blurring the distinction between reality and image. In the postmodern age, it becomes more difficult to define cultural differences by means of hegemonic colonialist notions of worth and possibility, and more difficult to define meaning and knowledge through the master narratives of "great men." The modernist emphasis on totality and mastery has given way to a more acute understanding of suppressed and local histories, along with a deeper appreciation for struggles that are contextual and specific in scope. In addition, in the age of instant information, global networking, and biogenetics, the old distinction between high and popular culture collapses, as the historically and socially constructed nature of meaning becomes evident, dissolving universalizing claims to history, truth, or class. All culture is worthy of investigation, and no aspect of cultural production can escape its own history within socially constructed hierarchies of meaning.

Another important aspect of postmodernism is that it provides a series of referents for problematizing some of the most basic elements of modernism, and for redrawing and rewriting how individual and collective experience might be struggled over, understood, felt, and shaped. For example, postmodernism presents itself as a critique of all forms of representations and meanings that claim transcendental and transhistorical status. It rejects universal reason as a foundation for human affairs, and poses as alternatives forms of knowing that are partial, historical, and social. In addition, postmodernism points to a world in which the production of meaning has become as important as the production of labor in shaping the boundaries of human existence. In this view, how we are constituted in language is no less important than how we are constructed as subjects within relations of production. The political economy of the sign does not displace political economy; it simply assumes its rightful place as a primary category for understanding how identities are forged within particular relations of privilege, oppression, and struggle. Similarly, postmodernism serves to deterritorialize the map of dominant cultural understanding. That is, it rejects the European tradition as the exclusive referent for judging what constitutes historical, cultural, and political truth. There is no tradition or story that can speak with authority and certainty for all of humanity. A postmodernism of resistance argues that traditions should be valued for their attempts to name the partial, the particular, and the specific; in this view, traditions demonstrate the importance of constituting history as a dialogue among a variety of voices as they struggle within asymmetrical relations of power. Traditions are not valued for their claims to truth or authority, but for the ways in which they serve to liberate and enlarge human possibilities. Tradition does not represent an all-embracing view of life; instead, it serves to place people self-consciously in their histories by making them aware of the memories constituted in difference, struggle, and hope. Tradition, in postmodern terms, is a form of counter-memory that points to the fluid and complex identities that constitute the social and political construction of public life.

Finally, and at the risk of great simplification, a postmodernism of resistance challenges the liberal humanist notion of the unified, rational subject as the bearer of history. In this view, the subject is not unified, nor can such a subject's action be guaranteed in metaphysical or transhistorical terms. Postmodernism views the subject as contradictory and multilayered, and rejects the notion that individual consciousness and reason are the most important determinants in shaping human history. It posits instead a faith in forms of social transformation that understand the historical, structural, and ideological limits that shape the possibility for self-reflection and action. Postmodernism points to solidarity, community, and compassion as essential aspects of how we develop and understand the capacities we have for experiencing the world and ourselves in a meaningful way. More specifically, postmodernism offers a series of referents for rethinking how we are constituted as subjects within a rapidly changing set of political, social, and cultural conditions.

What does this suggest for the way we look at the issue of pedagogy? We believe that by combining the best insights of modernism and postmodernism, educators can deepen and extend what is generally referred to as critical pedagogy. We need to combine the modernist emphasis on the capacity of individuals to use critical reason in addressing public life with a critical postmodernist concern with how we might experience agency in a world constituted in differences unsupported by transcendent phenomena or metaphysical guarantees. In that way, critical pedagogy can reconstitute itself in terms that are both transformative and emancipatory. This is not to suggest that critical pedagogy constitutes a monolithic discourse and a corresponding set of robotlike methods. In fact, the discourse of critical pedagogy as it has developed over the last decade incorporates a variety of theoretical positions that differ in both methodological focus and ideological orientation (Apple and Beyer, 1988; Giroux and McLaren, 1989; Pinar, 1988).

At its worst, critical pedagogy as a form of educational criticism has been overly shaped by the discourse of modernism. Increasingly reduced to a modernist emphasis on technique and procedure, some versions of critical pedagogy reduce its liberating possibilities by focusing almost exclusively on issues of dialogue, process, and exchange. In this form, critical pedagogy comes perilously close to emulating the liberal-progressive tradition in which teaching is reduced to getting students merely to express or assess their own experiences. Teaching collapses in this case into a banal notion of facilitation, and student experience becomes an unproblematic vehicle for self-affirmation and self-consciousness. Within this perspective, it is assumed that student experience produces forms of understanding that escape the contradictions that inform them. Understanding the limits of a particular position, engaging its contradictory messages, or extending its insights beyond the limits of particular experiences is lost in this position. It overprivileges the notion of student voice, and refuses to engage its contradictory nature. Moreover, this position lacks any sense of its own political project as a starting point from which to define both the role of the teacher, and the role that the school should play with respect to the larger society. In this version of critical pedagogy, there is a flight from authority and a narrow definition of politics that abandons the utopian project of educating students to locate themselves in their particular histories, and simultaneously to confront the limits of their own perspectives as part of a broader engagement with democratic public life.

At its best, critical pedagogy enables teachers and others to view education as a political, social, and cultural enterprise. That is, as a form of engaged practice, critical pedagogy calls into question forms of subordination that create inequities among different groups as they live out their lives. Likewise, it rejects classroom relations that cause difference to be seen as an object of condemnation and oppression, and it refuses to subordinate the purpose of schooling to narrowly defined economic and instrumental considerations. This is a notion of critical pedagogy that equates learning with the creation of critical citizens, rather than merely good ones. This is a pedagogy that links schooling to the imperatives of democracy, views teachers as engaged and transformative intellectuals, and makes the notion of democratic difference central to the organization of curriculum and the development of classroom practice.

In what follows, we want to advance the most useful and transformative aspects of this version of critical pedagogy by articulating a theory of what we call a border pedagogy of postmodern resistance. In this perspective, the issue of critical pedagogy is located within those broader cultural and political considerations that are beginning to redefine our traditional view of community, language, space, and possibility. It is a pedagogy that is attentive to developing a democratic public philosophy that respects the notion of difference as part of a common struggle to extend the quality of public life. In short, the notion of border pedagogy presupposes not merely an acknowledgment of the shifting borders that both undermine and reterritorialize different configurations of power and knowledge; it also links the notion of pedagogy to a more substantive struggle for a democratic society. It is a pedagogy that attempts to link an emancipatory notion of modernism with a postmodernism of resistance.

Border Pedagogy as a Counter-Text

Border pedagogy offers the opportunity for students to engage the multiple references that constitute different cultural codes, experiences, and languages. This means educating students to read these codes critically, to learn the limits of such codes, including the ones they use to construct their own narratives and histories. Partiality becomes, in this case, the basis for recognizing the limits built into all discourses, and necessitates taking a critical view of authority. Within this discourse, students must engage knowledge as border-crossers, as people moving in and out of borders constructed around coordinates of difference and power (Hicks, 1988). These are not only physical borders, they are cultural borders: historically constructed and socially organized within maps of rules and regulations that limit and enable particular identities, individual capacities, and social forms. In this case, students cross over into realms of meaning—maps of knowledge, social relations, and values that are increasingly being negotiated and rewritten as the codes and regulations that organize them become destabilized and reshaped. Border pedagogy decenters as it remaps. The terrain of learning becomes inextricably linked to the shifting parameters of place, identity, history, and power.

Within critical social theory, it has become commonplace to argue that knowledge and power are related, though the weight of the argument has often overemphasized how domination works through the intricacies of this relationship (Foucault, 1977b). Border pedagogy offers a crucial theoretical and political corrective to this insight. It does so by shifting the emphasis of the knowledge/power relationship away from the limited emphasis on the mapping of domination and toward the politically strategic issue of engaging the ways in which knowledge can be remapped, reterritorialized, and decentered in the wider interests of rewriting the borders and coordinates of an oppositional cultural politics. This is not an abandonment of critique as much as it is an extension of its possibilities. In this case, border pedagogy incorporates the postmodern emphasis on criticizing official texts and using alternative modes of representation (mixing video, photography, and print). It also incorporates popular culture as a serious object of politics and analysis, and makes central to its project the recovery of those forms of knowledge and history that characterize alternative and oppositional Others (Said, 1983). How these cultural practices might be taken up as pedagogical practices has been demonstrated by a number of theorists (Scholes, 1985; Giroux and Simon, 1988; Cherryholmes, 1988; Brodkey and Fine, 1988).

One example of how a postmodern pedagogy of resistance might inform the notion of border pedagogy can be found in some of the recent work being done on educational theory and popular culture (Giroux and Simon, 1988; Giroux and Simon, 1989). Two important issues are being worked out. First, in this work there is a central concern for understanding how the production of meaning is tied to emotional investments and the production of pleasure. In this view, it is necessary for teachers to incorporate into their pedagogies a theoretical understanding of how the production of meaning and pleasure becomes mutually constitutive of students' identities, of how they view themselves, and of how they construct a particular vision of their future. Second, the nature of how students make semantic and emotional investments needs to be rethought in the light of a number of important pedagogical considerations. One such consideration is that the production and regulation of desire must be seen as a crucial aspect of how students mediate, relate, resist, and create particular cultural forms and forms of knowing. Another concern is that popular culture be seen as a legitimate aspect of the everyday lives of students, and be analyzed as a primary force in shaping the various and often contradictory subject positions that students take up. Finally, popular culture needs to become a serious object of study in the official curriculum. This can be done by treating popular culture either as a distinct object of study within particular academic disciplines such as media studies, or by drawing upon the resources it produces for engaging various aspects of the official curriculum (Giroux and Simon, 1989).

Central to border pedagogy informed by postmodern criticism is the need to point to ways in which those master narratives based on white, patriarchal, and class-specific versions of the world can be challenged and deterritorialized. That is, by offering a theoretical language for establishing new boundaries with respect to knowledge most often associated with the margins and the periphery of the culturally dominant, postmodern discourses open up the possibility for incorporating into the curriculum a notion of border pedagogy in which cultural and social practices need no longer be mapped or referenced solely on the basis of the dominant models of Western culture. In this case, knowledge forms emanating from the margins can be used to redefine the complex, multiple, heterogeneous realities that constitute those relations of difference making up the experiences of students who often find it impossible to define their identities through the cultural and political codes of a single, unitary culture.

The sensibility that informs this view of knowledge emphasizes a pedagogy in which students need to develop a relationship of non-identity with their own subject positions and the multiple cultural, political, and social codes that constitute established boundaries of power, dependency, and possibility. In other words, such a pedagogy emphasizes the nonsynchronous relationship between one's social position and the multiple ways in which culture is constructed and read. That is, there is no single, predetermined relationship between a cultural code and the subject position that a student occupies. One's class, race, gender, or ethnicity may influence, but does not irrevocably predetermine, how one takes up a particular ideology, reads a particular text, or responds to particular forms of oppression. Border pedagogy recognizes that teachers, students, and others often "read and write culture on multiple levels" (Kaplan, 1987, 187). Of course, the different subject positions and forms of subjugation that are constituted within these various levels and relations of culture have the potential to isolate and alienate instead of opening up the possibility for criticism and struggle. What is at stake here is the development of a border pedagogy that can fruitfully work to break down those ideologies, cultural codes, and social practices that prevent students from recognizing how social forms at particular historical conjunctures operate to repress alternative readings of their own experiences, society, and the world.

Border Pedagogy as Counter-Memory

Postmodernism charts the process of deterritorialization as part of the breakdown of master narratives. It celebrates, in part, the loss of certainty and the experience of defamiliarization even as it produces alienation and the displacement of identities (Deleuze and Guattari, 1986). In opposition to conservative readings of this shifting destabilizing process, we believe that such a disruption of traditional meaning offers important insights for developing a theory of border pedagogy based on a postmodernism of resistance. But this language runs the risk of undercutting its own political possibilities by ignoring how a language of difference can be articulated with critical modernist concerns for developing a discourse of public life. It also ignores the possibilities for developing, through the process of counter-memory, new and emancipatory forms of political identity. In what follows, we address some of the important work being done in radical public philosophy and feminist theory, paying particular attention to the issues of identity and counter-memory. The brief final section of this chapter will offer some considerations of how the critical insights of a postmodernism of resistance can be deepened within a theory of border pedagogy.

Postmodernism has launched a major attack on the modernist notion of political universality (Ross, 1988). By insisting on the multiplicity of social positions, it has seriously challenged the political closure of modernity, with its divisions between the center and the margins, and in doing so has made room for those groups generally defined as the excluded others. Postmodernism has reasserted the importance of the partial, the local, and the contingent, and in doing so it has given general expression to the demands of a wide variety of social movements. Postmodernism has also effectively challenged the ways in which written history has embodied a number of assumptions that inform the discourse of Eurocentrism. More specifically, it has rejected Eurocentric assumptions such as the pretentious claim to "speak" for all of "mankind" and epistemological claims to foundationalism.

Laclau (1988) rightfully argues that an adequate approximation of the postmodern experience must be seen as part of a challenge to the discourses of modernity, with their "pretension to intellectually dominate the foundation of the social, to give a rational context to the notion of the totality of history, and to base in the latter the project of global human emancipation" (71–72). But Laclau also points out that the postmodern challenge to modernity does not represent the abandonment of its emancipatory values so much as it opens them up to a plurality of contexts and an indeterminacy "that redefines them in an unpredictable way" (72). Chantal Mouffe (1988) extends this insight and argues that modernity has two contradictory aspects: its political project is rooted in a conception of the struggle for democracy, while its social project is tied to a foundationalism that fuels the process of social modernization under "the growing domination of relations of capitalist production" (32). For Mouffe, the modernist project of democracy must be coupled with an understanding of the various social movements and the new politics that have emerged within the postmodern age. At the heart of this position is the need to rearticulate the tradition of liberty and justice with a notion of radical democracy; similarly, there is a need to articulate the concept of difference as more than a replay of liberal pluralism or a pastiche of diverse interests with no commonality to hold them together.

This is not a liberal call to harmonize and resolve differences. It is an attempt to understand differences in terms of the historical and social grounds on which they are organized. By locating differences in a particular historical and social location, it becomes possible to understand how they are organized and constructed by maps of rules and regulations, and located within dominant social forms that either enable or disable such differences. Differences exist only relative to the social forms in which they are enunciated—that is, in relation to schools, workplaces, families, as well as in relationship to the discourses of history, citizenship, sex, race, gender, and ethnicity. To detach them from the discourse of democracy and freedom is to remove the possibility of either articulating their particular interests as part of a wider struggle for power or understanding how their individual contradictory interests are developed within a historically specific conjuncture. Educators need to fashion a critical politics of difference not outside but within a tradition of radical democracy. It is imperative for critical educators to develop a discourse of counter-memory, not as an essentialist and closed narrative, but as part of a utopian project that recognizes "the composite, heterogeneous, open, and ultimately indeterminate character of the democratic tradition" (Mouffe, 1988, 41). The pedagogical issue here is the need to articulate difference as part of the construction of a new type of subject, one that would be both multiple and democratic. Chantal Mouffe (1988) writes on this issue:

> If the task of radical democracy is indeed to deepen the democratic revolution and to link together diverse democratic struggles, such a task requires the creation of new subject-positions that would allow the common articulation, for example, of antiracism, antisexism, and anticapitalism. These struggles do not spontaneously converge, and in order to establish democratic equivalences, a new "common sense" is necessary, which would transform the identity of different groups so that the demands of each group could be articulated with those of others according to the principle of democratic equivalence. For it is not a matter of establishing a mere alliance between given interests but of actually modifying the very identity of these forces. In order that the defense of workers' interests is not pursued at the cost of the rights of women, immigrants, or consumers, it is necessary to establish an equivalence between these different struggles. It is only under these circumstances that struggles against [authoritarian] power become truly democratic. (42)

Mouffe's emphasis on difference as central to any democratic society is important but it does not go far enough. We would like to offer a more substantive theoretical and political analyses by linking democracy to citizenship understood as a form of self-management constituted in all major economic, social, and cultural spheres of society. Democracy in this context takes up the issue of transferring power from elites and executive authorities, who control the economic and cultural appartuses of society, to those producers who wield power at the local level. At stake here is making democracy concrete through the organization and exercise of horizontal power in which "knowledge must be widely shared, through education and free information-flows, so that scientific and technological decisions are not made exclusively by people who possess capital or credentials; moreover, the basis of productive activity must be radically dispersed, not only to facilitate control but also to provide the necessary conditions for the achievement of a grassroots-generated society and ecological relations that improve the quality of life" (Aronowitz, 1990). We believe that questions of democracy and citizenship occupy the center of an emancipatory project designed to provide a "significant restructuring of social relations so that horizontal and vertical power flows from the base of society and representative institutions, to the extent that they are a necessary outgrowth of popular assemblies which are delegated and not constituted by elites who derive a mandate from electoral victories or alliances" (Aronowitz, 1990, 302). Not only does such a position dissipate the discourse of liberal pluralism in its call for democratic struggles and the construction of popular public spheres, it also places the issue of power, politics, and struggle at the heart of the debate over radical democracy.

How might the issue of democracy and difference be taken up as part of a border pedagogy informed by a project of possibility? We want to argue that the discourses of democracy and difference can be taken up as pedagogical practices through what Foucault calls counter-memory. For Foucault (1977a), this practice "transforms history from a judgment on the past in the name of the present truth to a counter-memory that combats our current modes of truth and justice, helping us to understand and change the present by placing it in a new relation to the past" (Arac, 1986, xviii). Counter-memory represents a critical reading of how the past informs the present and how the present reads the past. Counter-memory provides a theoretical tool to restore the connection between the language of public life and the discourse of difference. It represents an attempt to rewrite the language of resistance in terms that connect human beings within forms of remembrance that dignify public life, while at the same time allowing people to speak from their particular histories and voices. Counter-memory refuses to treat democracy as merely inherited knowledge; it attempts, instead, to link democracy to notions of public life that "afford both agency and sources of power or empowering investments" (de Lauretis, 1987, 25). It also reasserts as a pedagogical practice the rewriting of history through the power of student voice. This points to the practice of counter-memory as a means of constructing democratic social forms that enable and disempower particular subjectivities and identities; put another way, democracy in this instance becomes a referent for understanding how public life organizes differences differently, and for understanding what this means for the ways in which schools, teachers, and students define themselves as political subjects, as citizens who operate within particular configurations of power.

In effect, the language of radical democracy provides the basis for educators to understand how differences are organized, and also how the grounds for such difference might be constructed within a political identity rooted in a respect for democratic public life (Giroux, 1988b). What is being suggested here is the construction of a project of possibility, in pedagogical terms, which is connected to a notion of democracy capable of mobilizing a variety of groups to develop and struggle for what Linda Alcoff (1988) calls a positive alternative vision. She writes, "As the Left should by now have learned, you cannot mobilize a movement that is only and always against: you must have a positive alternative, a vision of a better future that can motivate people to sacrifice their time and energy toward its realization" (Alcoff, 1988, 418–419). If radical democracy is to work as a pedagogical practice, educators must allow students to comprehend democracy as a way of life that consistently has to be fought for, has to be struggled over, and has to be rewritten as part of an oppositional politics. This means that democracy has to be viewed as a historical and social construction rooted in the tension between what Bruce James Smith (1985) calls remembrance and custom. We want to extend Smith's argument by developing remembrance as a form of counter-memory and custom as a form of reactionary nostalgia rooted in the loss of memory.

Custom, as Smith (1985) argues, constructs subjects within a discourse of continuity in which knowledge and practice are viewed as a matter of inheritance and transmission. Custom is the complex of ideologies and social practices that views counter-memory as subversive and critical teaching as unpatriotic. It is the ideological basis for forms of knowledge and pedagogy that refuse to interrogate public forms and that deny difference as a fundamental referent for a democratic society. According to Smith (1985), custom can be characterized in the following manner:

> The affection it enjoys and the authority it commands are prescriptive. The behavior of the person of custom is, by and large, habitual. To the question "why?" he is apt to respond simply, "This is the way it has always been done." . . . A creature of habit, the person of custom does not reflect upon his condition. To the extent that a customary society "conceives" of its practice, it is likely to see it, says Pocock, as "an indefinite series of repetitions." If the customary society is,

in reality, a fluid order always in the process of adaption, its continuity and incrementalism give rise to perceptions of changelessness and of the simple repetition of familiar motions. . . . Indeed . . . custom operates as if it were "a second nature." . . . Custom is at once both more and less inclusive than remembrance. It includes things that are remembered and things that are forgotten. It is almost a definition of custom that its beginnings are lost. (15, 16)

Remembrance is directed more toward specificity and struggle; it resurrects the legacies of actions and happenings, it points to the multitude of voices that constitute the struggle over history and power. Its focus is not on the ordinary but the extraordinary. Its language presents the unrepresentable, not merely as an isolated voice, but as a subversive interruption, a discursive space, that moves "against the grain" as it occupies "a view . . . carved in the interstices of institutions and in the chinks and cracks of the power-knowledge apparati" (de Lauretis, 1987, 25). Remembrance is part of a language of public life that promotes an ongoing dialogue between the past, present, and future. It is a vision of optimism rooted in the need to bear witness to history, to reclaim that which must not be forgotten. It is a vision of public life that calls for an ongoing interrogation of the past that allows different groups to locate themselves in history while simultaneously struggling to make history.

Counter-memory provides the ethical and epistemological grounds for a politics of solidarity within difference. At one level, it situates the notion of difference and the primacy of the political firmly within the wider struggle for broadening and revitalizing democratic public life. At the same time, it strips reason of its universalist pretensions and recognizes the partiality of all points of view. In this perspective, the positing of a monolithic tradition that exists simply to be revered, reaffirmed, reproduced, or resisted is unequivocally rejected. Instead, counter-memory attempts to recover communities of memory and narratives of struggle that provide a sense of location, place, and identity to various dominant and subordinate groups. Counter-memory as a form of pedagogical practice is not concerned with simply marking difference as a historical construct; rather, it is concerned with providing the grounds for self-representation and the struggle for justice and a democratic society. Counter-memory resists comparison to either a humanist notion of pluralism or a celebration of diversity for its own sake. As both a pedagogical and a political practice, it attempts to alter oppressive relations of power and to educate both teachers and students to the ways in which they might be complicitous with dominant power relations, victimized by them, and how they might be able to transform such relations. Abdul JanMohamed and David Lloyd (1987b) are instructive on what counter-memory might mean as part of a discourse of critique and transformation:

> Ethnic or gender difference must be perceived as one among a number of residual cultural elements which retain the memory of practices which have had to be and still have to be repressed in order that the capitalist economic subject may be more easily produced. . . . "Becoming minor" is not a question of essence but a question of position—a subject-position that can only be defined, in the final analysis, in "political" terms, that is, in terms of the effects of economic exploitation, political disfranchisement, social manipulation, and ideological domination on the cultural formation of minority subjects and discourses. It is one of the central tasks of the theory of minority discourse to define that subject-position and explore the strengths and weaknesses, the affirmations and negations that inhere in it. (11)

Remembrance as a form of counter-memory attempts to create for students the limits of any story that makes claims to predetermined endings, and to expose how the transgressions in those stories cause particular forms of suffering and hardship. At the same time, remembrance as counter-memory opens up the past not as nostalgia but as the invention of stories, some of which deserve a retelling, and which speak to a very different future—one in which democratic community makes room for a politics of both difference and solidarity, for Otherness stripped of subjugation, and for others fighting to embrace their own interests in opposition to sexism, racism, ethnocentrism, and class exploitation. Counter-memory is tied in this sense to a vision of public life that resurrects the ongoing struggle for difference, and situates difference within the broader struggle for cultural and social justice.

Counter-memory provides the basis and rationale for a particular kind of pedagogy, but it cannot on its own articulate the specific classroom practices that can be constructed on the basis of such a rationale. The formation of democratic citizens demands forms of political identity which radically extend the principles of justice, liberty, and dignity to public spheres constituted by difference and multiple forms of community. Such identities have to be constructed as part of a pedagogy in which difference becomes a basis for solidarity and unity rather than for hierarchy, denigration, competition, and discrimination. It is to that issue that we shall now turn.

Border Pedagogy and the Politics of Difference

If the concept of border pedagogy is to be linked to the imperatives of a critical democracy, as it must be, it is important that educators possess a theoretical grasp of the ways in which difference is constructed through various representations and practices that name, legitimate, marginalize, and exclude the cultural capital and voices of subordinate groups in American society.

As part of this theoretical project, a theory of border pedagogy needs to address the important question of how representations and practices that name, marginalize, and define difference as the devalued Other are actively learned, interiorized, challenged, or transformed. In addition, such a pedagogy needs to address how an understanding of these differences can be used in order to change the prevailing relations of power that sustain them. It is also imperative that such a pedagogy acknowledge and critically interrogate how the colonizing of differences by dominant groups is expressed and sustained through representations in which Others are seen as a deficit, in which the humanity of the Others is either cynically posited as problematic or ruthlessly denied. At the same time, it is important to understand how the experience of marginality at the level of everyday life lends itself to forms of oppositional and transformative consciousness. This is an understanding based on the need for those designated Others to reclaim and remake their histories, voices, and visions as part of a wider struggle to change those material and social relations that deny radical pluralism as the basis of democratic political community. For it is only through such an understanding that teachers can develop a border pedagogy, one that is characterized by what Teresa de Lauretis (1987) calls "an ongoing effort to create new spaces of discourse, to rewrite cultural narratives, and to define the terms of another perspective—a view from 'elsewhere' " (25). This suggests a pedagogy in which occurs a critical questioning of the omissions and tensions that exist between the master narratives and hegemonic discourses that make up the official curriculum and the self-representations of subordinate groups as they might appear in "forgotten" or erased histories, texts, memories, experiences, and community narratives.

Border pedagogy confirms and critically engages the knowledge and experience through which students author their own voices and construct social identities. This means it takes seriously the knowledge and experiences that constitute the individual and collective voices by which students identify and give meaning to themselves and others, and draws upon what they know about their own lives as a basis for criticizing the dominant culture. In this case, student experience has first to be understood and recognized as the accumulation of collective memories and stories that provide students with a sense of familiarity, identity, and practical knowledge. Such experience has to be both affirmed and critically interrogated. In addition, the social and historical construction of such experience has to be affirmed and understood as part of a wider struggle for voice. But it must also be understood that while past experiences can never be denied, their most debilitating dimensions can be engaged through a critical understanding of what was at work in their construction. It is in the critical engagement of such experiences that they can be remade, reterritorialized in the interest of a social imaginary that dignifies the best traditions and possibilities of those groups who are learning to speak from a discourse of dignity and self-governance. In her analysis of the deterritorialization of women as Other, Caren Kaplan (1987) astutely articulates this position:

> Recognizing the minor cannot erase the aspects of the major, but as a mode of understanding it enables us to see the fissures in our identities, to unravel the seams of our totalities. . . . We must leave home, as it were, since our homes are often sites of racism, sexism, and other damaging social practices. Where we come to locate ourselves in terms of our specific histories and differences must be a place with room for what can be salvaged from the past and what can be made anew. What we gain is a reterritorialization; we reinhabit a world of our making (here "our" is expanded to a coalition of identities—neither universal nor particular). (194–95)

Furthermore, it is important to extend the possibilities of the often contradictory values that give meaning to students' lives by making them the objects of critical inquiry—and by appropriating in a similarly critical fashion, when necessary, the codes and knowledges that constitute broader and less familiar historical and cultural traditions. At issue here is the development of a pedagogy that replaces the authoritative language of recitation with an approach that allows students to speak from their own histories, collective memories, and voices while simultaneously challenging the grounds on which knowledge and power are constructed and legitimated. Such a pedagogy contributes to making possible a variety of social forms and human capacities that expand the range of social identities that students may carry and become. It points to the importance of understanding, in both pedagogical and political terms, how subjectivities are produced within those social forms in which people move but of which they are often only partially conscious. This pedagogy raises fundamental questions regarding how students make particular investments of meaning and affect; how they are constituted within a triad of relationships of knowledge, power, and pleasure; and why students should be indifferent to the forms of authority, knowledge, and values that we produce and legitimate within our classrooms and universities. It is worth noting that such a pedagogy not only articulates respect for a diversity of student voices, it also provides a referent for developing a public language rooted in a commitment to social transformation.

Central to the notion of border pedagogy are a number of important pedagogical issues regarding the role that teachers might play at the interface of modern and postmodern concerns taken up in this chapter. Clearly, the concept of border pedagogy suggests that teachers exist within social, political, and cultural boundaries, which are both multiple and historical in nature, and which place particular demands on a recognition and pedagogical appropriation of differences. As part of the process of developing a pedagogy of difference, teachers need to deal with the plethora of voices, and the specificity and organization of differences, that constitute any course, class, or curriculum, so as to make problematic not only the stories that give meanings to the lives of their students, but also the ethical and political lineaments that inform their students' subjectivities and identities.

This suggests a pedagogy that does more than provide students with a language and context by which to critically engage the plurality of habits, practices, experiences, and desires that define them as part of a particular social formation within ongoing relations of domination and resistance. Border pedagogy also provides opportunities for teachers to deepen their own understanding of the discourse of various others in order to effect a more dialectical understanding of their own politics, values, and pedagogy. What border pedagogy makes undeniable is the relational nature of one's own politics and personal investments. But at the same time, border pedagogy emphasizes the primacy of a politics in which teachers assert rather than retreat from the pedagogies they utilize in dealing with the various differences represented by the students who come into their classes. For example, it is not enough for teachers merely to affirm uncritically their students' histories, experiences, and stories. To take student voices at face value is to run the risk of idealizing and romanticizing them. The contradictory and complex histories and stories that give meaning to the lives of students are never innocent, and it is important that they be recognized for their contradictions as well as for their possibilities. Of course, it is crucial that critical educators provide the pedagogical conditions for students to give voice to how their past and present experiences place them within existing relations of domination and resistance. Central to this pedagogical process is the important double task of affirming the voices that students bring to school, and challenging the separation of school knowledge from the experience of everyday life (Fine, 1987). But it is crucial that critical educators do more than allow such stories to be heard. It is equally important for teachers to help students find a language for critically examining the historically and socially constructed forms by which they live. Such a process involves more than "speaking" one's history and social formation. It also involves engaging collectively with others within a pedagogical framework that helps to reterritorialize and rewrite the complex narratives that make up one's life. This is more than a matter of rewriting stories as counter-memories; it is what Frigga Haug (1988) and her colleagues call memory-work, a crucial example of how the pedagogical functions to interrogate and retrieve, rather than merely to celebrate, one's voice:

> By excavating traces of the motives for our past actions, and comparing these with our present lives, we are able to expand the range of our demands and competences. Admittedly, this is not as easy as it sounds. Our stories are expressed in the language we use today. Buried or abandoned memories do not speak loudly; on the contrary we can expect them to meet us with obdurate silence. In recognition of this, we must adopt some method of analysis suited to the resolution of a key question for women; a method that seeks out the un-named, the silent and the absent. Here too, our experience of education maps out a ready-made path of analysis; we have been taught to content ourselves with decoding texts, with search for truth in textual analysis, complemented at best by the author's own analysis. "Re-learning" in this context means seeing what is *not* said as interesting, and the fact that it was not said as important; it involves a huge methodological leap, and demands more than a little imagination. (65)

The different stories that students from all groups bring to class need to be interrogated for their absences as well as for their contradictions, but they also need to be understood as more than simply a myriad of different stories. They have to be recognized as being forged in relations of opposition to the dominant structures of power. At the same time, contrary to Elizabeth Ellsworth's (1988) argument, differences among students are not merely antagonistic. She suggests that there is little common ground for addressing these differences and that separatism is the only valid political option for any kind of pedagogical and political action. Regrettably, this represents less an insight than a crippling form of political disengagement. It reduces one to paralysis in the face of such differences. It ignores the necessity of exploring differences for the specific, irreducible interests they represent; for the excesses and reactionary positions they may produce; and for the pedagogical possibilities they contain, for helping students to work with other groups as part of a collective attempt at developing a radical language of democratic public life. Moreover, Ellwsorth's attempt to delegitimate the work of other critical educators by claiming, rather self-righteously, the primacy and singularity of her own political project appears to ignore both the multiplicity of contexts and projects that characterize critical educational work and the tension that haunts all forms of teacher authority, a tension marked by the potential contradiction between being theoretically correct and pedagogically wrong. By ignoring the dynamics of such a tension and the variety of struggles being waged under historically specific educational conditions, she degrades the rich complexity of the pedagogical processes that characterize the diverse discourses in the field of critical pedagogy. In doing so, she succumbs to the familiar academic strategy of dismissing others through the use of strawman tactics and excessive simplifications that undermine the strengths of her own work and the very nature of social criticism itself. This is "theorizing" as a form of bad faith, a discourse that has become an all too familiar characteristic of many left academics.

At stake here is an important theoretical issue that is worth repeating. Knowledge and power come together not merely to reaffirm difference but also to interrogate it, to open up broader theoretical considerations, to tease out its limitations, and to engage a vision of community in which student voices define themselves in terms of their distinct social formations and their broader collective hopes. As teachers we can never speak inclusively as the Other, though we may be the Other with respect to issues of race, class, or gender, but we can certainly work with diverse Others to deepen their understanding of the complexity of the traditions, histories, knowledges, and politics that they bring to the schools (Giroux, in press). This means, as Abdul JanMohamed and David Lloyd (1987a, b) point out, that educators need to recognize the importance of developing a theory of minority discourse that not only explores the strengths and weaknesses, affirmations and negations that inhere in the subject positions of subordinate groups but also "involves drawing our solidarities in the form of similarities between modes of repression and modes of struggle which all minorities separately experience, and experience precisely as minorities" (JanMohamed and Lloyd, 1987a, 11). To assume such a position is not to practice forms of gender-, race-, or class-specific imperialism, as Ellsworth suggests; rather, such an assumption creates conditions within particular institutions that allow students to locate themselves and others in histories that mobilize, rather than destroy, their hopes for the future.

The theoretical sweep may be broad, the sentiment utopian, but better this than wallowing in guilt or refusing to fight for the possibility of a better world. The avoidance of sentimentality is no excuse for the absence of any vision for the future. Like Klee's angel in the painting *Angelus Novus*, modernity provides a faith in human agency while recognizing that the past is often built on the suffering of others. In the best of the Enlightenment tradition, reason at least offers the assumption and hope that men and women can change the world in which they live. Postmodernism frays the boundaries of that world and makes visible what has often been seen as unrepresentable. The task of modernity, with its faith in reason and emancipation, can perhaps renew its urgency in a postmodern world, a world where difference, contingency, and power can reassert, redefine, and in some instances collapse the monolithic boundaries of nationalism, sexism, racism, and class oppression. In a world whose borders have become chipped and porous, new challenges present themselves not only to educators but to all those for whom contingency and loss of certainty do not mean the inevitable triumph of nihilism and despair but rather a state of possibility in which destiny and hope can be snatched from the weakening grasp of modernity. We live in a postmodern world that no longer has any firm boundaries, but has ever-flexing ones. It is a time when reason is in crisis, and new political and ideological conditions exist for fashioning forms of struggle defined in a radically different conception of politics. For educators, this is as much a pedagogical issue as it is a political one. At best, it points to the importance of rewriting the relationship between knowledge, power, and desire. It points as well to the necessity of redefining the importance of difference, while at the same time seeking articulations among subordinate groups and historically privileged groups committed to social transformations that deepen the possibility for radical democracy and human survival.

References

Alcoff, L. (1988). "Cultural Feminism vs. Poststructuralism: The Identity Crisis in Feminist Theory." *Signs, 13*(3), 405–36.

Apple, M. and Beyer, L., eds. (1988). *The Curriculum: Problems, Politics and Possibilities.* Albany: State University of New York Press.

Arac, J., ed. (1986). *Postmodernism* and Politics. Minneapolis: University of Minnesota Press.

Aronowitz, S. (1990). *The Crisis in Historical Materialism.* 2nd ed. Minneapolis: University of Minnesota Press.

Brodkey, L., and Fine, M. (1988). "Presence of Mind in the Absence of Body?" *Journal of Education, 170* (3), 84–99.

Cherryholmes, C. (1988). *Power and Criticism: Poststructural Investigations in Education.* New York: Teachers College Press.

Deleuze, G., and Guattari, F. (1986). *Kafka: Toward a Minor Literature.* Minneapolis: University of Minnesota Press.

de Lauretis, T. (1987). *Technologies of Gender.* Bloomington: Indiana University Press.

Dews, P. (1987). *Logics of Disintegration.* London: Verso Books.

Dienske, I. (1988). "Narrative Knowledge and Science." *Journal of Learning about Learning, 1*(1), 19–27.

Ellsworth, E. (1988). "Why Doesn't This Feel Empowering? Working through the Repressive Myths of Critical Pedagogy." Paper presented at the Tenth Conference on Curriculum Theory and Classroom Practice, Bergamo Conference Center, Dayton, Ohio, October 26–29, 1988.

Fine, M. (1987). "Silencing in the Public Schools." *Language Arts, 64*(2), 157–74.

Foucault, M. (1977a). *Language, Counter-memory, Practice: Selected Essays and Interviews.* Ed. D. Bouchard. Ithaca: Cornell University Press.

Foucault, M. (1977b). *Power and Knowledge: Selected Interviews and Other Writings.* Ed. G. Gordon. New York: Pantheon.

Giroux, H., and Simon, R. (1988). "Critical Pedagogy and the Politics of Popular Culture." *Cultural Studies, 2*(3), 294–320.

Giroux, H., and Simon, R., eds. (1989). *Popular Culture, Schooling, and Everyday Life.* Granby, Mass.: Bergin & Garvey Press.

Giroux, H. (1988a). *Schooling and the Struggle for Public Life.* Minneapolis:University of Minnesota Press.

Giroux, H. (1988b). *Teachers as Intellectuals.* Granby, Mass.: Bergin and Garvey Press.

Giroux, H. (in press). "The Politics of Postmodernism: Redefining the Boundaries of Race and Ethnicity." *Journal of Urban and Cultural Studies.*

Giroux, H., and McLaren, P. (1989). Introduction in H. Giroux and P. McLaren, eds., *Critical Pedagogy, the State, and Cultural Struggle.* Albany: The State University of New York Press.

Haug, F., et al. (1987). *Female Sexualization: A Collective Work of Memory.* London: Verso Press.

Hicks, E. (1988). "Deterritorialization and Border Writing." In R. Merrill, ed., *Ethics/Aesthetics: Post-Modern Positions.* Washington, D.C.: Maisonneuve Press, 47–58.

Hooks, B. (1989). *Talking Back.* Boston: South End Press.

Jameson, F. (1984). "Postmodernism or the Cultural Logic of Late Capitalism." *New Left Review, 146,* 53–93.

JanMohamed, A. (1987a). Introduction: Toward a Theory of Minority Discourse." *Cultural Critique, 6,* 5–11.

JanMohamed, A., and David, L. (1987b). "Introduction: Minority Discourse—What Is to Be Done?" *Cultural Critique, 7,* 5–17.

Kaplan, C. (1987). "Deterritorializations: The Rewriting of Home and Exile in Western Feminist Discourse." *Cultural Critique, 6,* 187–98.

Kellner, D. (1988). "Postmodernism as Social Theory: Some Challenges and Problems." *Theory, Culture and Society, 5* (2 and 3), 239–69.

Kellner, D. (in press). "Boundaries and Borderlines: Reflections on Jean Baudrillard and Critical Theory." *From Marxism to Postmodernism and Beyond: Critical Studies of Jean Baudrillard.* Oxford: Polity Press.

Kolb, D. (1986). *The Critique of Pure Modernity: Hegel, Heidegger, and after.* Chicago: University of Chicago Press.

Laclau, E. (1988). "Politics and the Limits of Modernity." In A. Ross, ed., *Universal Abandon? The Politics of Postmodernism.* Minneapolis: University of Minnesota Press, 63–82.

Laclau, E., and Mouffe, C. (1985). *Hegemony and Socialist Strategy.* London: Verso Books.

Lash, S., and Urry, J. (1987). *The End of Organized Capitalism.* Madison: University of Wisconsin Press.

Lunn, E. (1982). *Marxism and Modernism.* Berkeley: University of California Press.

Lyotard, J. (1984). *The Postmodern Condition.* Minneapolis: University of Minnesota Press.

McLaren, P. (1986). "Postmodernism and the Death of Politics: A Brazilian Reprieve." *Educational Theory, 36*(4), 389–401.

McLaren, P. (1988). *Life in Schools.* New York: Longman.

Morris, M. (1988). *The Pirate's Fiancee: Feminism, Reading, Postmodernism.* London: Verso Press.

Mouffe, C. (1988). "Radical Democracy: Modern or Postmodern?" In A. Ross, ed., *Universal Abandon? The Politics of Postmodernism.* Minneapolis: University of Minnesota Press, 31–45.

Peller, G. (1987). "Reason and the Mob: The Politics of Representation." *Tikkun, 2*(3), 28–31, 92–5.

Pinar, W., ed., (1988). *Contemporary Curriculum Discourses.* Scottsdale, Ariz: Gorsuch Scarisbrick.

Piñon, N. (1982). "La contaminacion de La Lenguaje: Interview with Nelida Piñon." *13th Moon, 6* (1 and 2), 72–6.

Richard, N. (1987/1988). "Postmodernism and Periphery." *Third Text, 2,* 5–12.

Ross, A., ed., (1988). *Universal Abandon? The Politics of Postmodernism.* Minneapolis: University of Minnesota Press.

Said, E. (1983). "Opponents, Audiences, Constituencies, and Community." In H. Foster, ed., *The Anti-Aesthetic: Essays on Postmodern Culture.* Port Townsend, Wash: Bay Press, 135–59.

Scholes, R. (1985). *Textual Power.* New Haven: Yale University Press.

Shor, I. (1979). *Critical Teaching and Everyday Life.* Boston: South End Press.

Smith, B. J. (1985). *Politics and Remembrance: Republican Themes in Machiavelli, Burke, and Tocqueville.* Princeton: Princeton University Press.

CHAPTER 6

THE PUNISHMENT OF DISCIPLINES: CULTURAL STUDIES AND THE TRANSFORMATION OF LEGITIMATE KNOWLEDGE

Introduction

Schools and universities are plagued by a litany of complaints that threaten to dominate the debate until the end of this century. While students are frequently blamed for the sad state of affairs of public literacy, educators, employers, and other critics are increasingly blaming the culture. Western civilization's decline may be traced by such critics to the ubiquity of electronically mediated culture; to the excess of democratic practices that have cropped up in our polity since the sixties; to the rise and triumph of pleasure; to the postmodern condition in which the past is devalued, particularly the literary and philosophical markers of what is called the West. Critical theory, left and right, bemoans the "eclipse of reason," the "closing of the American mind," the "culture of narcissism"; and it assails contemporary culture from the point of view of a discourse referring to an anterior state of affairs that, even if suffused with suffering, is alleged to have put high value on the search for Truth.

The decision made by the 1980s by major colleges and universities to reintroduce a required Western civilization sequence into the undergraduate curriculum was overdetermined by these developments, the most important of which was academic reaction to postmodern critiques of legitimate, if not reliable, knowledge that appeared in the sixties as part of student-generated reform of postsecondary education. The collective academy, still wedded to the idea that the canon of Western thought constituted the basis for liberal education, was horrified by the disrespect for these achievements, exemplified in subaltern discourses that challenged, on various grounds, the idea that the life of the mind begins with Plato and ends with (take your pick) Hume, Kant, Hegel (remember Trilling's Matthew Arnold?), or even Marx. By requiring students to become reverentially familiar with some version of the canon, scholars believe they are engaged in saving the Great Tradition from the advancing barbarians.

As recent experience has demonstrated, we simply cannot retain the documents of the past twenty-five hundred years intact. Plato should be read, but simultaneously deconstructed—an effort that would go beyond the usual Marxist critique that citizenship in the Greek city-state relied on the slave mode of production. The examination would begin with an analysis of the rhetoric of the Socratic "dialogue"—that is, the distance between polyphonic discourse and a monologue that admits the Other, but not as an interlocutor. Even the top hits of the last century—Phenomenology of the Spirit, Capital, Origin of Species, the Will to Power—appear somewhat shopworn in the wake of sea changes in our linguistic understanding, in mass-mediated culture, and equally in high art. Or, as in Hegel's case, elements of the canon must be reread in the light of what we have learned since the beginning of the nineteenth century about the position of the subject, lest we succumb to the fallacy of historicism. Postmodernism has produced a phobic reaction, and not only among bona fide conservatives who could be expected to oppose curricular changes that would accommodate new voices and discourses, particularly those of women and people of color. Liberals and leftists, wedded to the proposition that mastering the canon of Western culture is the condition of genuine education, have similarly recoiled at the idea that that cultural legacy is fraught with ideological presuppositions about class, race, and gender. As with their unqualified support of modern science as the best antidote to interested inquiry, the secular left is prepared to support the demands of the oppressed for "rights," and even for a measure of political power, but has, on the whole, erected a cordon around legitimate intellectual knowledge against the advances of the "barbarians." The hesitancy of secular humanists to embrace knowledge claims by subaltern cultures may be traced to the historical experience of fascism, which, in its own manner, mounted an assault against liberal culture. What the last several decades reveal with unmistakable clarity is that educational conservatism knows no conventional ideological bounds. Postmodernism, whose chief characteristic in this context is to deny the idea of sacred, unassailable texts, including those proposed by the inheritors of the classical traditions, realigns ideology. Among other things, we have learned that the struggle between left and right since the French Revolution may have been a family quarrel; that is, both sides shared bourgeois values, particularly the values of modernity. The struggle within the third estate was strategic: how to achieve the common goals of industrialization, scientific and technological progress, political freedom, and greater equality? It was not a struggle over whether these ends were intrinsically worthwhile. For with some exceptions, the radicals were not contesting modernity; on the contrary, they claimed to be its "true" legatees. Moreover, Western culture was understood to be the highest achievement of humankind, and the left wanted only to extend its many virtues to the subaltern classes: to separate high culture from property, to open the museums and libraries to the poor, to translate the treasures of Western literature into the vernacular (even though written language was, itself, always a marker of class and status). Even that great democratic communist, Antonio Gramsci, regretted that Latin and Greek could not be part of popular education in the new society. Acquiring a classical education presupposed both free time unencumbered by the weariness wrought by excessive manual labor and a social context that simply could not be reproduced in industrial or peasant societies. Nevertheless, in concert with Lunacharsky, Lenin, Trotsky, and other leading Marxists of the interwar period, Gramsci favored transmitting high culture to the masses as the best guarantee of creating a public sphere that would embrace the hitherto excluded.[1] When A. Bogdanov tried to impose an explicitly proletarian culture on the ruins of bourgeois high culture, Trotsky vehemently opposed this effort as both futile and anti-intellectual. Reflecting the consensus among Marxists of this period, he urged a massive educational effort to bring the "best" of the bourgeois literary and other artistic traditions to the workers. For the Bolsheviks no less than for Gramsci, creating the "organic" working-class intellectual did not entail a cultural alternative to that of the bourgeoisie. Imparting bourgeois high culture to the masses was itself a subversive act, and creating intellectuals of working-class origins who were familiar with the canon was considered a major step forward for humanity as a whole.[2]

Of course there is, sadly, no question of creating space for the appearance of organic intellectuals among workers, blacks, women, and other subaltern groups in Western countries. The democratization of higher education opens up new technical and professional options for some, and chances for lateral mobility and somewhat higher incomes for many, but does not offer a chance, on a grand scale, to reproduce the traditional intellectual. This situation is underscored by some of the difficulties currently faced by elite universities in the United States with respect to their Western civilization curriculum. For example, at Stanford students are able to enter at least ten different tracks in this subject; only one offers a facsimile of the literary/philosophical canon (*facsimile* because the readings are truncated in some respects: Descartes is excluded, among other notables). Other tracks focus on the social and historical influence on various canonical texts; scientific and technological aspects of Western history; and literature (excluding philosophy). For the moment, I do not want to comment on the justice of this pluralism, only to note that both faculty and students are rent concerning the validity of the track, which requires close textual analysis of both philosophical and literary works, even though it enjoys the highest status. Minorities and women claim that the canon excludes their traditions, which were accommodated after considerable protest—a reform that entailed some fairly important (male) exclusions.

To some degree, the humanities have suffered relative eclipse because of what Max Weber called formal, instrumental rationality.[3] In a word, culture is dominated by the scientific and technological imperative that knowledge be justified in terms of its practical uses. Arguably, even philosophy, once called the highest form of human knowledge, has been obliged to turn its attention to science as the object of its inquiry, or to ethics, construed increasingly in recent times as the normative considerations concerning the effects of science and technology. Speculation suffered in the wave of modernity that began in the sixteenth century, but has regained some glitter in our time, when mass education has prompted a new quest for grounds for distinction.

Cultural Studies

Slowly, against incredible resistance, denigration, and ultimately co-optation by the traditional disciplines, a post-1960s faculty and graduate student generational intellectual tendency is emerging within universities. In consideration of academic constraints, the movement often assumes an older, more respectable label: critical theory, history of consciousness, or one of those grab-bag headings—Philosophy, Literature, and Social Theory—intended to signify multidisciplinary studies. But increasingly the term "cultural studies," borrowed from the pioneering program of the Birmingham Centre for Contemporary

Cultural Studies, is used as a signal of a wider alternative to the under-lying logic of the disciplines.[4]

"Cultural studies" is an indefinite signifier for its own novelty. But it dare not answer the question "What is it?" too precisely in a time when institutions demand of any new paradigm that it adapt its more radical specifications to the realities of academic power. For cultural studies must survive in institutional contexts within which academic power is inevitably won or lost. However, in its manifold appearances several directions have surfaced. We discern three distinct but closely related positions:

1. The historical basis of the disciplines has been largely over-turned. Following several tendencies in critical social and cultural theory, it is claimed that the foundations of legitimate knowledge have collapsed. There are new, socially constructed objects of knowledge, and new ways of seeing them, that radically transgress disciplinary boundaries. But the new paradigm of social and cultural knowledge also challenges the Enlightenment conception that knowledge be constructed on irrefutable foundations that are the irreducible starting point of inquiry, as well as older methods by which this knowledge may be adduced.

2. The paradigm shifts in cultural knowledge have been fomented, in part, by emergent, subaltern, and otherwise marginal discourses—feminism, nationalism, ecology, and gay and lesbian insistence on the idea of heterosexuality as one among several options—and critiques of the methodological foundations and the results of science and technology. The new discursive practices insist on the irreducibility of political and ontological difference, rejecting the universalist claims of mainstream Western values. Or, in another register, subaltern discourses challenge humanism to align its allegiance to political pluralism with arguments for intellectual diversity.

3. What has been named postmodernism interrogates the privileged space of High Art in the panoply of aesthetic discourses. Cultural studies investigates the degree to which what is privileged in art may be historically and conventionally prescribed. The postmodern turn places the commodities produced by the culture industry on the same plane as those that construct their spectatorship from among elite forms. Sometimes this attack appears vulgar, because postmodernism argues that differential positions in the market become the basis of subject positions. This is a scandal from the perspective of the defenders of Western civilization from mass capitalist culture. For those who castigate the culture industry as a marker of the decline of the West, Benjamin's statement that mass reproducibility democratizes art is

nothing less than a betrayal of civilizing criteria themselves.[5] On the other hand, if there is no place outside the system from which criticism may derive, we are obligated to find the spaces for resistance and for alternative visions in the swamp of "degraded" intellectual and cultural forms.

Simultaneously, the humanities have become the repositories of the putative rebirth of high culture—putative, because even in philosophy and literary theory postmodern discourses have challenged the modernism of scientific philosophy and the pristine literary text. New movements such as cultural studies bid us to return the text to its interaction with the context that gave it birth. This idea of context— social, historical, and cultural—may not be equated with that in the older literary history, in which social life was taken principally as "background" but the work itself retained its privileged position as a nonreducible artifact whose intrinsic meaning was exemplified by its mythic or symbolic signifiers. This idea of context also differs from that in the Marxist incarnation of literary theory, in which social life is seen as a "cause" of the text, corresponding to the base/superstructure model of nineteenth-century thinking. That is, cultural studies does not read historically in order to discover immutable laws underlying social life, to impose order on chaos, or to create new myths about the past that can be appropriated in an interested way by the present. Rather, the text is read as discourse, disrupted by the multiplicity of voices that inhabit it. Moreover, the familiar distinction between the work of art and social knowledge becomes ambiguous; or to be more exact, the better the work functions as art the more reliable it is as social knowledge. This argument may be seen in Bakhtin's readings of Dostoevsky and Rabelais, where, contrary to the formalist notion that art is primarily or exclusively self-referential, Bakhtin sees it not as a reflection of society as in epistemological realism but as a terrain within which the social voices fight to construct the social world.[6] The artist employs the materials of utterance to exemplify the prose of the world—surely not a sociological report, but a "representation" of everyday life both in its banal aspects and in its wildly parodic features—which is, in any case, systematically ignored by formalisms of all sorts. Similarly, Sarah Faunce and Linda Nochlin have placed Gustave Courbet's painting in the cultural and political climate of mid-nineteenth-century French life, linking his aesthetic transgressions to the multiplicity of his situations: as a man of the left, as an artistic iconoclast, and as a gendered individual. Courbet's art is "gendered": woman and nature become "interchangeable"; their images are those of Otherness. The virtue of the Brooklyn Museum's 1989 Courbet show and its catalogue is to link text to context without reductive relations of determination, to show the multiplicity of Courbet's realities and their reception both in his time and in ours.

Cultural studies arises as a critique of the barriers erected by the disciplines, in the first place, that between humanities and social sciences, constructed in the last century as a signifier of the refusal of art to be subsumed under scientific rationality. Similarly, in philosophy ethics becomes separated from both ordinary language study and work on the theory of scientific knowledge. If the wall separating the two cultures is no longer tenable, nevertheless the battle continues, not only between science and art but within critical studies of literature, film, and painting, among other arts. The "French turn" in literary studies signaled in part a will to scientificity among critics by means of the incorporation of linguistics and its premier offshoot, semiotics, into its discourse. In contrast to the older mold, the new theoretically oriented criticism becomes really a series of microstudies meant to elucidate methodological issues; the text becomes pretext for advancing the precision of the discipline. Of course, this reading of poststructuralism is not necessary to the move to deconstruction, but seems vital to its appropriation by the American humanist academy. Under siege for both economic reasons and reasons of status, the humanities have increasingly constructed themselves in the image of theoretical disciplines, the works of literature and art taken as case studies illustrating, if not verifying, a series of refutable propositions.

We can observe the convergence of literary studies with significant trends in sociology, for example. In both, the object of knowledge is subordinated to explorations of ways of knowing; the epistemological project has taken over, but is frequently framed in the language of technique. While the older criticism was quintessentially a series of aesthetic, ethical, and historical studies, the latest tendency, led by Macherey, Barthes, Eagleton, and others, is toward a science of the text. The work itself becomes merely an occasion for a display of methodological skill on the lower levels and for a broader discussion of categories of knowing in the more philosophical works. The elite critics become interested in metatheory, particularly that concerning problems of a more general type, such as voice, genre, and—in these days of identity crises for criticism of all varieties—biography and autobiography, the constitution of the subject, the implied reader. Whereas semiotics has been relegated to the status of handy tool, Derrida has pushed criticism toward philosophy, just as philosophy, having lost its status as the universal signifier, survives in Richard Rorty's terms as criticism. But literary critics have been reluctant to take the turn, except insofar as criticism in several modes has redefined itself as "theory" without the scientific requirement that it provide explanation. Instead, properly, cultural theory addresses philosophy, science, and social relations from the perspectives of form, rhetoric, and discourse—a practice that is shedding new light on the social world and also on the traditional moves of philosophy.

Social sciences are frequently mired in sterile methodological debates, and seem to have lost sight, at least provisionally, of the real questions associated with understanding social life. Indeed, methodologists often protest that the turn to complex mathematical calculation is just a prelude to addressing these problems with scientific precision, free of the speculative sloppiness characteristic of the older practitioners. For now, social science, particularly sociology, has abandoned theory to philosophers and other humanists, at least in the United States. In western Europe, particularly in Germany, social scientists are split between those like Habermas and Offe, for whom the older conception of the *Geisteswissenschaften* describes the ongoing parameters of social investigation, and those like Luhmann, who wish to revive general sociological theory as description of a "real" social world by reinventing its categories.[7]

In some ways, cultural studies has affinities with the older conception of the human sciences rather than with the modernist invocation of natural science as the model for social and cultural investigations. We cannot here resolve the question of the specificity of the human raised by Dilthey and his colleagues. We might acknowledge that humans are part of natural history, a judgment implying that the distinction between nature and history is analytic.[8] In any case, cultural studies raises two fundamental issues about knowledge: How are its objects constructed? Can we distinguish method from object if we hold theory construction and object construction to be aspects of the same process? Thus cultural studies takes itself as its object even as it interrogates the social construction of objects. This procedure constitutes, of course, a way of seeing in which the process of investigation is part of the object of knowledge and itself becomes an object. We want to suggest some differences between an approach we have been calling "cultural studies" and traditional classifications of legitimate knowledge.

We may distinguish intellectual knowledge from four other types: practical knowledge, small talk, spiritual knowledge, and unwanted knowledge. These other forms of knowledge suffer from their lack of codifying practices such as canons, credentials, and methodologies, in comparison to intellectual knowledge. The university has become the dominant site of intellectual knowledge in the past two centuries, progressively incorporating independent intellectual production.[9] The process of incorporation is well known: more or less rapidly, areas of knowledge production that may have been considered practical (business, crafts, politics, social services) are endowed with a canon from which curriculum derives; credentials are attached to the acquisition of knowledge as a condition of practice; if the practical knowledge exercises considerable social power, it becomes a "discipline" (business, social work, political science), otherwise it becomes an applied science (as opposed to a conceptual or academic science). Consequently, the professions associated with these differentially placed sciences are treated differently. (With the rise of practical nursing, registered nurses are increasingly required to complete a bachelor's or even a master's degree; sociology has higher status than social work; psychiatry is held superior to psychoanalysis, which, in many places, is still a lay discipline.) The second transformation is that intellectual knowledge is produced, increasingly, by salaried professionals rather than by talented amateurs or independent artisans. Thus career trajectories in the sciences and the humanities lead, for the elite of knowledge producers, to the universities or to specialized research institutes and "think tanks" whose staffs move freely in and out of universities. Although some large corporations, notably AT&T and IBM, have retained their own capacities for intellectual knowledge production (though this production is limited, in the main, to natural science that can be transformed into technologies), the degree to which legitimate intellectual knowledge has been socialized by public and private universities through the agency of the federal government is a major characteristic of the postwar era.

Fritz Machlup's study of the production and distribution of intellectual knowledge, the first edition of which was completed in the late 1950s, shows clearly that the production of new knowledge in the natural and social sciences is intimately linked with its technical uses, hence the phrase "research and development."[10] He finds that schools are already major sources of new knowledge production, but are overwhelmingly the dominant institution for the production and distribution of knowledge in general, including the transmission of what is known. As early as 1958 the ratio of GNP spent for education was nearly 13 percent, before the explosion of the 1960s, when it increased to nearly 20 percent by the end of the decade. Clearly, if knowledge has become our leading productive force, a conclusion amply demonstrated in Machlup's study and many others since the 1960s, and schools are the sites of its production, the social organization of education bears on the configuration of knowledge production, for ideas, old and new, are not merely floating in the culture but are located in specific institutional sites that are also sites of power. In turn, these sites are linked with other power centers, principally the state and corporations. Thus the social organization of schools, in which academic labor is divided by disciplines, is not external to the kinds of knowledge that are likely to be produced. To the extent that the organization of knowledge bears on its content (leaving aside, for the moment, the economic, political, and broad ideological influences on the constitution of the knowledge object), the construction of knowledge in terms of disciplinary boundaries that usually prescribe algorithms of investigation, canonical knowledge inscribed in sacred texts, becomes an object for investigation by cultural studies. Disciplinary conventions therefore determine what may be considered legitimate and reliable knowledge and what must be marginalized. It is not chiefly that some piece of "information" is inappropriate to the discipline's conception of knowledge, but that its mode of presentation may not correspond to the way in which the discipline construes the object, and the appropriate ways of seeing. For it is increasingly clear that postmodern discourse is forcing profound shifts in the receptivity of established disciplines to new knowledge objects, but it is still not evident that these objects may be investigated outside the established procedures that have become markers of legitimate knowledge. The debates, then, seem to have moved from objects to methods: for literature, "close readings" that pay little attention to context versus readings that see the text constituted not only by language and formal elements but also by the degree to which it embodies culture, history, and social structure; for philosophy, analytic versus synthetic readings (although there is a debate between those for whom language is the object and those for whom, increasingly, the proper object of speculation is irreducible social and cultural norms); for social science, quantitative methods as the limit of legitimate inquiry and ethnographic and speculative inquiry whose characteristic modes of presentation are narration and the essay. (Of course these lines are rarely, if ever, hard and fast; they signify fundamental orientations by which knowledge may be obtained.)

The academic system exists on a world scale, organized along disciplinary lines. This is the dominant form of social organization of legitimate intellectual knowledge today. If it is correct that the constitution of legitimate objects and approved methods determines, in large measure, the configuration of knowledge, including what and how learning occurs, the disciplinary context for knowledge production as the key organizational form of intellectual knowledge is not innocent—

that is, not free of power considerations. One might expect that, globally, the disciplines form a power complex, mandating certain canonical texts, ways of knowing, and institutional contexts as the a priori conditions of knowledge production.

Therefore, the disciplinary basis of social, scientific, and cultural knowledge is conventional. That is, disciplines correspond neither to unique objects nor to methodologies that are uniquely tied to them. Instead, the academic division of labor that resulted in the formation of intellectual communities demarcated from others may be said to rest on associations, rituals, and journals that together constitute a culture that has successfully claimed turf in the panoply of arts, sciences, and humanities.

Scientific and intellectual practices are in the process of forcing modifications in the claim of these systems of classification to "objective" status—to a status, that is, of taxonomies that correspond to what is called the "real." (Here "objectivity" connotes the historically evolved reification of turf and community as types of social knowledge not subject to boundary crossing by those lacking specific training and credentials within an established discipline.) In the so-called hard sciences (i.e., empirically based experimental and mathematical modes of knowing) the Enlightenment-generated conventional boundaries of physics, chemistry, biology, and experimental pyschology have undergone a series of concatenations in the last century: biology merges with chemistry and physics, psychology with biology and chemistry, physics with chemistry and biology, and each merger constitutes a new discipline whose boundary conditions consist in newly constituted objects as well as methods. Surely, the atom is no longer the pristine object of physics, nor are particles. Here we may observe the partial breakdown of Aristotle's taxonomic typology of the natural sciences. Even though he posited no psychology and no distinct chemical object, the basic distinctions he established between physics, biology, metaphysics, ethics, politics, and poetics survived the revolt against the substantive theories of Aristotelean physics and biology beginning in the sixteenth and seventeenth centuries. However, the most important survival of Greek philosophy after Plato is its penchant for classification—that is, the adoption of a mode of knowledge production that vertically ensconced physics and mathematics at the foundation of all possible empirical knowledge and horizontally organized knowledge according to boundaries that purported to correspond to the organization of the natural world, in which the division between humans and nature, mind and body, became the second nature of all intellectual effort. Thus the leading presuppositions of knowledge were: the concept of levels corresponding to social hierarchies; and the idea of methodological distinction, particularly between the true sciences and the humanities.

However, methods are by no means discipline-bound. The experimental method is common to all natural sciences, except mathematics. Historical, hermeneutic, and theoretical ways of knowing not only cross disciplinary boundaries but differentiate themselves within conventional humanistic disciplines. One may suggest a taxonomy of methods classifying modes of knowledge according to their own conventions. And at one time it was possible to identify biblical studies with hermeneutics; literary studies, including biography, with the historical method; and natural sciences with observation and experiment. As for the social sciences, these were grouped under philosophy in its various branches, especially economic, political, and social philosophy. Thus the method appropriate to philosophy, namely immanent critique of first principles (the synthesis of presuppositions with acquired knowledge), applied to many forms of human inquiry.

Philosophies of social relations became sciences after Comte declared that the critical mode of social inquiry be abandoned in favor of positive (i.e., historical and experimental) inquiry. As Marcuse has shown, Comte understood positive philosophy as a way to abandon the project of historical transformation; by refusing to interrogate and challenge the givens of the social world, but instead to classify them, establish their relations, and describe them, Comte hoped to verify the existing state of affairs.[11] Today human sciences are no longer characteristically critical, although it may be observed that the once marginal fields of social and political theory have been edging to the (absent) center as empirically based social inquiry becomes more fragmented, specialized, and self-consciously incapable of synthetic reason.

We are in the midst of the revolt of post-Kantian philosophy, which, among other things, abjures taxonomies and wishes to return to a kind of hermeneutic/immanent critique of positivism, including the latent positivism of critical theory. Its claim is that positive science cannot escape metaphysical presuppositions, even in the form of rules of inquiry such as logical principles of thought and formal procedures for investigation. One wing, the new religiously based hermeneutics, bids us return to transcendental reason on the ground that science has failed to liberate thought from its a prioris.[12] Thus, given the ineluctability of the a priori, the return to ethical foundations of all knowledge provides, at the least, a moral basis for being-in-the-world. The second, led by French skepticism (which is both more and less than an adaptation of Nietzsche, and, in a somewhat different register, of German phenomenology), wants to abolish (or at least suspend) the foundational basis of thought, wants to return to the things themselves. As did Husserl, Derrida, having discovered the task to be beyond the capacity of culturally bound inquiry, has retreated into research on the cultural configurations of law and knowledge, a task close to that of Foucault.[13]

Richard Rorty has proposed a solution to the problem of the tyranny of taxonomies. Philosophy becomes a heurism for restoring the critical capacities of all forms of human knowledge: its demand that knowledge become reflexive provides philosophy with a role quite different from that assigned to it by medieval Schoolmen. It can no longer provide superior knowledge of the spirit, nor can it be replaced by the natural or human sciences. But this plea for philosophy without foundations as a kind of criticism is merely a restatement of the proposition that method replaces substance as taxonomic justification. For even if philosophy, as distinct from literary studies, proposes to explore the metaphoric presuppositions of any possible knowledge, claiming to do no more than make the sciences aware of their own a prioris, it does not follow that this task is unique to philosophy. In the social sciences and the humanities, as much as in the natural sciences, practitioners and theorists have been drawn to the interrogation of the foundations that was once largely the province of philosophy. In physics Heisenberg, Bohm, and Weiszaker come to mind; in sociology, Gouldner, Luhmann, and Giddens; Dahl advanced from the case-study, pluralist approach to a fundamental critique of the structures of political power; Eagleton's *Criticism and Ideology*, Jameson's *Marxism and Form*, and the interest in Derrida and Foucault among literary critics, all indicate the breakdown of taxonomic distinctions between philosophy, science, and the humanities. To be more precise, the disciplines have recently been obliged to do Rorty's version of philosophy—that is, a metacritique of classifications that in some instances becomes a discourse on the intersection of social and cultural theory, and in others becomes a reflection on the adequacy of scientific understanding.

At the same time, in the 1980s, we witnessed a counteroffensive to reassert the hegemony of disciplinary configurations of knowledge. This attempt is the outcome of three distinct developments: the threat posed to turf by the economic contraction of some universities; the rear-guard defense within disciplines against the critique of erstwhile marginal writers who have gained an audience; and the intrinsic neglect of valid aspects of taxonomies by their critics. In history, the dispute concerning the replacement of narration with cliometrics on the one side, and a deconstructive critique of narration on the other; in literature, the disappearance at the most prestigious levels of both historically and textually based critical studies by the literary theorists; in the social sciences, amid sweeping critiques of the positivist bent that has predominated since the late 1940s, critical theory has argued that sociology, economics, and political studies are mired in positivist constraints in which method becomes the criterion against which the objects of inquiry are measured. Thus the counterreaction builds on the weaknesses of grand theory, while the critical tendency argues for a theoretically informed discourse in which text and context become intrinsic to an examination of truth claims.

There is, however, no possibility for the return of traditional classifications within which knowledge can be contained. But it is not a question of interdisciplinary studies replacing traditional departments. More likely is the persistence of departmental boundaries within which a permanent crisis exists, a crisis that has already produced efforts to co-opt the new cultural studies. This is accomplished by declaring, even when there is little or no comprehension, that the given discipline is prepared to accommodate the new without surrendering an inch of ground except under extreme duress. The incommensurability of discourses will remain ubiquitous and processes of academic socialization will periodically break down as younger intellectuals discover nontaxonomic frameworks like deconstruction, Marxism, phenomenology, and so on, which seem to make more sense to them than mainstream disciplinary canons and methods for explaining the world. To be sure, young scholars remain attached to the old academy, if only by economic threads. Where argument fails, coercion may succeed in holding the line against the invasion of the new "barbarians." But a growing minority chooses to work in second- or third-rank institutions rather than wait for the front-rank universities to make room for the new. And the ranks of the converted among senior scholars grows as the generation born after 1940 comes into its majority. In short, even though the tyranny of the disciplines will remain an important deterrent to innovation and may retard the return of the repressed, the broad integrative tendency of modern knowledge, abetted by technologically generated breakdown of specialization, has already established itself as a more or less permanent opposition.

We are not arguing for some kind of technological determinism, or for the idea that new frameworks are equivalent "methodologies" of integration. Rather, we are asserting that we are on the precipice of profound and radical changes in the division of academic labor, changes that are likely to transform the conditions of the production of knowledge on a wider scale than ever before. In this context, discourses will not be viewed as comfortably commensurable either at the methodological level or in the construction of the objects of knowledge. Yet the more the processes of knowledge production dedicate themselves to interrogating their own presuppositions, the less they can claim a unique object or method. Rather, scrutiny of this sort buttresses the conventionalist thesis. However, Foucault's idea of the epistemé, the array of statements that forms a unity, constitutes the basis for historico-epistemologic commensurabilities.

The Nietzschean intervention is to point to historical breaks, to show that the idea of progress is itself mythic and science takes command as the master discourse that subsumes all others, and that discursive incommensurability displaces historical law. Hence the real situation is that faith in history turns out to be a cruel and "reactive" deception. We cannot rely on objective processes as means of rectifying the errors of human action. Historical culture thwarts the movement toward self-determination by occluding the present. In this sense, the disciplines are the guardians of the past, or to be more precise, they take the past as a model for the future.

What's Left?

There are various modes of discursive understanding, none of which, except science, holds a privileged place in the pantheon of knowledge acquisition and production. But the distinctions—say, between history and literature, for example—turn out to be entirely conventional. History is a fiction constructed from the vantage point of the present but whose telos concerns power over the future. Its object, to reconstruct memory from a specific standpoint, always entails forgetting what is left out. The synchronic moment, the examination of social and "natural" structure, is at best a necessary corrective to the excesses of historical reason. We can see the hegemony of synchronic discourse not only in literary and philosophic fields but in biology as well. The partial eclipse of the older evolutionary perspective in favor or micromolecular studies attests to the epistemological break that accompanied the 1960s. Still, as Kurt Hubner has argued, even physics discovers that the meaning of natural law cannot be discerned without a search for "origins"—without comprehending the history of discovery. The disputes between the scientists who have held out for a unified field and those who derive from quantum mechanics the conclusion that scientific law describes the unity of the observer and the observed and contains no small degree of indeterminacy rages sixty years after Bohr and Heisenberg suggested that the inferential significance of relativity theory subverted Einstein's own classical intention. It turns out that spec-ification is intrinsic to the enterprise, and no amount of mathematical precision can put Humpty Dumpty together again.

When philosophers of science discover ethics as internal to episte-mological inquiry and literary critics are obliged to do sociology, when sociologists discover semiotics and discourse as a vital way of seeing the social object, we will know cultural studies has arrived and, even if grand discourses are no longer possible, we will have the chance to share our perplexity.

On Intellectuals

In the late 1960s French intellectuals began to free themselves from the hegemony of a stultifying party Marxism that had dominated politics and culture for a generation after the war. Among other things, post-structuralism renounced determinate agents for historical change, and in the later incarnation declared any "standpoint" from which inquiry might proceed to be "essentialist." In the United States and the United Kingdom, many intellectuals have taken the "French turn" as an occa-sion for depoliticizing their own discourse. While Marxism has never enjoyed the dominant position among intellectuals and in the labor movement in English-speaking countries that it held in France or Ger-many, it had gained considerable academic weight in the 1960s and 1970s. In the 1980s, faced with conservative pressure, poststructuralism offered a new opportunity to legitimate "theory" in literary disciplines without suffering direct political consequences. No matter that the re-jection of Marxism was somewhat premature since many who declared themselves "post" had never really been Marxists. The many uses of poststructuralism and postmodernism as signifying practices are mu-tated by context, not by the letter of the ideas themselves. However, even as the idea of the working class as history's redeemer was de-clared null and void (a judgement not borne out by events in Eastern Europe or the Third World), new agents appeared on the scene. When confronted with this most recent instance of nihilism (albeit, contextu-ally speaking, it was reasonable), feminists and nationalists bitterly ob-served that the white males who announced the end of history tacitly abolished the new social movements that belied their judgment. For just as Derrida and Foucault, the leading theorists of antiessentialism, recognized that they were caught, insofar as writing is action, in its consequences (people are mobilized or demobilized by discourse), the most ardent post-Marxism is obliged to ask "What are the conse-

quences of giving up agency?" One implication is that, having elimi-
nated all competitors, or having relegated those that exist to "specialized discourses," the white male intellectual is the only recognizable
agent and writing becomes the privileged subject-position. Another is
to occupy a halfway house. Laclau and Mouffe insist that discourse displaces essentialist concepts such as "the social" and "historical agent,"
insofar as "discourse" becomes a verb—that is, constitutes "subject-
positions": a term coined by Foucault to connote agency without
agents.[14] They speak of new social movements as subject positions,
from which a new pluralism may arise that replaces the monologic discourse of really existing Marxism, whose metaphysical baggage weighs
intellectuals down. But one cannot escape the nagging feeling that
discourse/writing, the work of intellectuals, occupies a privileged place
in the pantheon of subject positions.

Events in Eastern Europe and China amply verify the contention, first
enunciated by Gramsci, that intellectuals occupy crucial places in political life.[15] As in May 1968 in France, when students detonated a process that threatened the existence of the authoritarian Gaullist regime,
Chinese students and intellectuals spearheaded the democratic movement that suffered a tragic defeat in spring of 1989. A Christian intellectual is head of state in the new Poland; the playwright Vaclav Havel
is the very symbol of the breathtaking movement for Czech freedom;
lawyers were named head of state in East Germany and Czechoslovakia
after the party monopoly was broken; and, of course, right-wing intellectuals such as William F. Buckley, Henry Kissinger, and Zbigniew
Brzezinski have been crucial for the resurgence of conservative political hegemony in the United States in the last forty years. Clearly, both
ruling groups and opposition movements require articulations of ideologies with which they contend for "moral and intellectual" leadership of society.

In contrast to the naive dichotomy between thought and action often posited in left and liberal circles, we insist that cultural political
struggle is waged in the universities as much as in the industrial or clerical workplace or in geographic communities. In an epoch in which
knowledge has become the central productive force in virtually all societies, and becomes the legitimating term in the state form, the
schools—their curricula as well as their modes of governance—are objects of intense debate. In this book we try to make a contribution to
furthering a democratic, postmodern standpoint in that debate. Here
and elsewhere we argue that teachers are intellectuals, but the space
they have occupied in the hierarchy of school power has diminished
over the past half-century.[16] Until recently, teachers have raised their

voices to protect their rapidly deteriorating economic position, but in return for union protections they often abdicated administrative control to others. In consequence, business groups, acting as conservative intellectuals, and school boards, frequently composed of people recruited from the business world, have demanded that schools be transformed into training institutes. Lacking a language to compete for the moral and intellectual high ground, teachers and their unions have been intimidated by the concentrated assault of these interests on the schools.

In the past several years, teacher organizations have begun to acknowledge that the deteriorating economic situation of their members is ineluctably linked to their subordinate intellectual position within the schools. Traditionally, teachers in elementary and secondary schools were relegated to the role of transmitters of knowledge producers by others. But this mode of subordination has spread to many colleges and universities. Since 1957, when University of California chancellor Clark Kerr enunciated his master plan, advising the state on how to accommodate increasing demands for mass higher education, the professoriate in public universities has witnessed the emergence of a virtual power monopoly by regents and administration over the curriculum and other issues of governance, and the concomitant erosion of the traditional right of the professoriate to collegial determination of these issues. For Kerr's proposal was in tune with increasing bureaucratization of university administration. The faculty has, in effect, become advisers to officials who have the final authority to hire, fire, and determine the curriculum and the budget. And this pattern is only slightly less true of private institutions. The broad historical trend for teacher disempowerment corresponds to the relative proletarianization of professionals, signified by their loss of considerable autonomy in institutional affairs and even in the classroom. In this respect, the emergence of union programs for more teacher participation in governance signals that teachers mean to regain power in schools. In the first place, teacher empowerment entails that teachers demand a voice in the production of school knowledge and that they be recognized as knowledge producers.

What is at stake is nothing less than the terms of inclusion and exclusion in the constitution of power. Intellectuals are not merely technicians, servants of power held by others. Insofar as they are the bearers of legitimate intellectual knowledge, they have become social actors rather than adjuncts of "primary agents," such as classes, in the Marxist sense. On the other hand, although intellectuals have developed a capacity for self-representation, they can rarely hold power without linking themselves to other social actors. For example, in the recent democratic struggle in Czechoslovakia, intellectuals invented the discourse of the movement, but it was not until workers staged the remarkable two-hour general strike in November 1989 that the movement became, in effect, a political "party," whose claim to replace Communist rule suddenly was palpable and legitimate. Similarly, recall that it was the Solidarity labor union that sparked the revolt in Poland. The Polish example is almost a textbook illustration of Gramsci's thesis that intellectuals gain their social pertinence when they are "organic" to leading class actors: capitalists and workers. But the Czech and East German cases do not support the claim for the universality of this proposition. There, the literary intellectuals are plainly key components of the mass movement and have provided the necessary articulation of demands and direction without which the movement would not have achieved its status as a viable political alternative, a situation that does not obtain in Poland where the role of intellectuals has been far more circumscribed. In none of these cases, however, do we observe the phenomenon of universal intellectual hegemony. Depending on the concrete historical and cultural conditions, differentially placed social actors hold different degrees of power. "The movement" is the name given for a multiplicity of voices whose unity is always fragile, especially after the illegitimate and arbitrary power against which it arose is deposed. Inevitably, there will be internal struggles for hegemony as well as persistent efforts to consolidate the movement's position against other contending forces, primarily the Communist Party and the Catholic church. In any case, it is uncertain whether intellectuals will exercise the dominant political voice.

Foucault has argued that there are no universal intellectuals, only "specific" intellectuals—literary, scientific, political, and so on. We have added that their political and, one may add, intellectual effectiveness depends on the circumstances in which they attempt to act; what opposing or alternative "discursive formations" (the Foucaultian name for subjectless social actors) contend within the same or adjacent spaces; and the degree to which they succeed in cementing alliances to exercise power. This configuration has been constituted by the breakup of humanist hegemony, itself formed by the Enlightenment. Humanism survives as a conservative counterculture in the West, and as an extremely important component of radical democratic discourse in the East. It does not possess, therefore, intrinsic ideological content.

In the light of this discussion, cultural studies' insistence on postsecondary educational spaces that are really plural in their curriculum, governance, and pedagogies presents a powerful counterpoint to the still dominant conservative humanism of the academy. At the same time, it cannot dislodge the disciplines for reasons that are intimately connected to its democratic purposes; it does not seek hegemony, for this is a category of domination. Instead, this kind of postmodern discourse is radically democratic insofar as it renounces all forms of power monopoly. Thus it is antihegemonic, and does not resemble Marxism's counterhegemony to liberalism or dictatorship. In educational terms, democratic postmodernism defends the right of intellectuals to question the foundations of their own training, to undertake practices in which canonicity is not a crucial pedagogical category, even when the canons in question are those of Marxism, poststructuralism, and phenomenology, for example. Taken together, these discourses that we have somewhat arbitrarily grouped under the name cultural studies constitute a standpoint that may be named radical democracy—radical because of its sharp critique of the prevailing theory of representation, according to which the people propose and the elites dispose. We acknowledge the crisis of representation to consist in the problematic position of administration, parties, and other self-contained bureaucracies. This perspective points out the ambiguous position of those, whether elected or not, who speak for others and at the same time retain powerful ties to parties, professional standards, or bureaucracies. This ambiguity may not prevent these elites from supporting good things. Yet, as new movements emerge, even the most far-sighted and enlightened power holders, including the intellectuals who are their adherents, are increasingly unable to legitimate their power monopoly. This is the lesson of Eastern Europe's democratic upsurge; this is the crucial importance of the new feminist and other social movements of the last two decades. These movements provide the social context for the array of challenges to liberal practices in contemporary higher education.

Notes

1. Antonio Gramsci, *Selections from the Prison Notebooks* (New York: International Publishers, 1971).

2. A. Lunacharsky, *On Literature and Art* (Moscow: Progress Publishers, 1975); Leon Trotsky, *Literature and Revolution* (New York, Pathfinder Books, 1978).

3. Max Weber, *Economy and Society*, trans. Guenther Roth (Berkeley and Los Angeles: University of California Press, 1978), vol. 1, 24.

4. For a founding statement of the idea of cultural studies see Richard Hoggart, *Uses of Literacy* (London, 1957); for a recent statement by the current director of the Birmingham Centre, see Richard Johnson, "What Is Cultural Studies, Anyway?" *Social Text*, 16 (1988).

5. The debate is joined in Walter Benjamin, "The Work of Art in the Age of Mechanical Reproduction," in Hannah Arendt, ed., *Illuminations* (New York: Schocken Books, 1969); and Max Horkheimer and Theodor Adorno, "Culture as Mass Deception," in *Dialectic of the Enlightenment* (New York: Seabury Press, 1972).

6. Mikhail Bakhtin, *Rabelais and His World* (Bloomington: Indiana University Press, 1984); *Problems of Dostoevsky's Poetics* (Minneapolis: University of Minnesota Press, 1984).

7. Niklas Luhmann, *The Differentiation of Society* (New York: Columbia University Press, 1982).

8. This is Adorno's position. See Theodor Adorno, *Negative Dialectics* (New York: Seabury Press, 1973).

9. Fritz Machlup, *The Production and Distribution of Knowledge in the United States* (New York: Columbia University Press, 1962, 1969).

10. Ibid.

11. Herbert Marcuse, *Reason and Revolution: Hegel and the Rise of Social Theory* (New York: Columbia University Press, 1942), part 2, chapter 2.

12. Hans Georg Gadamer, *Truth and Method*. (New York: Seabury Press, 1975).

13. Michel Foucault, *Power/Knowledge* (New York: Pantheon Books).

14. Ernesto Laclau and Chantal Mouffe, *Hegemony and Socialist Strategy* (London: Verso, 1986).

15. Gramsci, "On Intellectuals," in the *Prison Notebooks*.

16. Aronowitz and Giroux, *Education under Siege* (South Hadley, Mass.: Bergin & Garvey Press, 1985).

CHAPTER 7

WORKING-CLASS DISPLACEMENTS AND POSTMODERN REPRESENTATIONS

Introduction

One of the crucial political innovations of the emergent social movements of the last twenty years is to enlarge the scope of what is subjectively perceived as oppression. To the time-honored struggle against the material effects of exploitation and domination manifested in jobs and public accommodations—discrimination, official violence, and social indignities—feminists and people of color, especially, have called attention to the question of *representation* in a great variety of contexts. Critics have scrutinized film and television, mass circulation newspapers, magazines, and textbooks. They have conclusively demonstrated the astonishing range of distorted images with which subordinate groups have been depicted. Armed with new weapons of criticism, notably the widely disseminated social semiotic borrowed from structural linguistics and also from the anthropological-literary understandings of the uses of myths and symbols, cultural domination has been chronicled in a rich critical literature.

Images are not only transformed into private property by the rise of mass media; they also constitute collective perceptions and even conceptions of subjects and their positions in the social order. So the reproduction of economic and social inequality and repression depends as much on the cultural system as it does on everyday practices on the job and in public life. For example, beyond the older, widespread use of caricature to depict subordinate groups, we have learned to detect perhaps the more contemporary use by the media of code reversals. Representations of the male shibboleth "women own the world" by means of images of the powerful, scheming woman; the beautiful woman as the embodiment of evil; the portrayal of blacks as oppressors of innocent merchants and other middle-class strata in television crime shows; the close identification of working-class characters with bigotry and violence—all of these have become familiar objects of cultural critique. More sophisticated critiques trace the processes of code violations less to blatant ideological manipulation than to subtle changes in the political culture. Increasingly, cultural criticism is influenced, unevenly, by one or another post-Kantian theoretical framework—notably Marxist structuralism, Bakhtin's conception of artistic texts as social knowledge, discourses of social construction, and post-structuralism.[1] Each of these perspectives insists on shifting the epistemological ground from denotative relations between representations and their "real" structural foundation (economic and political power) to a standpoint that posits discourses as constitutive of social relations. These theories grasp the rise of visual images as crucial, even dominant forms of discourse, which in their contradictory and indeterminate interactions constitute the contemporary world. Thus the study of popular culture and forms of media representation has become a profoundly political undertaking, for it seeks to enter the public debate about race and gender.

In Gramscian terms, the new cultural politics of race and gender has spawned a critical mass of intellectuals organic to the new social movements who have entered, in different ways, the public struggle for "moral" leadership, and who have profoundly influenced the discursive environment in which these issues are considered.[2] Although Reaganism and Thatcherism regained some political ground on cultural issues in the 1980s, the moral ground, still contested, has been more difficult to win back for conservatism because feminists and people of color have often combined a powerful pedagogy with a new discursive agenda on questions of representations. That is, avant-garde intellectuals who link themselves to new social movements have effectively broadened the definition of the political to embrace representation. The rejection of the narrowly economistic perspectives of earlier movements has made subalternity a new moral force.

As much as we have become familiar with textual criticism that addresses the constitution of subjects through juxtapositions, reversals, and caricature, we are less attentive to displacement as representation.

As we shall argue below, the representation of workers, for example, in film and television has been transformed by the political and cultural processes of marginalization of the past fifteen years. Until then working-class representations were typically construed in the model of the dominant male in family settings. The worker's subordination to capital was represented only in its displaced forms: slave in the factory (or in the case of "The Honeymooners' " Norton, Ralph Cramden's interlocutor, in the sewer), but king of (his) castle. The ideological content of working-class exploitation is culturally displaced to the home, but the subject, the worker, is still represented as a denotative and connotative sign.

In post–modern culture of the 1980s, the sign "floats" and lands on other social/discursive positions — particularly cops and sports figures — and the scene of action experiences a counter-displacement back to workplaces. In such television shows as "Hill Street Blues," the station house is the main setting; we never see cops at home. Unlike Ralph Cramden, Chester Riley, and Archie Bunker, earlier representations that presented workers as middle-aged ideological Neanderthals whose center is the imperial home, Hill Street precinct inhabitants are typically younger participants in male culture. As we shall demonstrate, this culture is situated in bars as almost exclusively male preserves, while in the office, which even in a police station is a heterosexual workplace, women and men labor side by side but share few if any extraoccupational cultural spaces. As if to comment on the persistence of cultural segregation, the recent hit television series "Cagney and Lacey" features two women police officers whose bonding closely articulates with their mutual antagonism to the prevailing male police culture.

Until recently the dominant radical discourse on working-class representation attributed the general absence of working-class heroes in mainstream movies and television, or the distorted images of workers, to media "manipulation," a reflection of the patterns of media ownership that overlap with large-scale financial corporations. In this reprise, the media are more or less direct instruments of ruling-class domination. Instead, in this chapter we want to locate displaced representations in the transformed subject positions of the working class in American economic, political, and cultural life. Ours is both a historical and a material perspective, which stipulates the contributions of Armand Mattelart, Herbert Schiller, and others who have provided a welcome antidote to the culturalist orientation of a media criticism derived wholly from literary/critical inspiration.[3] For us, a political economy of the media is, however, a necessary but not sufficient condition for understanding the question of subaltern representation. Rather, we view the media as an arena of contestation constituted by a multiplicity of determinations, including those of the history and conventions of art forms themselves. Clearly, we cannot accept "the determination of the economic in the last instance" of media representations; but to abstract the specifically internal features of artistic representation, to fashion a purely internalist discourse, is equally unacceptable. Moreover, this view adopts a conception of the political as an obstacle, rather than as one possibility for addressing power. In this connection, critical practices take on particular significance when they are linked, however indirectly, to the emergence of social movements. We would not want to make these links a condition of criticism, but we call attention to the difference between critical practices within a transformative context and those that remain content to integrate themselves as part of the legitimation of academic and other dominant cultural institutions. As we will argue in the concluding chapter, even though discourse is a politics insofar as the knowledge/power concatenation is constitutive of social structure, we refuse to reduce social structure to discourse.

Yet in what follows we will concentrate on showing the tacit displacements in forms of representation that result from working-class marginalization, a marginalization that we take as a crucial marker of the shift from cultural modernity to postmodernism. For the postmodern does not consist chiefly in decentering practices; these were already present in modernism. Displacements do not mean obliteration, for representations must still strive to incorporate working-class images even as these are driven underground. We speak here of migration, of the transgressions of discursive borders rather than code reversals and distortion. For the migration of signifiers to historically situated contexts contains elements of both continuity and discontinuity. The familiar sites such as the bar and its crucial male sign—beer— are supplemented by the appearance of new subject positions. This combination, in linguistic terms, constitutes a kind of ideological oxymoron insofar as the "working-class" cop violates the dichotomous codes of labor doctrine. Such are the ambiguities of postmodernism.

Individual and collective identities are constructed on three sites: the biologically given characteristics that we bring to every social interaction; givens that are often covered over by social relations, family, school; and the technological sensorium that we call mass or popular culture. In Western culture these givens assume meaning over which individuals have some control, but they are often beyond the powers of individuals to reverse. Our race and gender confer boundaries as well as possibilities in various relations, particularly the kind of friends we can make, work we can do, mates that are available to us. Surely, the meanings of race and gender, like those of class, are socially constituted; there is no inherent significance to these identities as social signs. However, we are born into these identities, given the social arrangements. The second crucial social site is our interaction with family, school, the workplace, and other conventional institutions such as the church. These relationships are often conceived as self-determining, that is, free of biological givens. Obviously, parents and teachers differentiate between boys and girls. Boys and girls are treated differently; we might say they enjoy/suffer a different moral development regardless of class membership or race. As many writers have argued, the family remains perhaps the crucial site for reproducing gender difference. Schools are important secondary institutions in this regard; they play a major part in the reproduction of racial difference, the forms of which remain to be fully explored. It is enough here to point out that schools are the first places children experience as racially segregated. It is in school that children experience themselves as white or black; needless to say, most textbooks make clear to blacks their subordinate status, apart from any overt content. Images of blacks, even when they appear, are tokens of the power of the civil rights movement over the past thirty years, but black history and culture remain absent, a silence that signifies relations of domination.

Of course, there are less subtle signs of difference. The failure of racial integration since the 1954 Supreme Court decision outlawing school segregation is an overwhelming feature of public schooling. White kids learn that they are of a specific race simply by the absence of blacks in their classrooms; blacks understand this by parental instruction, but also realize that race means subordination by virtue of second-class education and inferior resources made available to them, and finally come to know that their individual and collective life chances were decided long before they entered the work world, a realization only working-class white kids have by secondary school.

Class representations are largely constructed by mass-mediated culture, especially since the working-class community, like the urban-based mass production industries that created it, passed into history. We do not want to devalue the importance of the school for determining "how working-class kids get working-class jobs" (in Paul Willis's account in *Learning to Labor*, mostly by rebelling against middle-class curriculum). This process still occurs in schools, but the working-class kids' culture, at least among whites, is acutely marginalized in an era when, in the older cities of industrial capitalism, the traditional working class is being wiped out.

In this chapter we want to trace the historical displacement of representations of the working class in mass-mediated culture. There are, for instance, no longer direct representations of the interactions among workers in American television, but these have been refracted through the police shows that still dominate prime-time television in the United States and have become increasingly important, even crucial, in British and French television as well. In this connection it may be argued that television shows that are made in the United States have become important exports. As American-made durable goods no longer dominate world markets for these products, the ingression of American culture in world communications markets has grown. This inverse ratio can be seen in new films in Paris, for example. In any given week, of the dozen new films opening in that city, between four and six are American imports. "Miami Vice," "Hill Street Blues," "LA Law" are among the top twenty shows on English and French television; only advertising remains truly national—but signs of Americanization are appearing even in French commercial videos, including ads.

Here we will focus on mass-media representations and claim that they can no longer be grouped under institutional socializations, which include the family, peer interactions, and schools. The media are unique sites precisely because of the specific space of technology in the production of culture. More to the point, mass-mediated visual culture occupies the "objective" space of the dream work, and constitutes its double. If Althusser claims that the school is the chief ideological state apparatus, this may hold for the production of the symbolic system, the constellation of signs and codes out of which what counts as reliable knowledge is constructed;[4] but the mass media construct the social imaginary, the place where kids situate themselves in their emotional lives, where the future appears as a narration of possibilities as well as limits.

We also want to argue that what is called popular culture has become technologically mediated, even as the acoustic guitar (formerly a vehicle for the expression of popular sentiment) is now an instrument for the production of high or esoteric music. The popular is still produced by the people, but can no longer be appropriated directly, just as the biologically given returns in a subsumed form, that of social construction. We can no longer, if we ever could, distinguish what really counts as a popular form from the electronically produced culture that is consumed as records, television programs, or movies. (I exclude film from this list because of the market distinction made between the art film and movies in the last two decades, e.g., the cinema of Erich Roemer, Louis Malle, Yvonne Rainer, Agnes Varda, and the late John Huston, compared with that of Steven Spielberg; Sidney Lumet, whose position is a bit ambiguous; and Oliver Stone, whose location is not.) Television is not just a manipulation of popular culture; it constitutes a crucial element in the construction of imaginary life and is appropriated, just like rock music for young people, as popular culture, in the same manner as were songs and dances for rural populations in the preindustrial era. Thus a further claim: the electronic media can determine, to some degree, how social life is represented—their autonomous field of action consists in modes of representation—but not *whether* a social category will be represented. Therefore, it is literally not possible to exclude working-class representation, but it is equally improbable that these representations would remain direct under conditions where the cultural traditions of workers disappear or occupy smaller social spaces. Moreover, modes of representation are themselves refracted narratives of working-class history. So, if we find representations of working-class life assuming the configuration of police shows or, in the case of Bruce Springsteen, nostalgia for the absent subject, we can take these forms as social knowledge subject to critical deciphering, like all fictions.

One of the crucial functions performed by schools since the turn of the century has been to erase the memory of a self-representing popular culture. Concomitantly, schools, at all levels, are constituted to devalue popular culture, including its electronically mediated forms. Just as science occupies a space of privileged knowledge even if the student never succeeds in learning any, so high art, including the literary canon and especially that of the national culture, displaces the popular as a source of valid aesthetics. The objective of schooling, conscious or not, is among other things to strip away what belongs to the student, to reconstitute his or her formation in terms of the boundaries imposed by hegemonic intellectuals acting for the prevailing social order. The students who succeed in these terms must be stripped of their ethnicity, race, and sex; if they are of working-class origin, their submission to the curriculum already signifies probable social mobility. Those who fail or otherwise rebel must recognize that their own subculture is not the real thing, even if they own it. We insist that central to the issue of ownership of images are the products of electronically mediated art, which for all intents and purposes must be treated by school authorities as much as by the producers of dominant ideologies as illegitimate. Cultural histories could be written about this process of erasure in the United States and other late industrial societies. They would chronicle the degree to which English became a cultural ideal for immigrant generations in the first half of the twentieth century and how the American language was imposed on the whole world in the second half. These studies would focus on the induction of whole populations into this language, and would also narrate the emergence of the representations in electronic media as the new aesthetic norm against which their own forms—both those inherited from earlier high and popular aesthetics and those that developed out of these aesthetic forms in the earlier years of film. For it is evident that European filmmakers—East and West—modeled their art on their literary traditions, which in turn emanated from popular peasant and working-class cultures, as well as from bourgeois appropriations and transformations of these in that unique bourgeois cultural form, the novel. One of the great twice-told tales of film history is the revolution made by D. W. Griffith and Charlie Chaplin, a revolution in image that paralleled those in more material industries initiated by Henry Ford and Frederick Taylor.

The great forgotten aspect of these transformations is the debt they owe to American popular cultural forms such as vaudeville: the birthplace of a dozen or more major film comedians, and in the case of Griffith, of the American pageant, itself derived from a Catholic church spectacle. Under the extreme pressure exerted by avant-garde critics and the audience itself, film became a proper object of academic study.[5] A canon has been proposed that distinguishes art from spectacle; directors have been made authors, despite the fact that film is crucially a collective process of production; the critical community is divided between those charged with the task of providing a consumer guide and those whose ruminations count as literature—or even science, as in the case of semioticians.[6]

But television and rock music, forms that remain the chief repositories of contemporary popular culture, await their true co-optations and their resultant institutional legitimacy. After all, there are no departments of rock music in the academies, and certainly no provision for the study of this form in music departments. Nor, except in some newly founded media studies programs, is television accorded the status of an art form. Its claim to legitimacy is clearly contested on the right as well as on the left, and in the midst of the current ideological offensive by conservatives who aggressively assert their counterclaim as Keepers of the Faith of High Art, the chances for a breakthrough remain dim.

Clearly, for those who want to generate an emancipatory pedagogy the task has changed since the days when the judgments of the Frankfurt School dominated their thinking about mass culture. It is not a question of unmasking television or rock music as forms of domination that reproduce the prevailing set-up. Instead, we are engaged in a program of reclamation, to rescue these forms as the authentic expressions of generations for whom traditional culture is not available. Certainly one cannot be unambiguously enthusiastic about television or popular music since they are, after all, highly mediated, and are presented to their audiences as objects of consumption rather than spheres of participation. Nevertheless, the notions of deconstruction do not apply in the usual way. Rather, critical work should uncover the utopian, popular elements of what are considered debased expressions, in order to invent a different set of aesthetic criteria by which to comprehend electronically mediated products.[7] These inventions necessarily cannot be performed by teachers alone, not only because it is bad pedagogy, but because teachers have been cleansed of the popular elements of their own cultural formation and must, therefore, reflexively recover them. This process becomes a necessary prelude to reforging collective identities, which in any case are not on the surfaces of representation, at least for the last decade in rock and even longer in television.

Appropriation entails production as much as critical analysis. For the real innovation in teaching popular culture is the reintroduction of a theme raised in the midst of 1960s political and educational movements: the idea that we are all authors of the text and that art should be popularly produced. This aspect of the work involves the struggle for resources: video production costs money (but not as much as it did before miniaturization), and musical training is a formidable regimen. The point is that critical work without an effort to produce the popular art forms remains a peculiarly intellectual take on cultural life which is already distant from the experience of students. What we are saying is this: there can be no cultural pedagogy without a cultural practice that both explores the possibilities of the form and brings out students' talents. Otherwise, the statement that the artifacts of electronically mediated art are forms of popular culture descends to rhetorical flourish, or worse, reproduces criticism as high art behind the backs of the critics.

Rock music and television work because they reach down to the erotic dimension of human character, and the depth of that reach marks them as antagonistic to the precepts that control high art. As cultural forms they are consonant neither with the old model of art as subversive activity, according to which the utopian dimension of aesthetic experience consists precisely in its distance from the grubbiness of everyday life in consumer society, nor with Brecht's proposal that theater disengage the mind from emotions. Rather, popular culture both reconciles us to the social order and threatens it because it puts us in touch with pleasure, even when we have to buy it. So critical pedagogy is, among other virtues, a *discourse on pleasure*. And school is an activity, from the point of view of all of its participants, that systematically denies pleasure; in fact, one of its most valuable features from the view of the dominant anticulture is its regime of discipline and the conversion of play into labor. Together with the effort to purge children of their own culture, to recreate the vain old dream of capitalist production, humans as tabulae rasae, the respect for the sovereign authority of the state as represented by school officials forms the place of the school in the division of labor. School offers a reward as the price for the surrender of the underground culture of the youth community, an exchange that substitutes work and consumption for the pleasures associated with subcultures. Since television and rock music both reinforce these values but also undermine them with dreams of communal life and sexual pleasure, their reproductive functions are not sufficiently reliable to warrant authoritative approbation. Thus a pedagogy of popular culture finds itself in the interstices of the contradictory elements that constitute the forms of the wider society.

One of the crucial moves of the more recent versions of a critical theory of culture was to group all electronically mediated popular culture under the rubric "culture industry." Having determined that none of the products of this industry merits characterization as art, critical theory thereby frees itself of the obligation to read popular culture, not merely in terms of aesthetic problems but even as ideology critique. One can refuse to listen to rock music or watch television without cost, since these do not qualify for cultural analysis. In stark contrast to its critique of Marxist orthodoxy's tendency to reduce art to its so-called social determinations, the major writers in the critical theory tradition simply dismissed popular culture as just another kind of commodity production. However, it is not enough merely to assert the value of popular culture.

Before looking at specific representations it is necessary to recognize that television and film portray class, race, and gender in a differentiated way. These forms are constructed, to some extent, by the location of these social categories within the discursive formations in a specific place and time. These representations correspond to patterns that have been established both in the medium's own discourse and in the social formation of which it is a part; the two are not always in sync, as the differences between television and rock music illustrate. With the important exception of recent work by women in rock music, this form and its various genres are marked historically by the absence of women as subjects. Unlike television, in which this tendency is contested, at least at present (by "Cagney and Lacey," notably), rock music has presented songs of working-class male life (of course, black popular music has been the basis for this idiom, which is intimately intertwined with black proletarian culture in many variations). Although it can be argued that rock's assertion of male worker as subject is largely nostalgic, as in the case of Bruce Springsteen, or that it signifies the growing marginality of workers in late capitalist societies, as illustrated in the bitter, sardonic songs of the Clash and the Gang of Four as well as those of American heavy metal, these are all examples of male white worker as signifier while, in contrast, in the past decade, television has systematically displaced direct working-class representation, whatever the particular ideological content.

So the first task is to open the discussion by refusing the simple characterization of popular culture as culture industry, and by delineating difference.

We want to discuss briefly the representations of women and blacks in the media. Despite their marginality, the existence of recent movements for sexual and racial equality have made a difference in the ways these categories are treated. Even in a relatively dismal era, the late 1970s and 1980s, blacks and women occupy visible and, relatively speaking, direct space in media representations. The race and gender questions have by no means been resolved in American society and culture; indeed, there is considerable evidence that, in the absence of powerful protest and contestation of these issues, racism and sexism have reinserted themselves in public discourse in the last decade. Nevertheless, even in the presence of residual racism, it is virtually impossible for television to present blacks as racially skewed comic figures (although their subordination is once more asserted), and since revival of the genre of docudramas about social "problems" in which the position of women is a constant topic, women have emerged as moral agents, albeit ambiguously. This ambiguity is expressed in the absence of women's voices, even when they become subjects of film or television.

As feminist analysts of film have shown, women are presented in this medium as objects of the male gaze—that is, their subjectivity is simply absent.[8] This lack is exemplified by the rarity of women as protagonists in films, by the standpoint of both enunciation and utterances from which the mise-en-scène emanates. The male voice is heard; that of the woman is not, if by "voice" we mean not simply speech but the declaration of a standpoint; women appear, but the camera gaze is from above, whereas in contrast male power is presented by the angle shot, which magnifies the male image.

One can argue that the absence of the female voice in popular cultural representations does not apply to images. There are female cultural images but most of them exclude woman from historical and moral agency, that is, from the role of world maker. This situation is egregious, but it is not the same as the problem facing black and working-class people. Blacks are rarely if ever represented, and when they are, they are typically devoid of agency, even in the television cop shows where they often are given the position of sidekick to an agent. Although a brief period—1965 to 1970—witnessed a partial reversal of this tendency as media corporations revised the agencyless presentation of blacks, the fate of workers' representation in film and television is somewhat different. Until the early 1960s a small number of films and television shows offered direct representations of white workers (usually in a comic or pathetic mode), but the mode of this presentation changed in the next decades. Workers became the object of liberal scorn; they were portrayed as defenders of the status quo, racist and sexist, and equally important, politically and socially conservative. Archie Bunker ("All in the Family") was not only a comic character, as were Chester Riley ("Life of Riley") and Ralph Cramden ("The Honeymooners"), he was also a moral agent suffused with evil, a direct violation of the code according to which the working-class man, however scarce his media image, was invariably a hero. In contrast to Marlon Brando's 1954 portrayal in *On the Waterfront*, of a benighted but brave longshoreman who, in the last analysis, comes down for truth and justice, Bunker is a troglodyte, a "hard hat" whose wrath is aimed at the young, the poor, and blacks.

It was hard for working-class kids to identify with Archie in "All in the Family," but he was, as late as the mid-1970s, a palpable working-class figure, recognizable by his syntax, his body language, his gruff, semiarticulate speech that parodied the results of working-class culture. As we shall argue in this chapter, Archie proved to be a rear-guard character. After his demise (or, as we shall show, his good fortune to have moved up the social ladder), specifically working-class representations disappear. Today, working-class kids may still look forward to getting working-class jobs, but forging a class identity is more difficult than ever. They confront a media complex that consistently denies their existence, or displaces working-class male identity to other, upwardly mobile occupations—for example, police work, football, and other sites where conventional masculine roles are ubiquitous.

The message is clear: working-class identity, always problematic in American mass culture, is no longer an option in media representations.[9] We live in a postindustrial service society in which the traditional markers of working-class culture survive—especially the barroom, where waves of male industrial workers have congregated to share their grievances against the boss, their private troubles, their dreams of collective power and individual escape, their visions of women, their power displacements to the sports arena. But working-class men do not inhabit these television or movie precincts; they are the watering holes of off-duty cops, of derelicts, of miscellaneous white-collar administrators. The working class is absent among these signifiers, even as the sites and the forms of conviviality correspond to typical working-class culture.

Electronically mediated culture forms play an enlarged role in the formation of cultural identities. Of course, the claim that media are so hegemonic that they may exclude the influence of family, peers, and schools appears excessive. But it would be a serious error to conclude that it is an even match. We claim that electronically mediated cultural forms have the upper hand because they carry the authority of a society that, over the last half-century, has displaced patriarchal authority. For the discourse of social authority promises what family and friends can't deliver: a qualitatively better life, consumption on an expanded scale, a chance to move beyond the limits of traditional working-class life.

No institution represents the promise of this type of transcendence more than the school. Its curriculum is widely understood as a ticket to class mobility. But the content of that alternative is offered working-class kids by the situation comedies of television, the celluloid dreams of the movies, and especially by the advertisements that evoke lifestyles considered worthy of emulation. The relationship between schooling and media representations of vocational and cultural aspirations has become symbiotic, to the extent that the curriculum is almost entirely geared to presumed occupational requirements of modern corporations and the state. The dependence of what counts as education on the collective cultural ideal is almost total. These occupational requirements, especially in large parts of the service sector, are not so much technical as they are ideological. That is, just as many advertisements sell not products but capitalism, so school learning is organized around behaviors required by types of bureaucratic work, as well as around the rewards offered by consumer society for performance according to established corporate norms. Students are no longer (if they ever were) enthusiastic about discovering new things to know, much less Truth; rather they want to find out how the real world works, especially what it takes to achieve a certain level of consumption. And the high school is the major site in which the "real" world of work is discovered. Students retain little or nothing of the content of knowledge (facts of history, how to perform algebraic equations, the story line of *Silas Marner*) but do remember how to succeed in receiving good grades, how to gain admission to a decent college or university, and how to curry favor with authorities, teachers, counselors, and employers.

Working-class kids often fail to get the message right. As Paul Willis tells us in *Learning to Labor*, their rebellion against school authority, manifested as the refusal to internalize the two parts of the curriculum—its "knowledge-based" content and its latent demand for discipline and respect for authority—insures that they will get working-class jobs rather than make it up the ladder of economic and social mobility. But, as Aronowitz has argued elsewhere, while assembly-line, construction, and other heavy industrial labor was available for school leavers until the early 1970s in the United States and United Kingdom, these options are today largely foreclosed by the restructured world economy.[10] Parents, especially fathers, can no longer serve as substitute representations of viable occupational alternatives to those imposed by school and the media. And this ideal erases working-class representations—the class sensorium has disappeared.

We see this problematic replayed in the film *Dirty Dancing*. An upper-middle-class family in the early 1960s goes to a Borscht Belt Catskills resort for a short vacation. Two daughters are immediately plunged into the social life, mostly with waiters and entertainers. The waiter chosen by one of the daughters is a Yale law school student; he turns out to be a philanderer. The other daughter commits the transgression that provides the dramatic grist for the narrative: she falls in love with the resort's star attraction, a working-class youth who has succeeded in learning Latin, ballet, and other "exotic" dances. He gives lessons, performs, and fools around with the women who work as entertainers or in the kitchen, similarly of lower-class background. Unlike other films of this developing genre of class indiscretion (working-class men and upper-class women), the film has a happy ending because the young woman chooses to become a dancer—she exercises her option to downward mobility, to be declassed. The working-class man has become a professional; he may be working in the Catskills but he certainly is talented. And this class movement has already separated him from his roots, so the relationship is acceptable.

We shall amplify on the theme of displacement later in this article. For now, it is enough to ask how to engage in a pedagogy among working-class students concerning their social identity. Indeed, if identification is a basis for the forging of a personal identity, school and media consort to persuade, cajole, and (by the absence of representations) force working-class kids to accept middle-class identities as the only legitimate option available to them. However, it is obvious that many will choose not to accept this course or, having bought into the aspiration, will fail to make the grade. The result for both groups is cultural homelessness. Clearly, the task of a pedagogy that addresses this dilemma is to critically examine its contours, its motivations, and its consequences.

Several issues come to mind: the ineluctability of the merger of masculinity with working-class identity; the question of displacement and its effects on self-images; and the class/gender reversals in contemporary representations in film and television—that is, the degree to which male conquest becomes the power equivalent of class difference. It is time to address these issues.

When I worked in the steel mills,* the barroom was far more than a place to have a casual beer or to get drunk. It was the scene of union politics, the site of convivial relationships that were hard to sustain on the shop floor because of the noise, frequent speedups, and the ever-watchful eye of the foreman. Of course we had the john, but only for twenty minutes at a time; as the metal was heating up in furnaces, we often took a break. Sometimes, the john substituted for the barroom. We had animated arguments about baseball, women, or an incident that had just occurred, usually one in which one of our fellow workers was hurt (I remember Felix, who caught a hot wire in his leg). But, inevitably, the warning buzzer would interrupt our discussions—metal was nearly ready to come out and be drawn into wire.

So the gin mill was the place where our collective identity as a community was forged and reproduced. Even when we had harsh disagreements about things that really mattered (should we stop work over a safety grievance or was Jackie Robinson a better second baseman than Billy Martin, a tinderbox of an issue in 1960), we knew that the next day we would have to pull together in the hot mill, that our disputes were in the family. We knew also that we had to fight the boss together, not only for the ordinary reasons of better pay and benefits but for our sur-

---

*While this chapter presents our collective views, this section is written in the first person, reflecting Aronowitz's personal experience.

vival. The mill was a dangerous place, and for most of us, losing a limb meant losing the best-paying job we were ever likely to own. In the union shops of the 1950s and early 1960s, the job was a property right. As we used to say, the only reason you could get fired was if you punched the foreman while sober.

Steelwork was definitely male culture. As in Freud's essay on femininity, women were the mysterious Other. We did not know much about them and, apart from the incessant desire that occupied our prurient conversations, they did not enter into working lives. Women were obscure objects of our desire, but desire also reached out for a secure collective identity. For even as early as fifteen years after the war, the neighborhoods of Newark, Elizabeth, and Jersey City, within which working people saw in the faces of others part of their own selves, a self that was recognized in the local grocery store, at bingo games held in the basements of the Catholic churches (which became the place where the women's community was formed), were in the process of dissolving. I remember meeting shopmates at the movies, in the neighborhood Chinese restaurant where we took the kids for dinner some Sunday evenings, in the bar on South Orange Avenue where a diemaker named John hung out (we became friends because we were both interested in music; he played the accordion professionally at Polish weddings on weekends).

I went to christenings and confirmations in the area around the plant, which was located in an industrial suburb. Most of the families were of eastern and southern European backgrounds: not only Italians and Poles, although they were in the majority, but also Czechs, Russians, and Greeks. People lived around the northern New Jersey plants in wood-frame, one-family houses or in "uppers" (the second and third floors of multiple dwellings). Those of us who were not veterans either of the Second World War or the Korean War did not qualify for special mortgage deals, so we rented apartments that ate about 25 percent of our monthly pay or less. However, a growing minority of my friends were moving to the middle-class suburbs where single-family housing developments were mushrooming (or, more graphically, springing up like weeds). These were more modern homes, often built without firm foundations even though they were constructed on landfill. They surely did not fulfill the letter of James Truslow Adams's "American Dream," but they were an acceptable facsimile until something better came along.[11]

Suburban flight was made feasible by low-interest mortgages, but also by the federal highway program initiated by President Harry Truman and fulfilled by the Eisenhower administration. In earlier years, living fifteen or twenty miles from the plant was simply not an option because the roads were invariably local. Such a trip could take more than two hours. Now, barring traffic jams, night-shift workers could make it to work in twenty minutes. And those working days simply left home before rush hour and came back late. For many, being away from the wife and kids presented few, if any problems; male culture excluded women, and the notion that men should share child care was simply unthought in most families in those days. Certainly, many workers were left behind—blacks, Hispanics, the young, those not yet able to raise a down payment or still unmarried, and older workers who had never recovered from the Depression.

White working-class flight was engendered, in part, by the influx of southern and Caribbean blacks into large northern cities; it was also driven by the failure of federal and state lawmakers to expand the federal housing program beyond the poor. In fact, the choice of the home mortgage program was the alternative to new multiunit housing for workers. Housing for large families was simply unavailable in the cities at rents that even relatively well-paid steel and auto workers could afford. Racism was not the "cause" of white flight in the sense that individuals who harbored these attitudes decided to move to get away from blacks. Racism was the result of a combination of developments. In addition to the urban housing shortage (because virtually no new one-family moderate-income homes were constructed after the war), the era was marked by a precipitous decline in services—schools, hospitals, and amenities such as recreation and child care were either in serious disrepair or overcrowded.

In historical retrospect, the deterioration of the urban regions after the war was the result of federal and corporate policy. By the mid-1960s, center city industrial plants were closing down. From Harrison, the industrial suburb of Newark, General Motors removed its roller-bearing plant to the Union County suburb of Kenilworth; General Electric closed its lamp factory in the black section of Newark. By the end of the decade, no major industrial plant remained in that city. Jersey City and Hoboken suffered similar fates; industrial expansion was still a powerful spur to economic growth, but not in the big cities. Capital and white working-class flight, together with federal housing and highway programs and the enthusiasm of local communities, gave away the keys to the town to any corporation willing to build a plant, office building, or research facility.

The dispersion of white workers into the suburbs did not immediately destroy working-class communities, although they were considerably weakened by the late 1950s. The gin mill next to the production mill retained its pride of place. Sometimes this function was performed by a bar located in a local union hall or in a fraternal association of, say, Poles or Ukrainians. Typically, after going off shift a worker would stop at the bar for an hour or two before going home, even a home as far as forty miles away. There, he would play darts, shuffleboard, or pool, or just sit at the bar and drink and talk. Those who worked days arrived home at six o'clock (the shift ended at three o'clock). After supper, if there were no chores, the family might sit in front of the television set.

The television explosion of the 1950s is generally acknowledged to have changed the leisure-time activities of Americans. The simulations that film brought to theater audiences now became daily fare. The stimulation of the unconscious by imaging (the term is Teresa de Lauretis's from *Alice Doesn't*) consists in a simulacrum of the dream work, so that identities are formed through identification with the gendered characters that appear on the screen. Aural media also are powerful desiring machines, but sound is burdened with an enormous load because images must be produced by the listener. Identification can be fomented, but with difficulty. The film form invokes the stark real-life character. De Lauretis argues that women do not insert themselves into film culture, that they are absent in imagining. They cannot identify with the actual representations of women on the screen, for these women are the objects of male desire, they do not occupy subject positions from which emanate distinctive female voices. That is, there is no chance for identification unless women accept the object space to which they have been assigned.

Males identify with characters (protagonists, heroes) who are the subjects of narratives; women are objects of desire/exchange/conflicts among males and only assume distinctive character when they occupy male subject positions from which, in both comedies and drama, they must inevitably fall (the Spencer Tracy and Katharine Hepburn comedies such as *Woman of the Year* and *Desk Set*, the Joan Crawford soap opera *Mildred Pierce*, in which women who speak as male characters find that adopting these personae invites self-destruction). Male workers do find representations in film and television in the 1950s. The characters of Ralph Cramden and Ed Norton and William Bendix's Chester Riley are comically absurd, the situations often artificial and juvenile, but family relationships articulate with the prevalent war between the sexes, the distinctiveness of male culture, the absence of a corresponding women's community.

Cramden is a bus driver, and like many working-class men, he dreams of escaping his routine, relatively low-paid job by entering a constant succession of imagined business schemes. His driving ambition for wealth is lodged entirely in the imaginary (male) fantasies that are widely shared. His wife can barely disguise her contempt for these wildly improbable desires, most of which serve not to enhance the opportunity for real social mobility, but instead are Ralph's pathetic efforts to establish his dominance in the home. On the other side, Norton, a sewer worker, harbors neither illusion nor the desire to flee his job. The sewer affords him a considerable measure of autonomy, at least in comparison to factory work or bus driving. He enjoys the lack of responsibility his job entails but fervently asserts its dignified character against the constant chidings of his quixotic friend.

As with most television situation comedies, the characters have a cartoon quality; there is no room for complexity in the representations. And the stripped-down sets evoke 1930s Depression decor rather than that of the postwar era. The Honeymooners have been left behind by the white urban exodus; they are transhistorical working-class types. Norton is invariably dressed in a T-shirt and wears his hat indoors. Cramden dons the uniform of a bus driver, signifying the ambiguity of his situation; clearly, he is a wage laborer, but his will is that of a petty official, since genuine wealth has been foreclosed to him. Cramden displaces his frustration onto intrafamilial quarrels. His wife Alice's housework never counts as real work; his characteristic posture is that of an inquisitor ("What have you done all day?"). Since Alice rarely awards him the deference he urgently needs, given his relatively degraded social position, his usual gesture is the verbal threat of violence (against women), "One of these days . . . pow, right in the kisser!" Alice seems bored by his remonstrations, and we, the audience, know that Ralph is simply too henpecked (or, in the male vernacular, pussy-whipped) to follow through.

"The Honeymooners" retains its large audience after thirty years because it displays the range of class and gender relations. Its class ideology is represented by the absence of the labor process except discursively. The family relations displace the class relations as Ralph seeks to dominate Alice, and she, the real proletarian, remains recalcitrant. Here we see the inner core of male fantasies: lacking the individual power to achieve the freedom wealth presumably affords, domination becomes the object of male desire. As with Hegel's master, Ralph desperately covets Alice's recognition, but is denied such pleasures, except in the last instance when, at his wits' end, Ralph demands the approbation that she must grant.

"The Honeymooners" succeeds as a tableau of the sadomasochistic version of the family romance. Ralph's infantile behavior generates Alice's maternal role even as there are no children in the household. Ralph plays master, insofar as he trumpets his breadwinner status, but also is the emotionally dependent male for whom sexuality is identical with submission. Alice is not a moral agent, only a mirror to the absurdity of male will.

Caricature notwithstanding, working-class life demanded representations in the 1950s and early 1960s. By the later years, the dispersion of working-class culture made direct representation improbable. Where the previous generation knew economic class as a regulating principle, including the real subordination of women by men, the generation of the 1960s was by comparison free-floating. The universalization of postsecondary schooling (misnamed higher education then, as now) brought many working-class kids in contact with ruling- and upper-class peers. The results from the point of view of the established social structure were potentially devastating. Surely class resentments and distinctions do not disappear in youth culture, but are explicitly challenged by the effort to invent new normative principles of social relations. These relations, which held equality as their highest cultural ideal, challenge generations of difference, not only of economic power but of sexually construed cultures.

But the worker as tragic hero is a transitional figure, for the tragedy is born of the disintegration already prefigured by consumer society, especially suburbanization. Working-class culture is preeminently urban; it belongs to the industrializing era, which by the late 1960s has passed. Postindustrial culture is already postmodern: it is marked by boundary crossing. While working-class culture still finds renewal on the shop floor, its residential base is dispersed. In the suburbs of major metropolitan centers, industrial workers mow their lawns alongside professionals, managers, and small-business neighbors.

By the early 1980s, Archie Bunker, the Queens, New York, political and social Neanderthal, had opened a bar. Having pushed himself up into the business-owning small middle class, Archie left his working-class roots behind, not only in his newly found proprietorship but also in his contacts. In this assimilation, he continued the tendencies of the earlier incarnation of the show: recall, the Bunker family lived in that part of New York that most resembled the suburbs. The only black family he knew owned and operated a dry-cleaning business. In other ways, he rubbed shoulders with those who had more completely achieved one of the crucial elements of the American dream, a business of one's own. So it is entirely reasonable that Archie should aspire to gaining a toehold on the social ladder. With that, the Archie of that show, "Archie's Place," lasted only two seasons, then disappeared into the middle class.

From the mid-1970s, there simply are no direct representations of working-class males (much less working-class women) in television. Representations are dispersed to beer advertisements, thirty-second images of football players hoisting their favorite brands, jostling each other in timid evocations of the ribbing characteristic of working-class bar culture; or to cop shows in which characteristic working-class culture is displaced and recontextualized in the station house, on the streets, in the bars where cops congregate. These are displacements, so we see only the remainders—conviviality, friendship that is overdetermined by the police buddy system, the obligatory partnership. It is in these interactions, when the partners of, say, "Hill Street Blues," discuss their personal problems or their troubles with the department, that the old class solidarity bonds are permitted to come to the surface, often against the captain or even the lieutenants who are a step above the line and possess some authority. We know that in these representations the patrolmen (and some women) may rise to sergeant but are not likely to make lieutenant, much less captain. These are not educated people. Their bravery entitles them to recognition, not rank. They have their own hangouts, their personal troubles (especially with women). In contrast, officials, whatever their origins, do not congregate in barrooms; they have no sharers of their troubles because they must observe the tacit code of hierarchy. In recent films, displacement of class to the police continues, but is joined by displacement of sex (gender) relations to class as well.

Hollywood movies of the late 1980s (*Someone to Watch Over Me*, *Barfly*) are marked by a conventional theme in contemporary narrative: the working-class man is powerfully attracted to an upper-class woman, disrupting not only the prohibition of interclass romance, but also the family romance. In these instances, to be working class is identified with masculinity, upper-class membership with femininity. This is exemplified in *Barfly*, the nonstory of a derelict writer who meets two women: one a derelict, apparently a renegade from upper-class life who names her profession as "drinking"; the second a publisher of a literary magazine who "discovers" the writer. The triangle is resolved by his choice of the woman barfly who, like him, lives to drink and engages in barroom brawls. Her masculinity allows him to hook up with her, to combine sex and male bonding. In contrast, his benefactor is a beautiful woman who cannot hold her liquor and, because she lives outside male lower-class culture, cannot hold him. The woman barfly engages the world like a man in other ways. She goes off with the writer's arch-enemy, a bartender in his favorite hangout, because he comes to work one day with a full bottle of bourbon. Like many males, her loyalty to people is always subordinate to loyalty to pleasure. In the end, the writer admires such priorities, for his own life has been conducted according to the precept that conventional morality is for the nerds.

Someone to Watch Over Me finds a cop of plainly working-class parentage married to a tough, feisty working-class woman; they live together with their kids in a modest single-family house in Queens. The cop is assigned to protect an upper-class woman, ensconced in a Manhattan townhouse. He is assigned the midnight shift and quickly has an affair with her, an event that disrupts his tension-filled, but stable, home life. As with the young publisher of *Barfly*, the woman is attracted by the merger of class identity and masculinity and he by the reverse class/sex combination. *Someone to Watch Over Me* reenacts a crucial male working-class fantasy, to dominate a beautiful rich woman, to make the "impossible dream" real.

These films address the insufficiency of middle-class comfort for the generation of upwardly mobile working-class kids born after the war. The protagonist of *Barfly* chooses the underlife, a degraded bohemia punctuated by the struggle for male honor even in the lower depths. The cop is socialized into a conventional honorific position—the centurion—but finds it suffused with mediocrity and, most important of all, marked by repetition and continuity with the anterior generation. What is new is adventure, which can be fulfilled only by sexual indiscretion, "penetration" into the forbidden territory of the upper class. For the cop, buried in the routine tasks dictated by a bureaucracy that seems entirely beyond his power to control, sex becomes, besides the exotic, the power that can propel him out of his own real-life subordination.

It may be that the discourse of sex refers today to class issues, but it is also true that class discourse refers to gender domination. The import of the image of the working-class cop engaging in sexual relations with a woman in an entirely improbable class position is not that American society is somehow democratic; these relationships end in disaster. They are themselves sundered, but more important, they wreck families, personal lives, and so forth. The significance is otherwise. Class is no barrier when upper-class women are involved. In current representations, the reverse is rarely portrayed. Femininity is not a universal signifier; the privilege is reserved for male culture.

There are, of course, no public representations of working-class culture other than the images associated with male bonding. In fact, one may read *Barfly* as a signal that one key site of class solidarity, the bar, has been declassed, or, more precisely, the lumpies are the legatees of what was once a marginalized but distinct subculture. And just as women are absent from media representations of social agents, they constitute no part of the representations of working-class culture. Working-class culture is almost always seen as white and male, even in its displaced forms. The community of women is generally denied, but as we have argued, women appear as the new proletariat insofar as maleness exercises itself as dominating power.

At first glance, *Flashdance* is an exception to the rule. A woman welder in a steel fabricating plant falls in love with the boss, himself cast as the self-made man rather than the MBA or accountant. Here class difference is mediated by other bonds of solidarity, particularly sexuality (itself a difference) and membership in the same occupational community. The film presents the "new" woman as both male and female; the relationship presupposes both her male and her female personae. As in *Barfly*, interclass sexual relations are possible only when the woman displays masculinity, which remains the privileged class position. In short, in contrast to the 1950s, when a viable working-class culture connected to powerful large-scale industry represented America's emergence as the leading world economic power, and when this work was accorded considerable status in media (*On the Waterfront, View from the Bridge*, and *Saturday's Hero* are just three films of this decade), class has been displaced in two ways—first, to other signifiers of masculinity, and second, to the code violations entailed in sexual relations between working-class or declassed men and upper-class women. In this case, sex/class relations are reversed. Men achieve class parity, despite lower-class roots, with women owing to the status conferred upon masculine sexuality and its powers by society.

In *Someone to Watch Over Me* and other examples of this relationship, the absent male is a businessman. His shadow existence is owed to the obvious fact entailed by the conditions of his own success: his real marriage is to the business, not to his wife. Sexuality of the traditional sort is confined to those without sublimations, which accounts for its relatively ambiguous role in the drinking woman's life in *Barfly*. Writing and booze are serious competitors, but for the working-class man, neither art nor business provides the channel for the discharge of erotic energies. At the same time, sex is not really an acceptable form of power, for unlike art or business (real work), its results are horrendous from a moral point of view. The message of this film is that transgression, although possible, is not desirable. Similar to nineteenth-century and early twentieth-century novels (Thomas Hardy, D. H.

Lawrence), love is forbidden by class difference, and when the barrier is transgressed dire consequences ensue. Yet, moral proscription aside, the sex/class/power axis in television and movies constitutes a critique of the cultural ideal of consumer society that passes for the 1980s equivalent of the mobility myth. The entrepreneurial ambition that drove two generations of immigrants has disappeared from public view; the remainder is the civil service, which has become the far horizon of well-being for a new working class that can no longer count on high-paying factory jobs. The army and the police force have replaced industrial labor for working-class men for whom professional options simply have never existed.

Male bonding persists in these contexts, but not the solidarity born of the mutual recognition among production workers that they share a common fate as well as a common existence. For the civil servant, existence is never identical to essence. There is always one place more in the bureaucratic hierarchy for which to strive. On this material foundation, a family could, as late as 1980, enjoy the prospect of owning a single-family home in the cop or noncommissioned-officers enclaves bordering on the suburbs. Such options are increasingly out of the question. And, because the concept of collective fate is constantly disturbed by the latest promotional examination, so is social solidarity, at least for younger officers.

The only vital life consists in dreams of power, the most vivid form of which is male sexuality. Contrasted to earlier direct representations in which sex is virtually absent from discourse, but class persists, today's movies and television code sex, class, and power interchangeably. As with earlier genres, women do not occupy subject positions; they remain the palpable objects of male desire and by this precise relation experience class reversal. In sum, the persistence of even these displaced representations of workers and their culture (Paul Schrader's *Blue Collar*, in 1980, may have been the last direct example) attests to the media's yearning for a source of vitality and renewal that clearly cannot be derived from depictions of ruling-class relationships, a genre that survives not in the drawing-room comedy but in the old tradition of portrayals of scandal and corruption (see the Oliver Stone movie *Wall Street*). This lack of credible ruling-class subjects occurs at a time when public confidence in business appears to be considerably higher than at any time since the Gilded Age. Yet what excited the old public's imagination, rather than admiration, was the degree to which the capitalist merged with the frontiersman earlier in the century. Despite his ruthlessness, he was a romantic figure, a conqueror, a risk taker, and, above all, sexy. This figure was displaced to that of the underworld boss in the 1930s and 1940s, when entrepreneurship had already passed to the hijacker, the bank robber, the gambler, figures revived briefly in the 1960s.

The working-class man is no longer viable as a mythic figure, but neither is Ivan Boesky; while politicians and investment bankers have lost any semblance of sexuality, male or otherwise, class culture survives as masculinity. What working-class culture may signify is the last hope for class equality, provided the object is a woman.

New Perspectives on Mass Culture

In the last two decades, converging intellectual movements in the critical theory of education and in cultural studies have, in different ways, rejected the idea, pervasive until the 1960s, that mass culture was an unmitigated disaster whose outcome was nothing less than the reshaping of the human personality along the lines imposed by technological domination. In education the works of Henry Giroux, Roger Simon, and Paul Willis stand out as complementary to the arguments advanced by feminists such as Teresa de Lauretis and Ellen Willis and critics such as Robert Christgau, Simon Frith, and others who have argued that rock music, film, and other popular forms express, in different ways (generational, feminist, working class), types of social and cultural oppositions. We are at the crossroads when our thesis that schools are sites of opposition must be integrated with the critique of critical theory's dismissal of popular culture.

In the most recent past, in *Education under Siege*, we have advanced the idea that the critique of schools was not enough, that radicals must learn to speak a language of possibility, while avoiding the illusion that a few school reforms could adequately alter the profound commitment of schools to reproduce the prevailing system of social power. Speaking a language of possibility entails speaking about the cultural experience of students as if their knowledge of rock and television and other electronically mediated popular forms was a type of reliable knowledge whose status, even though not legitimate in terms of the curriculum to which they are responsible, may be understood, at least in the classroom and among peers, as an appropriate starting point for cultural and intellectual formation. There are two ways to proceed with this project. One is to claim a rock and television aesthetic commensurable with, say, literature and classical music. A necessary corollary to this strategy is the claim that these forms embody moral and ethical values that school authorities, professional critics, and philosophers can recognize as plausible alternatives to those offered by so-called high cultural forms. This is a tricky path, for it entails an explicit acceptance of the criteria that have marked high culture since the early bourgeois era, an approach already suggested, for example, by the effort of proponents to argue that jazz is "America's classical music" or the already-mentioned distinction made between "film" and "movies" that claim mass audiences. In this undertaking, the distinction between high and popular culture is recognized only as a question of audience, not an intrinsic characteristic of the work of art. Thus placing pop art in the museum marks it off from its more commercial representations. Or the difference in the minimalism of Phillip Glass and Steve Reich from that of punk rock appears largely in that the former is presented in the concert hall while the latter plays in clubs and large sports stadiums and sell records in shops designed exclusively for the pop market. The first perspective also challenges the curriculum to make a place for popular culture, if it is proved that the work merits consideration as legitimate knowledge.

This approach is consistent with the dominant doctrine, rarely practiced in schools, of pluralism. It would not deny the validity of literature or film, or what is called classical music, but would demand that the repertoire of acceptable cultural objects be expanded. Further, this approach might claim that beginning from student experience, validating what students already know, is just good pedagogy that can influence the process of language acquisition, written expression—in short, the learning that is currently grouped under the rubric of literacy. This is, of course, an expression of "new realism" that increasingly characterizes left politics in an era when cultural radicalism is in retreat. The question posed by this strategy is whether its success undermines the radical content of the cultural project itself by facilitating its integration into the prevailing curriculum.

Obviously, the second perspective would insist that the popular forms possess significance lacking in contemporary high art, which, it can be easily shown, survives primarily as a weapon of distinction, part of the apparatus that maintains class and generational differences. The second strategy is to argue for the historicity of high culture as an avant-garde—those who propose through their art a utopian future—to be located chiefly, even if not exclusively, in such expressions as can be identified in popular culture. It would have to be demonstrated that popular expressions propose a new vision of the future as well as a different critique of the present, whether coded or not. And the fundamental issue is surely pleasure, for if rock music can be delineated from other forms it is precisely its evocation of pleasure as a mode of life that moves its detractors to the lengths of an Allan Bloom. Bloom castigates rock music for its suggestion of sexual intercourse as if this were an aesthetic crime. Presumably the representation of sexuality in art must remain a delicate matter, best exemplified, one supposes, by the muffled repressed invocations of Victorian literature, a Henry James perhaps, or even better, Gustave Flaubert.[12] In any case, the claim that youth culture possesses a radical alternative aesthetic of pleasure spills over to the critique of the schools as institutions of deprivation and, equally important, constitutes a harsh critique of the work world as necessarily opposed to the kind of life that rock dreams articulate. Cultural radicalism has absolutely no chance of being accepted, even on pluralist grounds, in the present conjuncture. It would not legitimate its ideology by reference to accepted educational norms. On the contrary, it would propose a new relationship between work and play that would posit their necessary integration rather than opposition; which given the current arrangements would ineluctably entail the subordination of the latter.

Clearly, either pluralism or cultural radicalism would integrate writing and reading with popular knowledge. But this integration would by necessity break the line between critique and practice. A curriculum in popular cultural studies would be required to include at its center video and music production and performance. Students would make videos that expressed their own ideas—writing the scripts, producing the documentaries, learning how to write and perform the music, and so forth. This departure from traditional humanities and cultural studies programs at the secondary and postsecondary levels is crucial if the privileged place of science over technique, of criticism over production, of intellectual over manual labor is to be overcome.

Notes

1. Louis Althusser, "Ideology and Ideological State Apparatuses," in *Lenin and Philosophy* (London: New Left Books, 1971).

2. Antonio Gramsci, *Selections from the Prison Notebooks* (New York: International Publishers, 1971).

3. Herbert Schiller, *Mind Managers* (Boston: Beacon Press, 1973); Armand Mattelart and Ariel Dorfman, *How to Read Donald Duck* (Paris: International General, 1977).

4. Althusser, "Ideology."

5. There are many sources for the shift of film studies from a journalistic subspecialty to an academic discipline. In this country credit must go especially to Siegfried Kracauer, whose *Theory of Film* (New York: Oxford University Press, 1960) established an important ontological and epistemological credential for film studies even as his *Caligari to Hitler* (Princeton: Princeton University Press, 1947) was a pioneer work in the cultural, psychological, and historical context for film.

6. Andrew Sarris, *The Film Directors* (New York: 1965); Christian Metz, *The Language of Cinema* (London and New York: Oxford University Press, 1977).

7. Fredric Jameson, "Reification and Utopia in Mass Culture," *Social Text*, 1 (1979).

8. Teresa de Lauretis, *Alice Doesn't: Feminism, Semiotics, Cinema* (Bloomington: Indiana University Press, 1981).

9. Some may object that the hit series "Roseanne" belies this judgment. While Roseanne is surely a working-class woman, this identity is overcoded by sex and gender relations. Plainly stated, in the contemporary political and cultural conjuncture, race and gender, regardless of other identities, predominate.

10. Stanley Aronowitz, *Working-Class Hero: A New Strategy for Labor* (New York: Pilgrim Press, 1983).

11. James Truslow Adams, *Our Business Civilization (New York: A. and C. Boni, 1930)*.

12. Bloom's outrage has been recently echoed by that leading art critic, Senator Jesse Helms (R-N.C.) whose critique as pornography of the Robert Mapplethorpe show at Washington's Corcoran Gallery has placed the National Endowment for the Arts in extreme jeopardy. The affair serves as one more grim reminder that America is still ensconced, in some respects, in its Puritan heritage.

CHAPTER 8
CONCLUSION:
POSTMODERNISM AS POLITICS — BEYOND DIFFERENCE AS TECHNOLOGICAL UTOPIANISM AND CULTURAL SEPARATISM

The last decade is marked by the emergence of two crosscurrents that appear paradoxical from the standpoint of traditional social and cultural theory. On the one side is the triumph of political conservatism in the West, concomitant with the end of the postwar economic boom in the wake of a long wave of recession and stagnation as well as the breakup of communist hegemonies in eastern Europe and Asia. From this perspective interventionist Keynesianism appears dead even as state expenditures continue to grow and the ubiquity of executive authorities within social life spreads. Similarly, the disparity between ideology and practice has never been more dramatic than in intellectual knowledge. Even as the conservatives have taken control over education, proclaiming the need for school renewal built on the basis of a rededication of the curriculum to canonical texts and recycled forms of accountability, they have ruthlessly slashed school budgets, demanded that education be subordinated to business needs, and implemented a more sharply etched tracking system in which the gap between upper-class and lower-class students' acquisition of cultural capital is widened.

At the same time, the opposing current, radical democracy and its intellectual expression, postmodernism, has gripped two generations of intellectuals. Since we have explored these themes in detail in this book, we will address them here in relatively general terms. On the one hand, Marxism and liberalism as master narratives of history and politics are challenged. On the other, the traditions of knowledge grounded in first principles are spurned, and rejected along with this is the idea of a master narrative that unifies all knowledge, whether philosophical, historical, or methodological. Since we can no longer stand on the foundations established by past savants, the canon that derives from these foundations must be interrogated. New intellectuals who refuse to preserve the tradition as a basis for shaping the future in favor of a new skepticism or in another register propose a counter-canon consisting of marginal discourses. Of course, the canon of the excluded is ironic, for postmodernism understands the notion of the sacred itself as suspect. The postmodern strategy of interrogation leads to an evaluation of the disciplines within which intellectual knowledge is configured. Holding these disciplines to be constructed under historically specific circumstances leads to the discovery that as these conditions have been surpassed the legitimacy of the forms of dominant knowledge is in doubt. Therefore, efforts to preserve the distinctions—between natural, social, and human sciences as well as between these fields and the arts—can be viewed as exemplars of the historicity of academic disciplines. Rather than holding knowledge in some kind of correspondence with a self-enclosed objective reality, postmodernism views the production of knowledge in the context of power. In the broader areas of cultural criticism and political theory, the consequences of these moves need to be highlighted. First, knowledge is being reshaped according to the strategy of transgression. It is no longer a question of interdisciplinary education but of nondisciplinary learning, the boundaries of which are to be constructed by the learner as well as the teacher. Second, traditional disciplines are defined as much by their exclusions as by their inclusions. Postmodern educational criticism insists on the intellectual equality of marginal discourses—feminism, sexuality, race, class—with those in which these discourses are occluded, when considered at all. These considerations exempt neither science nor social science from interrogation, thus removing the halo around science that has exempted it from all but internal criticism—that is, correction by other members of the scientific community. Third, among the markers of modernism is the distinction between high and low culture, a divide in which certain works qualify as art on the basis of criteria set by particular consensual conventions. What is at issue here is how aesthetic standards emerge, how they are authorized, and what is at stake in the idea of standards as such. Critical postmodernism insists that the products of the so-called mass culture, popular and folk art forms, are proper objects of study, not, as some modernist film criticism argues, to establish their aesthetic credentials, but to challenge aesthetics itself as a legitimate discourse of exclusion.

Regardless of whether critics see postmodernism as pastiche, parody, or serious cultural criticism, the postmodern temperament arises from the exhaustion of the still prevailing intellectual and artistic knowledge and the crisis of the institutions charged with their production and transmission—the schools. The "nihilism" of postmodern discourse does not signify its rejection of ethics, politics, and power, only its refusal to accept the givens of public and private morality and the judgments arising from them. Of course, we go further in this book and argue that critical postmodernism provides a political and pedagogical basis not only for challenging current forms of academic hegemony but also for deconstructing conservative forms of postmodernism in which social life is merely made over to accommodate expanding fields of information in which reality collapses into the proliferation of images. At its best, a critical postmodernism signals the possibility for not only rethinking the issue of educational reform but also creating a pedagogical discourse that deepens the most radical impulses and social practices of democracy itself.

It is important to remember that within the language of educational reform advocated by the right, democracy loses its once dynamic nature and is reduced to a set of inherited principles and institutional arrangements that teach students how to adapt to rather than question the basic precepts of society. Under such a regime, students rarely find themselves introduced to modes of knowledge that celebrate democratic forms of public life or that provide them with the knowledge and skills they will need to engage in a critical examination of the society in which they live and work.

We argue in this book that any viable educational theory has to begin with a language that links schooling to democratic public life, that defines teachers as engaged intellectuals and border crossers, and develops forms of pedagogy that incorporate difference, plurality, and the language of the everyday as central to the production and legitimation of learning. But this demands the reconstruction of a view of language and theory that establishes the groundwork for viewing schooling and education as a form of cultural politics, as a discourse that draws its meaning from the social, cultural, and economic context in which it operates.

Within the present period of conservative leadership and authority in many of the industrialized countries of the world, with its appeal to universality, its totalitarian view of history, its ethnocentric embrace of culture, and its celebration of greed and individualism, a number of important questions need to be asked by educators regarding the counterhegemonic role that a discourse of postmodernist educational criticism might assume. Questioning can begin by specifically addressing the need to develop forms of theoretical practice capable of retrieving history as the discourse of the Other, reclaiming democracy as a site of struggle within a wider public vision, and developing a radical ethic that rejects finality and certainty for the voice of difference and dialogue. Postmodern educational criticism offers the opportunity for a discursive practice whose identity and political value can only be understood in particular circumstances, informed by the historical conjuncture that gives it meaning. At issue here is whether postmodern educational criticism works in the interest of making the familiar strange, acknowledging difference as the basis for a public philosophy that rejects totalizing theories that view the Other as a deficit, and providing the basis for raising questions the dominant culture finds too dangerous to raise. What many educators often forget is that the importance of such a language as a theoretical practice derives from its power as a critical and subversive discourse. To judge educational theory with the simple yardstick of clarity or the immediate demands of practice more often than not represents a specific theoretical discourse incapable of reflecting on its *own* practice within the present historical conjuncture, a practice that has more to do with a defense of the status quo than it does with developing a viable politics of theory, language, and schooling.

Postmodern educational criticism points to the need for constructing a critical discourse to both constitute and reorder the ideological and institutional conditions for a radical democracy. In this view, the broader parameters of a postmodern educational criticism are informed by a political project that links the creation of critical citizens to the development of a radical democracy. This includes but goes beyond merely discursive struggles in order to transform nondiscursive and institutional relations of power—that is, a political project that ties education to the broader struggle for a public life in which dialogue, vision, and compassion remain critically attentive to the rights and conditions that organize different public spaces as democratic social forms. These must be capable of challenging the growing regimes of terror and oppression that are emerging throughout the world. It is important to emphasize that difference and pluralism in this view do not mean reducing democracy to the equivalency of diverse interests; nor does a critical postmodernism suggest situating difference merely within a politics of assertion and separatism. On the contrary, what is being argued for is a language and social practice in which different voices and traditions exist and flourish to the degree that they listen to the voices of others, engage in an ongoing attempt to eliminate forms of subjective and objective suffering, and maintain those conditions in which the act of communicating and living extends rather than restricts the creation of democratic public life. At stake here is a politics of difference that is constituted in dialogue and struggle around those articulations and social practices that inform a critical notion of democracy, citizenship, and the public sphere. In this case, differences are both transformed and unified, without losing their specificity, as part of a broader collective struggle. Within this perspective, postmodern educational criticism is located within those broader cultural and political considerations that are beginning to redefine our traditional view of community, language, space, and possibility. In short, postmodern educational criticism presupposes an acknowledgment of the shifting borders that both undermine and reterritorialize dominant configurations of power and knowledge; it also links critical postmodernism to the creation of a society in which there is available a multiplicity of democratic practices, values, and social relations for individuals and social groups to take up within different learning situations and political projects. The goal is a view of democracy and learning in which multiplicity, plurality, and struggle become the raison d'être of democratic public life.

The challenge that a critical postmodernism has to face in education is represented in part by the power of dominant narratives to frame the questions, issues, and problems of the day in ways that exclude oppositional and radical discourses and movements. For example, the national media consistently portrays the current educational reform movement as if it were exclusively about the discourse of accountability, certification, and testing. The agents of reform are state legislators, federal spokespersons, and educational bureaucrats. Amid the myriad problems faced by public schools, the solutions offered are conceived in top-down fashion and limited to approaches that are primarily technical in nature and trivial in substance. The ideology at work here is market-driven, the objective is to abstract schools from their public and civic functions in the interests of concerns derived from human capital theory, that is, the view that education is meaningful only in terms of job preparedness. Individual achievement replaces community struggle, and standardized testing transforms the conditions for teaching to the mechanics of deskilled workers. Of course, there are other movements for educational reform going on in this country. In Chicago and a number of other cities, there is a mass movement by teachers, parents, and others to decentralize the schools and to reclaim education as a community tradition linked to forms of self- and social empowerment. There is also a legacy of critical educational work that has significantly challenged the current ethos of schooling and has offered a trenchant critique of dominant approaches to educational reform. Not only have these movements been ignored, they have been relegated to the status of nonexistence in the popular and national media.

A critical postmodernism must provide the discursive tools to re-think the project of emancipatory schooling as a language of both cri-tique and possibility. The notion of a critical postmodernism may ring harshly in the ears of those who have decided that politics is really about the past; we don't agree with this tenet. Without a standpoint from which to develop an educational project there cannot be any form of political engagement. Put bluntly, an apolitical postmodernism articulates perhaps unwittingly with a right-wing political agenda. Of course, the term "right-wing" does not signify what is commonly un-derstood as political conservatism, but a cultural and intellectual galaxy of discourses that see themselves in the language of the historical avant-garde. In its right-wing manifestations this avant-garde presents itself most frequently as a new aesthetic that seeks to overcome the ba-nality of everyday life, the mechanical and bureaucratic politics of lib-eral pluralism, and in literature and art, counterposes high modernism to the conventions of traditional critical realism. What gives this van-guard a distinct right-wing hue is its bold assertion of the affirmative, even utopian character of culture and its attempt to make life a form of art.

Some elements of this vanguard are connected to new social move-ments, some are linked to what may be described as technological uto-pianism. In this regard, we are currently witnessing the rise of a dis-tinctly anticritical discourse that is seemingly postpolitical and, simultaneously, worshipful of the infinite possibilities for learning and teaching inherent in new computer technologies. This is not the place to enter into a detailed evaluation of either the aesthetics of electron-ically mediated hypertexts or of the possible benefits of computer-aided instruction (which in any case are necessarily limited). In the context of this book, it is important to note the shift from arguments that call attention to the instrumental value of computers for writing and reading and as an aid to instruction, to the emergence of a fully elaborated cultural theory that wishes to subsume pedagogy—indeed, the entire educational enterprise, under a new will to totalization. Hy-pertextuality links itself to the postmodern refusal of reverence for tra-ditional intellectual forms, to postmodern irony, and to the intellectual tendency that always wishes to transgress the distinction between aesthetics and everyday life. But technological ideology, whose refusal of the past as anything but an occasion for memoir is an article of faith, also ignores the historical memory of the link between fascist ideology and art predicated on the aestheticization of politics and everyday relations. Futurism, an art movement of the First World War period, was intimately linked to emergent posthistorical and modernist ideologies. Recall that the Futurists comfortably folded themselves into Mussolini's public sphere after he adopted aspects of their aesthetic/political manifesto as the offical cultural ideology of the Italian fascist state. Or Leni Riefenstahl's powerful epilogue to modernism, *Triumph of the Will*, in which traditional images of empire—marble Roman columns—are combined with long pans of Hitler's multitudes to conjure ecstasy. In the revolt against the banality of progressivist and old conservative politics as well as emerging consumer culture, the interwar right as well as important left art and intellectual movements agreed that the idea of progress remained little more than a justification for the status quo, and that bourgeois rationality, now so deeply embedded in politics, as much as science had turned from a public good to an evil. Surrealism, Dada, and various forms of critical theory challenged socialists as much as liberals to renounce the clichés of the Enlightenment, but not to become postcritical. Their argument—that science, technology, and mass politics had numbed public imagination by releasing and directing libidinal energy to pseudosatisfactions linked to technologically driven mass consumption—was surely one-sided, but it retained the significance of criticism for the achievement of freedom. Listening to the new vanguard, we are called to a technological utopia that promises to invent a new master discourse/technique but without the baggage or benefits of the accumulated intellect.

One of the more articulate expressions of the promise of technological utopia is J. David Bolter's recent study *Turing's Man* (1986). Bolter, who teaches classics, argues that we have, indeed, already entered the new age in which human agency can both overcome natural genetic limits through self-programming and adapt, with the help of the computer, to ever-changing environments. Recent neurological and genetic knowledge "shows how little we control those apsects of nature which affect thought and action." But, according to Bolter, Turing's man is unwilling to wait hundreds of years for natural processes to take root. "Turing's man is so caught up in the computer metaphor that he refused to wait for a genetic solution; he chooses to regard man as software more than hardware, as the program run by the computer more than the hard-wired machine itself." For Bolter and other technological utopians the familiar distinction between man and nature is overcome by regarding both as artifacts, simulations capable of infinite adaptation.

This is astonishingly pre-ecological thinking, in which the imperium of artificial (or, as Bolter would have it, "synthetic") intelligence becomes a model for abolishing the signifiers of the old culture: nature, human nature, emotional intensity. Bolter argues for the "synthesis of man and computer," in which computer game playing becomes the new form of life and the task of education is to invent languages of assimilation of man to the computer. In this regime nature (or human nature) is unbounded and is, therefore, subject to perennial colonization. But this new computer ideology shares with its rival, the bourgeois Enlightenment, a penchant to see only the mathematical dimensions of nature, to view "natural" environments as only raw materials for the production of machines, which in turn properly constitute the genuine environment within which synthetic interactions occur.

The left wing of the technological utopia wants to liberate the machine from the rituals of private ownership, understand the computer as a liberator of human knowledge, as the means to reintegrate knowledge and secure its universal dissemination. The technological left is bothered by problems of copyright and ownership and feels compelled to assure us of its democratic intentions. But such caveats do not detain Bolter. Rather, he is concerned to shake off the notion of limits, to reassert in the manner of the bourgeois Enlightenment the infinity of space and time and of scientific and technological possibility. Bolter's reflections on Western culture focus nearly exclusively on it as humanity's premier repository of power over nature, as a story of freedom through domination; his discourse is framed as a gleeful account of scientific progress. He bids farewell to the old humanists but carves out a new role for them. Like the transformation of philosophy from metaphysics to a nearly exclusive preoccupation with language and science in the late nineteenth century, humanism can survive as the faithful watchdog of computer science and technology, whose task is to "trim" the computer's "excesses"—to remind the hackers of the ethical implications of their diffusion.

Obviously, the new prophets of hyperreality range across the ideological spectrum. Some even argue that the computer is the final road to human freedom because it permits each of us to create our own worlds, to escape the straitjacket of linear text, to make of thought a collage of insight. In this new world Marshall McLuhan's (1964) most radical fantasy, the global village, is on the brink of realization. Politics exists, but it is viewed as a massive obstacle to the creation of the electronically mediated community in which we are all digitally linked. The struggle for social power, having been rendered obsolete by the now realized dream of total individual autonomy made possible by the machine, may be conceived as an illusion.

Another important postmodern tendency associated with, but not identical to, the new social movements insists on the absolute ineluctability of difference. While retaining a powerful political standpoint (feminism, ecology, race movements, gay and lesbian rights, animal rights), this position argues that the dialogic imagination identified with emancipatory discourses such as democracy and the traditional Enlightenment conception of a specifically human freedom are merely deceptions perpetrated by white male intellectuals in order to retain their own hierarchical, patriarchal power. In contrast to those who have advocated the possibilities of a technological dodge of the conventional politics of social imagination, this view reduced the "social" to particular discursive communities. The us-and-them politics of the class struggle is carried out with a vengeance, only class has been redefined to connote exclusions and incommensurabilities rather than inclusions. However, the most relentless expression of this position, exemplified by the work of cultural feminism, eventually takes the form of community-building without public politics, that is, separatism.

These tendencies, including a noninstitutional spiritualism, have their appropriate intellectual expressions which, despite their rejection of conventional "left" ideologies, retain a political cutting edge despite themselves. But the most widespread mood of postmodern antipolitics takes a distinctly aestheticist turn, a path most forcefully articulated by Jean Baudrillard (1988), whose influence on American architectural and literary theory is considerable. Irony is transformed into a passionate nihilism and, finally, a celebration of postindustrial consumer culture. Baudrillard has produced a simulacrum of social and cultural theory, a reproduction without a prototype because its "reflections" on everyday practices are in the final accounting descriptive because its standpoint, which may be mistaken for critique, is really that of the existing culture.

Postmodern political discourse needs to reformulate the relationship between difference and democracy, between the role of intellectuals and the creation of social and political spaces that speak to the needs of a broader public culture. This suggests more than a politics of discourse and difference; it also points to a politics of social and cultural forms in which new possibilities open up for naming in concrete terms what struggles are worthy of taking up, what alliances are to be formed as a result of these struggles, and how the relationship between issues and coalitions can deepen a postmodern politics of difference with a modernist struggle for justice, equality, and freedom.

Central to the notion of postmodern educational criticism is the need for educators to rethink the relations between the centers and the margins of power. That is, this view of educational criticism must not only call into question forms of subordination that create inequities among different groups as they live out their lives but also challenge those institutional and ideological boundaries that have historically masked their own relations of power behind complex forms of distinction and privilege. Of course, the theoretical framework presented here makes no claim to certainty; it is a discourse that is unfinished, but one that may help to illuminate the specifics of oppression and the possibilities for democratic struggle and renewal for those educators who believe that schools and society can be changed and that their individual and collective actions can make a difference.

References

Baudrillard, J. (1988). *Selected Writings*, ed. M. Poster. Stanford: Stanford University Press.

Bolter, J. D. (1986). *Turing's Man*. London: Harmondsworth.

McLuhan, M. (1964). *Understanding Media: The Extension of Man*. New York: McGraw-Hill

INDEX

Compiled by Eileen Quam and Theresa Wolner

Stanley Aronowitz is professor of sociology at the City University of New York Graduate Center and coordinator of cultural studies at the Graduate Center. He has also been employed as a steelworker, trade union organizer, and school planner. Aronowitz received his Ph.D. in sociology from Union Graduate School. He contributes to *The Nation*, *Social Policy*, and the *Village Voice*, and is the founder and editor of *Social Text*. He also is coeditor of Minnesota's American Culture series. Among his many books are *False Promises* (1973), *Science as Power: Discourse and Ideology in Modern Society* (Minnesota, 1988), *The Crisis in Historical Materialism: Class, Politics, and Culture in Marxist Theory*, second edition (Minnesota, 1990), and *Education under Siege*, with Henry Giroux (1985). *Education under Siege* was named by the American Educational Studies Association as one of the most significant books in education for the year 1986.

Henry A. Giroux has taught in the School of Education and Allied Professions at Miami University of Ohio since 1983; he is professor of education, Renowned Scholar in Residence, and director of the Center for Education and Cultural Studies. A secondary school teacher from 1969 to 1975, he earned his doctorate in curriculum theory, the sociology of education, and history at Carnegie-Mellon University in 1977 and subsequently taught at Boston and Tufts universities. Giroux's most recent books include *Schooling and the Struggle for Public Life: Critical Pedagogy in the Modern Age* (Minnesota, 1988), *Teachers as Intellectuals* (1988), *Popular Culture and Critical Pedagogy* (coedited with Roger Simon, 1989), and *Schooling, Politics, and Cultural Struggle* (coedited with Peter McLaren, 1989). He contributes to numerous journals, including the *Harvard Educational Review*, *Social Text*, *Cultural Studies*, and *South Atlantic Quarterly*. Giroux is a member of the consulting editorial boards of the *Journal of Education* and *College Literature*. He is coeditor, with Paulo Freire, of the series Critical Studies in Education, published by Bergin and Garvey Press, and coeditor, with Peter McLaren, of Teacher Empowerment and School Reform, a series published by SUNY Press. In addition to *Education under Siege*, four of Giroux's other books—*Ideology, Culture, and the Process of Schooling*, *Theory and Resistance in Education*, *Teachers as Intellectuals*, and *Schooling and the Struggle for Public Life*—were named by the American Educational Studies Association as significant books in education for the years 1982, 1984, and 1988.